TAX HAVENS TODAY

The Benefits and Pitfalls of Banking and Investing Offshore

HOYT BARBER

John Wiley & Sons, Inc.

Published by John Wiley & Sons, Inc., Hoboken, New Jersey.
Published simultaneously in Canada.

Library of Congress Cataloging-in-Publication Data

Barber, Hoyt L.
Tax havens today : the benefits and pitfalls of banking and investing offshore / Hoyt Barber.
p. cm.
Includes bibliographical references.
ISBN-13: 978-0-470-05123-8 (cloth)
ISBN-10: 0-470-05123-X (cloth)
1. Tax havens. 2. Tax planning—United States. 3. Tax planning—Canada. 4. Tax planning—Great Britain. I. Title.
K4464.5.B373 2006
343.05'23—dc22

2006030739

Printed in the United States of America.

10 9 8 7 6 5 4 3 2 1

"To the hunted, not the hunter;
to the passage, not the path."

Special dedication to my friend,
the late Manuel G. Espinosa, Esquire,
a true gentleman and a scholar.

Also, in memory of Harry Browne,
fellow author, economist, freedom fighter.

CONTENTS

PREFACE

Fifteen years have passed since I wrote a book on the subject of tax havens and offshore banking and investing. The year was 1992 and I was writing *Tax Havens: How to Bank, Invest and Do Business Offshore and Tax Free* for McGraw-Hill in New York. There weren't too many good books out on the subject, and I felt the timing was good for a book on these themes.

Offshore has transformed a lot since then, and many people have discovered, often recklessly, that there are pitfalls to avoid that could cause financial loss and even jail time. The more I thought about it, the more I liked the idea of a new book. But, I decided it couldn't be treated in the same way as last time, and that this time might be my last good opportunity to share what I know and what I have drawn from personal experience. So I would have to make it a real *tour de force*—the "Offshore Bible"—a single place where readers can find all the information they need on the topic, including reliable answers and important connections.

A new book of this nature seems more urgent with each passing day. National and world events are playing havoc with our personal sovereignty and freedoms. I hadn't planned to write this book, but it came to me overnight, and I realized that I could provide a valuable tool for Americans, and others, to get a quick lesson in alternative financial solutions and thereby increase their investment choices. Okay, I decided that I would write it. But it would have to be more than just another offshore book.

Since my first tax haven book was published, dozens of related titles have come and gone. Amazingly, mine stayed in print and remained on the market for a full decade. From my time in the business and from fresh new research, I realized there was huge public interest in these topics, and little material was getting out that was truly accurate and reliable. As for the Internet, the stuff found there is often entirely questionable and sometimes clean off the map.

The result: I have the pleasure of bringing you *Tax Havens Today: The Benefits and Pitfalls of Banking and Investing Offshore.* I have to give credit to my publisher, John Wiley & Sons, Inc., and specifically to my senior editor, Mr. David Pugh, who took a personal interest in this project, and who had the vision to recognize the timeliness, and need for a book on the topic, and indeed, one with deeper themes than the mere subject of tax havens.

Tax Havens Today is designed for easy use. In Part One: "The Offshore Controversy," you will find up-to-date information on the state of the offshore world, against the backdrop of current world events. Changes have occurred rapidly in this business in just the past few years, and more changes are coming. It is important to know what to expect so that you can avoid the pitfalls while implementing your plan of attack. After all, that is what it is all about today—the barbarians are standing at the gate, right now.

Part Two: "Building a Solid Offshore Financial Fortress" includes the reasons the offshore angle may be your best choice of methodology and defense, and it will provide you with valuable hands-on information and strategies for going offshore. There is a diverse selection of offshore banking and investment options to accommodate any investor and any set of goals as well as tax-planning ideas to provide inspiration. You will learn how to reduce taxes, defer taxes, and invest tax-free while protecting your assets and planning your estate, meanwhile staying out of the reach of creditors and growing confiscatory government practices. In Part Two, you will also learn how you and your spouse can earn up to $160,000 a year tax-free simply by relocating.

Part Three: "Today's Tax Havens" gives you an accurate picture of the advantages and drawbacks of 40 important tax havens. Twelve categories of information are provided so that you can make an intelligent decision on the best tax haven for you and your purposes. And, that is not all. This book contains over 500 contacts, including names, addresses, telephone, fax, e-mail addresses, and web sites of the most important investment, banking, and financial advisors in the world. These are organized by tax haven or other jurisdiction, and a brief description of their areas of expertise is included. After reading this book, no matter what questions you may have, an authority on the subject is just a phone call or e-mail away.

Part Four: "Resources—The Big Picture" provides contacts for developing new financial plans and includes other information sources to help you further pursue the concepts presented in this book, including exploration of tax-advantaged offshore retirement havens, and other countries, with strong appeal to aspiring investors and expatriates.

Ninety-five countries are profiled in Part Four as possible alternative places to live or retire. Thirty-one countries where you can secure residency and possibly naturalization are covered in detail, along with two very attractive Economic Citizenship Programs where you can get a second citizenship and passport just by writing a check. These countries are also reviewed with taxation in mind, as well as their individual and unique benefits. Then, an additional sixty-two countries are included where you can possibly live as an expatriate, either temporarily or permanently.

Now, does it sound like I left anything out? That's it, all rolled into one tight package. I believe you will find herein everything you need to get started on your road to reducing taxes, protecting assets, increasing your profits, and living a better life. And, as I uncover more opportunities, I'll gladly share them with you. Just send me your name and e-mail address, and I'll make sure you get my latest take on what's happening offshore—and elsewhere. You may e-mail me direct at BarberFinancial@hotmail.com or to my office at info@BarberFinancialAdvisors.com.

One last thought before I leave you to explore your new options. You have already contributed to some important causes by the mere action of looking into this topic: yourself, your family and a brighter future. And I *believe* in more action and less talk: In that spirit I decided while writing this book to contribute my royalties to a worthy organization known as DownsizeDC.org. It is a nonprofit organization co-founded by one of my long-time (since 1970) favorite investment writers and philosophers, Harry Browne and his associate, Jim Babka. Among a world of other things, Harry Browne was the 1996 and 2000 libertarian presidential candidate. When I heard the news while writing this book that Harry Browne had passed away, I was compelled to make my contribution to reducing bureaucracy. As they say, I may be a day late and a dollar short, but if enough people in this country really want to make an impact, then we can make a difference, and there is truly no time like the present. I hope this book will inspire others, the way Harry Browne and others have inspired me. For more information on DownsizeDC.org, please refer to Part Four.

Best of luck as you make your way through these pages. Only you hold the key to your future. Let me know how you fare on your voyage to a better, richer, and more independent tomorrow.

HOYT BARBER

PART ONE

The Offshore Controversy

1

WHY ARE SO MANY PEOPLE GOING OFFSHORE?

What in the *world* are these people *doing?* Well, there are as many reasons as you have dollars in the bank to take your finances and investments offshore, and then some. And the motive? Probably there are as many motives as there are people who go offshore; they cover the spectrum from excitement about valid new opportunities to legally reduce taxes and protect assets, all the way to down and dirty fear about the future. There are a multitude of excellent reasons to consider going offshore at some level, and as long as we are truly free people, these choices should always be available to us.

But will they? *Maybe.* For the moment, many options are still available, and scores of doors are still wide open to give savvy investors a chance to preserve and protect assets, ease tax burdens, and plan for the future.

Of course, you must plan carefully to avoid the pitfalls and dangers you might encounter along the way. To stay out of trouble with government and today's big brother mind-set, it is best to know which lines *not* to cross. The trick is that governments with certain behind-the-scene agendas regularly redefine those parameters in an attempt to control their taxable subjects and hang on to revenues for support of their ever-expanding plans and budgets. As James Bond said, "World domination, same old dream."

This intent is typically in direct competition with most decent folks who work hard and smart to increase their wealth and only wish to provide better financial and physical security for themselves and their families. These are valid aims, and in today's state-of-the-world, you are well advised to explore the many options for going offshore legally, while there is still time. Certain special interests in the world today are trying to close particular doors as we speak.

Like a jealous, insecure miser, the U.S. government has long speculated about missing tax dollars from the untold numbers of citizens who are suspected of evading taxes.

When identifying the suspects of so-called tax evasion, the Internal Revenue Service (IRS) may see little distinction between evasion and avoidance, the latter of which incidentally is still considered legal. But with 250,000 U.S. citizens voluntarily choosing to leave the United States permanently every year, largely due to the specter of taxes, it is clear that a significant number of disenchanted Americans are willing to try something new—an entirely new life. And these numbers don't even include the undoubtedly much larger segment of people who utilize offshore planning and strategies without leaving home.

Australia, another high-tax jurisdiction, also has a large number of suspected tax dodgers who have gone offshore, and the Australian government is cracking down hard to combat the pattern. They are even investigating Paul Hogan, creator of Crocodile Dundee, who has been implicated as a result of Operation Wickenby, a criminal tax investigation in that country. The British government is doing the same dance—and with a vengeance. In Italy, tax evasion is considered a way of life and is jokingly referred to as the national pastime.

The trend of citizens actively protesting their government's tax rates generally occurs in countries where the combined taxes of the local, state, and federal governments exceed 50 percent of a person's gross income. In the late 1970s and 1980s, the United Kingdom was grabbing a hefty 70 percent from the citizenry. This finally led to a tax rebellion of sorts as taxpayers began leaving the country in numbers. And their departures were less discreet than might have been expected, as some of the country's richest and most talented English citizens were quite expressive about their disenchantment of being gouged by the taxman. Reminds one of a certain Beatles tune!

Jean Baptiste Colbert put it eloquently when he said, "The art of taxation consists of so plucking the goose as to obtain the largest amount of feathers with the least amount of hissing."

Well, the English plucked one too many feathers, and the exodus gained such serious momentum that by the early 1990s the government decided to put the brakes on its excessively high tax stance by rolling it back to the previously high level of just 50 percent. There was a collective sigh of relief in many quarters, and gradually expatriates in Spain, the Canary Islands, and other common English hideouts began returning to the mother country.

Among the economic classes in a given country, the upper 2 percent (in part, the "national treasures") include businesspeople, entrepreneurs, industrialists, capitalists, inventors, writers, actors, singers, scientists, and other rich and creative types. They constitute much of the economic foundation on which wealth is created and from which the taxman can taketh. In England, these brightest flowers among her citizenry were often the very folks who had packed up and taken leave. When the government decided to back off, her patriots had to weigh the benefits of remaining expatriates against the lure of returning to their home country, including the welcome-home gift of a new reduced tax structure that now looked strangely like an actual tax incentive. Although 50 percent is still considered to be high taxation, history proves that it is about the maximum level with which citizens are generally willing to cope. And 50 percent is generally the level that taxpayers experience today in the United States, Canada, England, and other first-world industrial nations.

The taxman devised a new strategy for the returning English expatriates of the 1990s who thought they would come home to find things the way they had been before they left. Not so!

The English tax laws included a "foreign earnings deduction." In this scenario, if you were a U.K. citizen and worked overseas in excess of one year, *and* physically spent less than 62 days in the United Kingdom during that year, you were *exempt* from income tax on your foreign source income. No wonder there had been an exodus. The IRS wouldn't consider such an idea for a moment—they would have too many takers!

There was a slight wrinkle in the plans for certain former residents wanting to return to Jolly Old England. In all "fairness," Mr. Blair's government decided that these returning citizens, while in the United Kingdom, would now have to pay income tax on their worldwide income if they had any U.K. source income at all. Ouch! That likely felt like a penalty for leaving in the first place. And why did the taxman do this? Because he could.

The United States, as well as other countries, is well aware of this breaking point with taxpayers. As such, strategies are being formulated at a brisk pace, occasionally with an agenda toward a "one-world order," and in all cases to generally tighten the noose. What might governments do with tighter control of their citizens? Of course, they might tax them even more.

The countries and organizations with an agenda for eliminating tax havens because they see them as "unfair tax competition" include the United States, the United Kingdom, Australia, the European Union, the Organisation for Economic Co-operation and Development (OECD), the Financial Action Task Force (FATF), and the G-7—in other words, countries and groups with the greatest revenue and strongest economies.

Stop the presses: While writing this book in the spring of 2006, I learned that the United Kingdom's stance against tax havens and suspected tax avoiders has stepped up to a new level that I suspect will have an even greater negative effect on the 13 British overseas territories and their status as viable tax havens, particularly for British citizens and Americans.

2

WHIPPING THE TAXPAYERS INTO SHAPE

According to an estimate by the Internal Revenue Service (IRS), between one and two million Americans may be using offshore accounts with a debit card such as American Express, Visa, or MasterCard attached, allowing them to easily access their funds on deposit offshore. The estimate is likely correct, considering the previous numbers we reviewed in which we saw that a full quarter of a million Americans are physically leaving each year and untold further Americans are taking their money offshore. In fact, these "guesstimates" are based on records obtained from an investigation several years ago, during which MasterCard was served a summons to produce bank records on U.S. taxpayers from just three tax haven countries, which is only a handful of what is really out there. This limited "fishing expedition," as such investigations are commonly called, revealed over *230,000 bank accounts* held by Americans.

Among these figures, some were certainly blatant tax cheats whom the government no doubt rightly set about to identify and bust. But fortunately, simply having an offshore bank account or employing offshore investment and asset protection strategies does not mean that a person is cheating the taxman or committing any crime. On the surface, however, and in the fervor to realize more revenue from taxes, this is what the IRS would sometimes like to believe.

With the previously mentioned fishing exercise, the government surprised a lot of people who had thought they were safe offshore. The IRS gained immense publicity for their tax crusade; and knowing the effects of their efforts, the IRS began to flex its muscles, leveraging taxpayers to comply or else. Finally, in 2003 the IRS established an amnesty program, offering *not* to prosecute all those other taxpayers who were offshore but had not yet been discovered, if only they'd fess up by a given date. The convenient assumption was that if there were illegal accounts, then the account holders might have something to hide such as not having reported all their income from earned fees, profits, dividends, interest, and capital gains, which quite possibly the good citizens had simply and legally diverted offshore.

In an attempt to hide money from whomever—the government, ex-spouses, creditors, or others—U.S. taxpayers have often failed to file Treasury Form TD F 90-22.1. Whether they failed knowingly or not, this form is a mandatory requirement under most circumstances and must be filed annually, or the taxpayer risks facing civil and criminal penalties of up to five years in prison and $500,000 in fines for each account gone unreported by the signatory authority on the account. *More on reporting requirements later.*

By turning themselves in during the amnesty period, taxpayers who were operating outside the law avoided plenty of potential grief; and those who didn't take advantage of the opportunity took a further gamble if they were caught. Summoning bank records from credit card companies is only one of many methods the IRS can use to go after what they feel is theirs. This particular investigation netted $170 million, so fishing expeditions look mighty attractive, even when unconstitutional.

And just who were these big fish? According to the IRS, many of the account holders who were cheating on their taxes were business owners, executives, attorneys, doctors, Wall Street types, and even executives of publicly traded companies. Many of these folks were using their debit cards to pay for everyday living expenses directly from offshore and thus not paying taxes on otherwise reportable income. How is this possible? Well, deductions are typically not automatically taken for these earners because they report their income directly. Income that lands offshore and then gets spent with an offshore account debit card doesn't even need to show up in the earnings column, anywhere. The fishing trip results indicated that a majority of the offshore catch were in the top one percent of all U.S. taxpayers.

With the success of the MasterCard case, the IRS had all the incentive in the world to bait up and head out again. In April 2006, headline news released the story that the IRS had asked for and received approval from a federal court to request that PayPal turn over private financial information about its customers on the mere assumption that some customers might be evading taxes. In 2005, PayPal customers, individuals and businesses alike worldwide, had transferred $27.5 billion through the company's system. Many account holders access their money through credit and debit cards, and the IRS wanted to know which ones might have transferred unreported earnings offshore.

The outcome of this investigation remains to be seen, but in the meantime, an interesting factoid is that eBay owns PayPal and has a staggering one hundred million account holders throughout the world.

3

THE BIG SQUEEZE

Getting offshore legally, and staying there legally . . . that's the goal. So, it is best to start the process right and avoid any hard lessons. You will have plenty of opportunities as you go along with your plan to internationalize your finances and reduce those burdensome taxes, but you want to avoid breaking any laws with a quick fix or other strategy that could expose you to government attack or open another can of worms. Whether or not you approve of the government's methods and scrutiny, it's best not to justify away the facts and take an unnecessarily high risk. Save high-risk measures for when you really need them.

Avoiding taxes will likely not be your sole reason for wanting to move all or part of your money and assets to another country, although as we have seen, high taxation has had the net effect of driving people to offshore solutions.

Typically, pressures such as the ones in the following list provide strong incentives for seeking alternative solutions:

- Government oppression
- Dwindling privacy
- Discrimination
- Lawsuits
- Threat of crime
- Excessive government
- Terrorism

This list names just a few incentives. If we look back over the past few decades in the United States, we can see a pattern of social deterioration in our society at all levels. It may have started at the bottom, but it now seems to have reached the top—just look at the players today in business and in government. Would you buy a used car from some of these people?

There have been significant and rapid developments in the United States and elsewhere, especially in the new century. Problems just seem to get worse as we are forced into accepting a globalized society. But what does this mean?

Young people are more willing to accept the way things are because they haven't been around long enough to witness or feel the effects of change. In time, they, too, will realize that their futures will be marked by change, putting them in potential jeopardy; one day, they will reminisce about the past when they had more liberties, freedom, and opportunity. Fortunately, there are also plenty of offshore possibilities for young people, including foreign job opportunities.

Talk of global free markets and worldwide democracy gives us a warm fuzzy feeling, certainly. But shouldn't we look carefully at such fine-sounding concepts if they are coming at the expense of our sovereignty as individual citizens of an independent nation? This is the country that has guaranteed our rights and liberties under the U.S. Constitution and the Bill of Rights, and we have the good fortune and privilege to be the beneficiaries of this legacy. But the sad news is that these rights are in danger of vanishing—and quickly.

How? Let's look at one area: privacy. It is a bit unsettling to consider the erosion of our privacy. More and more, we are subject to new surveillance. We are unwittingly photographed in our automobiles at traffic lights and tollbooths, in parking garages and overpasses. Our persons are photographed on the street corners, in malls, in office buildings, in banks, at airports, sitting in a bus station, walking down the street minding our own business, you name it. And on occasion, these cameras are face-recognition devices that, unbeknown to us, may be running a check on our identities, and possible criminal records, as we go quite innocently about the business of our daily lives in what we consider to be our private little worlds. Is it so far-fetched to imagine that next, it could be the bedroom?

When we are at work, and even at home, it is now possible for our own government and others to spy on us through our phone conversations and e-mails. Our banking and other financial institutions can now be used as extensions of law enforcement efforts and government snoops to keep tabs, not only on our financial affairs, but on what the information may say about us. Today, the government is using libraries and bookstores to learn more about who we are and what we are doing, based on what we are reading—truly Orwellian.

Under broad legislation, much like the racketeering laws that were meant specifically to catch gangsters, the new powers are regularly used against ordinary citizens in the hopes of getting convictions. And the same applies to laws passed under the guise of eliminating certain bad elements such as drug traffickers, counterfeiters, smugglers, and money launderers, but then are used to better control the general population. The natural progression could be the potential criminalization of nearly everything.

Is this why we have a *secret* federal court in the United States, in direct violation of our Sixth Amendment rights? According to Associated Press, federal courts are keeping thousands of cases sealed so they never see the light of day. These are not cases against terrorists. These are cases against defendants in criminal cases. Since 2003, there have been over 5,000 such cases. And why are they being kept secret? The Justice Department was asked this question but remained conveniently silent. Maybe a liberal application of broad laws and powers would encourage more lenient plea bargains and eliminate the need for fair and speedy trials. Could that be why?

The fear of terrorism led to the passage of the Patriot Act in the name of "security." To paraphrase a famous American, it seems that what we need to fear is fear itself. We are letting the aura of fear become an excuse for surrendering our freedoms.

Of course, all rational people want to eliminate criminal activity as much as possible. But at the cost of violating the civil liberties of citizens who supposedly have rights, and who are taxpayers, too? The "War on Terrorism" starts to look suspiciously like a war on our very freedoms.

Incredibly, a recent poll of Americans turned up the interesting fact that the majority support these tactics in the name of antiterrorism because they believe that this is the price to pay for freedom. Well, if the American public is willing to believe this, then it is no wonder Congress rubber-stamps whatever the president wants to sell.

It is not too late, and there are still measures that each of us can take to preserve the key values of sovereignty, freedom, privacy, and individuality. These may require a conscientious effort, but the cause is worth it, and the degree of our success may depend on how seriously we view the threat. Bolder action may be required.

Privacy is an important commodity that helps to insulate us against all forms of oppression and intrusion from the government, or other persons and entities whose motives are unlikely to benefit us. At the core of the question is an individual's right to sovereignty, which in theory, should carry more credence than any rights bestowed on a government by its own citizenry, as in, "We the people . . . ," the very breath that gave our Republic life.

But, if we think we have already seen the worst on the subject of privacy, we need only to return to the news. A movement is afoot toward a single form of personal identity, and we aren't chatting just about the new idea for a national identification (ID) card. Indeed, the talk is also about the technology for a microchip—to be embedded in your body—and the uses of which are being seriously discussed in certain circles for identification and control. Who? You. There will be many "good" arguments, some truly well meant, to support such a plan, but once in place, like the "temporary" income tax of 1913, it will likely never go away and potentially it will be abused beyond our imagination.

Still other means of physical identification are being employed, aside from the good old fingerprint, such as the reading of the retina of your eye for positive identification. Sound like the movies? Well, technology is moving forward quickly and the subject of our privacy is of critical interest. My hope is that all of us will remain vigilant on the topic as we take positive action in our lives to preserve our other values, such as our freedom, our income, and our assets.

The real point is that awareness of changes and impending changes that can threaten or compromise your liberties, freedoms, and financial security should be a priority in these times, along with an interest in what you might do to minimize or avoid unnecessary trouble and undesirable potential outcomes. *Please refer to the many resources in Part Four of this book, including excellent sources of information about the current status of the field and the best options to respond and deal with it.*

Although the creative and legal ways to avoid excessive taxation provide a worthy theme, attacks on us can come in many forms such as our dwindling personal privacy. Any outside pressure (government oppression, economic woes, or whatever it may be), brings with it a host of issues that come with the territory, and we need to examine them in relation to our own existence. Is action required? It may help to think of protecting your freedom as a game that you intend to win. People have more power than they give themselves credit for, but, to be effective, you must identify the problem and exercise the solutions. Now is the time!

You might start by making a comprehensive list of your goals and build on it. Include the negative pressures that challenge you daily. Then list possible alternatives that are within your power to consider and that would ease these unpleasant elements. This book represents possibilities and, for those who want them, real solutions that are at hand.

4

THE CHANGING WORLD OF TAX HAVENS

In a perfect world, you wouldn't need this book. Life is not so, but the good news is that there are many interesting aspects of going offshore, and many benefits to gain.

There are also some pitfalls to avoid, and these can be circumvented by knowing what to look out for, and applying yourself and your knowledge to the challenge.

The world of tax havens has changed since its earliest beginnings, around the time the first tax dollar (or drachma, etc.) was collected. And, as the concept of safe havens from taxes has evolved and received more attention, more people have recognized the advantages. So, over time, the havens have become a threat to the emerging first-world nations and their greedy hunger for tax revenue.

Interestingly, as the big powers have pressured offshore venues into becoming more transparent, many now call themselves "International Financial Centers" (IFCs), instead of offshore financial centers or tax havens. And other first-world powers like Switzerland and Austria are not pure tax havens as we know them, but are important banking centers and safe and stable havens for money and assets. Aha!

And anyway, taxes should be only one of the many good reasons for going offshore.

The two oldest tax havens in the world are Liechtenstein and Panama, each dating back to the 1920s, and both have been two of my favorite tax havens for years. In fact, both are still at the top of my list.

The real development in tax havens got underway in the 1960s and 1970s, when tax haven legislation in these countries was still light but was quickly evolving under the fire of the venues and their individual self-governments. In the 1980s, foreign governments and international agencies started applying real pressure, which they then increased throughout the 1990s in the hope of legislating these jurisdictions off the planet. However, many tax havens weathered the turmoil well, a few simply became more determined not to be bullied, and a handful of these stand today as some of the best choices.

A few once important havens, like the Bahamas and the Cayman Islands, were hit the hardest. In the case of the Bahamas, this former headliner among tax havens can today no longer be considered even useful as it has allowed itself to be gutted by the influence of its huge and powerful neighbor, the United States. And anyway, there are too many other better places to go.

The individual country profiles in this book provide complete information on the status of each important tax haven available in these interesting times. I have profiled only the most significant ones. Places not mentioned (e.g., Nauru in the Central Pacific), do not register on my radar screen for very good reasons and are not worth further discussion. This applies to any other tax havens that are not included, with the exception of some extraordinarily unique places that might be useful under special circumstances, but would serve little purpose for most readers.

But to return to the historical perspective, let's look at the concept of owning your own offshore bank. As an example of the lack of internal legislation as recently as the 1960s and early 1970s, you could still obtain an offshore banking license to start your own bank—a topic and practice that is practically taboo today. In some tax havens, you needed simply to provide some basic information about yourself as the applicant, pay the fee for a local lawyer, cough up the nominal government license fee, and voilà, you were in the banking business! A couple thousand dollars could swing it. I know, because I have been a student of tax havens since the earliest of those heydays. Today, the requirements for conducting offshore banking are much stricter and are better enforced for the sake of the depositors and the general well-being of all.

Even the most casual observer knows that the subject of offshore is, and always has been, a hot topic. When I wrote my first book on the subject (*Tax Havens,* New York: McGraw-Hill, 1992), people I came into contact with would still ask, "What is an offshore bank?" And they weren't sure if Vanuatu was a real country, or just a scam. Times have changed immensely in just the past 15 years. With rapid developments in the world today and the war on tax avoidance—a tactic that, as mentioned, has always been accepted as legal—imagine what the prospects will look like in another decade if people don't exercise their rights and freedoms while they still have the options. Tax havens are in part an interesting reflection of a rapidly changing world.

The key to benefiting from these changes is to recognize the excellent choices and opportunities that still exist and capitalize on them while they last. By acting now, a person can be more prepared, and more secure, for an unknown future. The opportunities today may not be viable alternatives tomorrow. Of course, the future may be even better, but who knows for sure? The question should really be, are we willing to speculate with everything we have and wait until it's too late? Remember, if you use tax havens correctly, you have nothing to lose and much to gain.

5

THE INTERNATIONAL DRAGNET

The hard reality is that there's much effort extant from governments, and not just our own, as well as from international organizations, often working in tandem, to tighten the grip on the citizens of the world for the purpose of increasing taxes and implementing more effective tax collection measures. In fact, the focus is tremendous, as is the desire to plug the "loopholes," as they are viewed, and to create a "level playing field," on which to tax everyone to death. Why? Because they can—or so they would like to think. The problem with this plan, besides toying with our individual sovereignty, is that the sovereignty of individual nations is also jeopardized by other bigger nations, or more hideously, by international organizations that want to bully the smaller countries into telling them what to do. By hoping to eliminate tax competition between nations, which incidentally promotes economies and business for the benefit of these smaller countries, they are also hoping to reduce or eliminate the opportunities for their taxpayers to creatively and legally lower their taxes. Government oppression? Well, effectively, yes.

The United Nations, with its 191 member nations, is supportive of a global tax organization, presumably to eliminate "unfair tax competition" as part of their agenda, as if this were a noble cause. If they ever succeed, one thing will surely happen. Taxes will go up. Why? Because, there will be nothing to stop them. The sovereignty of individual nations is gradually being usurped by outside forces with special agendas, served up by organizations like the Organisation for Economic Co-operation and Development (OECD) and their redheaded stepchild, the Financial Action Task Force (FATF), and many others. They are beginning to work in concert, trying desperately to get everyone to comply with their wishes. There is plenty of talk of expanding global democracy and capitalism, free markets, and free trade, all of which sound great! Doesn't it? But, the consolidation of power is likely no matter what you call it, and the downside is potentially horrific. Imagine a world in which the current discussions to give the UN the power to create the ultimate global tax-collecting body become a reality. Imagine a single, worldwide UN-administered IRS, and no other options. Actually, this very scenario is a possibility, and this one, like others, is what we need to be thinking about when we blindingly support initiatives that are being touted as "good for us."

The big "D" word, "Democracy," is being peddled all over the world as the cure-all form of government that every foreign country should hope to achieve. President George Bush talks about democracy in general and continual terms, almost as if it were a religious experience. Why is democracy being trumped so hard on the world stage? Will fewer people die in wars, will the debt of nations go down, will the people of the world be freer and happier? Not likely? Well, then, why not?

Could it be because democracy is a more favorable environment to increase commerce and productivity worldwide and, in the globalization crusade, to tax the world? Free markets are music to a capitalist's ears, but they should not be attained at the expense of the sovereignty of nations and the sovereignty of individual human beings. And, what better way to finance the ultimate plan than through globalization? Former President George H. W. Bush put it on the table when he declared it a "New World Order," but he stopped short of telling us where that might lead us. These inconvenient details are often left undisclosed to the populace, particularly in advance of changes of this magnitude. Only later, through time and tide and our own reflection, can we perceive the amplitude of the true intentions and the bigger picture—and often when it's too late. Did the German population really know what plans Hitler had for them, and others?

A uniform global tax policy and unified collection methods will be necessary to fuel the ultimate plan that is not yet revealed to us. Once again, individual national sovereignties are at stake, and so is yours.

In this chapter, we review a few pitfalls that are directly related to anyone going offshore, and that were largely designed to reduce liberties and increase taxation. The latest tactic in the war on our liberties is action in the name of "security." The "anti-money-laundering" laws that are being passed worldwide are one mechanism to create a strong umbrella of control. We are told these laws are necessary to stop terrorists and other international criminals, but tax collection purposes are almost entirely the real reasons for this expansive global legislative move. The legislators might not actually recognize a terrorist if they saw one—in fact, all the funds uncovered from terrorist financing came through OECD member countries or Islamic nations, not, as the authors of this legislation have tried to imply, through the "bad boy" tax havens.

In fact, the high-handed tax regimes themselves are to blame, as they have provided their own citizens ample inspiration to become more creative and personally respond to this global epidemic. Protection from persecution at the hands of their own government is why folks have made tax havens so popular. Corporations have taken the same measures. Money, like water, still seeks its own level, and it will seek out safe havens regardless of the state of the world.

What the world governments really need is to have their taxpaying citizens hold them fiscally responsible. Only then will this spiraling problem modify and maybe end. Otherwise, the finale will be much more dramatic and few people will escape its consequences.

Why have tax havens become the brunt of these actions? Supposedly, they harbor vast amounts of criminal money and protect tax-dodgers of every description. The truth? More money is laundered through OECD member nations, and an even larger sum through the United States, than is supposedly laundered in all the world's tax havens combined. Laundered criminal proceeds are less easily detected flowing through huge financial centers like Tokyo, New York, and London. Curiously, the *United States is also the biggest tax haven in the world,* as it provides many tax incentives to foreign investment. Without this infusion of foreign capital, our economy would be in serious jeopardy, along with our future. Ironically, this is precisely why, in 2002, the United States backed off on giving the OECD its support. The United States could not be party to the idea of global harmonization as long as the truth is that our nation is greatly benefited by its status as the largest tax haven of all.

6

THE GLOBAL LAUNDROMAT

Anti-money-laundering legislation of all kinds is spreading worldwide, and its purpose is broader than its publicly stated reasons for being—to combat crime and terrorism. Money-laundering legislation, coupled with other dangerous legislation such as laws to allow the legal confiscation of private property and assets even under questionable circumstances and often without due process, has the potential to be a powerful and unbridled weapon to use against the average person.

As even grade-school kids know, the anti-racketeering laws were originally passed to corral underworld gangsters who were the villains in organized crime. Today, these laws are freely used on anyone, and are just an addition to the arsenal for those looking to put you away. When this legislation was originally drafted, the language was purposefully ambiguous, to make it easier to manipulate through future interpretation and application. The unsuspecting public does not necessarily consider this aspect of legislation at the time it is proposed and ultimately passed.

A closer look at the U.S. Patriot Act raises a similar specter. Six weeks after 9/11, we were led to believe that bureaucrats agreed to, and drafted, a 342-page piece of legislation supposedly designed to stop terrorists and rogue states and to keep us safe from our airplanes being wrangled and our buildings falling down around us. Was this possibly written in advance by those hoping to limit our liberties and other agendas, then dusted off, and put into place when the right moment came along? Maybe not, but why then did so few bureaucrats read it before it was passed? Many were later surprised to learn the scope of this document.

Approximately one-third of this legislation is targeted at offshore banking and finance under the label "anti-money-laundering." And, what have we learned is the real reason for anti-money-laundering legislation? In case you would like to read the United States Patriot Act for yourself, you will find it on the FINCEN web site at www.fincen.org. This Act, which was again passed in 2006, has been called the *anti-Constitution* by some observers since. In a subtle subtext, it brilliantly and deviously sneaks away with the rights granted to us and the liberties guaranteed to us in the documents of the founding fathers of this country.

Just what *is* the definition of money laundering? Of course, there are many. Here is the definition used in Article One of the European Communities Directive of 1990:

> *The conversion or transfer of property, knowing that such property is derived from serious crime, for the purpose of concealing or disguising the illicit origins of the property or of assisting any person who is involved in committing such an offense or offenses to evade the legal consequences of his action, and the concealment or disguise of the true nature, source, location, disposition, movement, rights with respect to, or ownership of property, knowing that such property is derived from serious crime.*

This leads the thinking reader to wonder what the definition of "serious crime" might be. Inevitably, it is open for further analysis and interpretation, making it convenient for those in power to define according to need.

There are numerous anti-money-laundering organizations around the world. Readers should be aware of the more active and outwardly spoken ones, and what they are doing. A few of the more prominent ones are covered here, and they are mentioned occasionally in this book and frequently in the media.

In fact, there are many references to money laundering these days. A quick search on the Internet will produce lots of reading material, although, of course, I wouldn't trust all of it.

7

THE TAX POLICE

The Organisation for Economic Development (OECD) is a Paris-based organization composed mostly of former tax collectors from various industrial nations, and it is charged with expanding the global powers of its membership, which comprises 30 democracies that "work together to address the economic, social and governance challenges of globalization as well as to exploit opportunities."

In 1998, the OECD came out with a report entitled *Harmful Tax Competition* in an aggressive move to thwart countries that promoted the tax advantages of their jurisdictions over those of others—the low-tax countries versus high-tax countries—and encourage them to raise their taxes so they wouldn't attract capital away from the big guys. They promoted their argument as "fairness" between countries.

But it is merely a strategy by OECD member nations to eliminate the loss of business and revenues as a result of their overtaxation. If this so-called fairness is believable, then every country is guilty of promoting *their* advantages over their neighbors, including the OECD countries. Yet only the non-OECD members are the ones being targeted.

In the United States, we call this type of scenario the "free market," or fair competition. And, ironically, although the United States at first embraced the OECD's underhanded methods, the government came to the conclusion that to support the OECD's cause would be detrimental to the U.S. economy. Why? Because as mentioned, the United States is actually the largest tax haven in the world, attracting trillions of tax-advantaged foreign investment capital annually. Clearly, and understandably, the United States supports the concept of tax havens. Just not for anybody else.

The OECD has also tried to hoodwink those who would listen into believing that having a more harmonized and balanced tax collection system between countries would not hurt underdeveloped nations, but the opposite is true. Indeed, the tax havens would suffer greatly as there is very little other industry to support their economies.

International and centralized tax collection is the name of the game. Taxpayers would be muscled into cooperation by the threat of antidrug and anti-money-laundering legislation with stiff civil and criminal penalties, which, in recent years, was touted as a means for many countries to enforce their own tax collection schemes. Fighting crime was the ploy dispensed to sell these pieces of legislation, just like terrorism was the justification for passing the Patriot Act with its comprehensive anti-money-laundering legislation and other oppressions built into it.

The Financial Action Task Force (FATF) is an intergovernmental body whose stated purpose is the development and promotion of national and international policies to combat money laundering and terrorist financing. The FATF states that it is a "policy-making body" created in 1989 that works to generate the necessary political will to bring about legislative and regulatory reforms in these areas. It is the anti-money-laundering wing of the OECD. The FATF has published the "Forty Plus Nine Recommendations" to meet this objective.

As with other governmental and quasi-governmental agencies, many have an agenda that is not revealed in their mission statement. On the surface, their purpose appears even noble, such as "good versus evil." Here, that inspiring purpose is supposedly to eliminate money-laundering and terrorist financing. Well, most of us would agree that getting rid of crime is good, even critical. But at what point can we allow overzealous bureaucrats to jeopardize the sovereignty of our nation, and other nations, or force us to relinquish our individual rights and sovereignty in return for advancing their agenda?

More laws are passed every day in the name of security, to protect us from terrorists and criminals. Whom do we really need to be protected from? As the philosopher Tacitus stated, "The more corrupt the state, the more numerous the laws."

The U.S. Constitution left criminal justice to the states. Only three federal crimes were written into the original Constitution, but they have increased exponentially in the past three decades. Today we have over four thousand federal crimes. Here is where we need a clear distinction, not broadly written legislation designed to criminalize everything and anyone, based on the whim or need of the moment. The inherent danger here occurs when this type of legislation is abused to convict people of otherwise minor infringements, or no crime at all. Is the purpose of the law to protect us from crime and criminals, or to gain greater control over us, and the implied threat of us as citizens and individuals? The question bears deeper examination.

These are the countries worldwide that have become members of the Financial Action Task Force:

- Argentina
- Australia
- Austria
- Belgium
- Brazil
- Canada
- Denmark
- European Commission
- Finland
- France
- Germany
- Greece
- Gulf Cooperation Council
- Hong Kong
- China
- Iceland
- Ireland
- Italy
- Japan
- Luxembourg
- Mexico
- Netherlands
- New Zealand
- Norway
- Portugal
- Singapore
- Spain
- Sweden
- Switzerland
- Turkey
- United Kingdom
- United States

The Financial Crimes Enforcement Network (FINCEN) is an arm of the U.S. Treasury, specifically created "to safeguard the financial system from the abuses of financial crime, including terrorist financing, money laundering, and other illicit activities."

So, crime and terrorism were the justification for setting up FINCEN in 1990, but one reason it exists is to go after your money. This agency *has* been effective in financial crime investigations and is linked to other government agencies. All the accumulated records required by law to be filed since the passage of the Bank Secrecy Act in 1970 are computerized and available to other agencies and law enforcement, including the Central Intelligence Agency and the Defense Intelligence Agency. The FINCEN computer system can also probe into all U.S. bank accounts.

8

BARBARIANS AT THE GATE

We should be concerned about preserving our liberties. Without our liberties, other attempts at preserving the quality of our lives will be hollow, if not quite difficult.

If we don't defend our Constitution and Bill of Rights, we will ultimately have nothing. *These* are our guarantees; they are precious, and our dedication to these concepts is what makes us true patriots. The U.S. Constitution and Bill of Rights are our very protection from totalitarianism. And a government out of control, and paranoid is a government that desperately wants to get even more control, often through the only means available to those without power—by instilling fear.

We should not stand aside while we are told that compromising our rights as citizens is in our best interest in the name of security. The implication here is, without giving up our rights, we will not be secure and protected by our government from the invisible enemy, known today as the *terrorist.* But, without personal sovereignty, national sovereignty cannot last long.

Our rights are spelled out in the founding documents of this nation, the United States of America. These rights are indivisible. They cannot be divided or edited for the benefit of any special interest or even for the government. Period. But, that is precisely what has been happening gradually for years, and is now advancing with a mission-like quality. It is your freedom on the line. And you and I must defend our rights to deserve the sweet bounty of freedom. You don't need to enlist in the military or fight a war to protect America. Defending your rights and liberties is even more important—without them, America won't be worth defending.

Terrorism is a convenient concept for intimidating us into cooperation. Historically, crime has been effectively used the same way. The fear of the "baddies," and jail, helps to keep the general populace in line, and the taxpayer is happy to oblige. Federal taxes were not even a reality until 1913 when the Internal Revenue Service was created. And then, citizens of the day were told, among other things, it was only a temporary measure to finance the war machine, and would be abolished soon thereafter. That was a lie and an excuse, and it worked. We have been in the government's clutches ever since.

A person could conceivably feel compelled and justified to "voluntarily" pay taxes if the funds were responsibly used to run the government in the best interests of the citizens of the country. Today, half of your earnings are going to taxes—local, state, and federal. But, are the billions of dollars in revenues wisely spent? Is your opinion even asked, or for that matter, considered?

Let's see. Were our massive intelligence agencies able to stop an attack in New York City on September 11, 2001? Tremendous intelligence and surveillance was in place and working hard prior to this historic date. In fact, we didn't need to have a terrorist attack of this magnitude to justify surveillance on foreigners and citizens—it was already being done. But now it is justified and is being sold to us as not only legal, but in our best interests.

This wonderful intelligence continues today, costing even more billions, and it cannot guarantee that we have any additional personal security. However, we are not only asked, but expected to give up our personal rights and liberties as some kind of righteous cause to save the nation.

Before we went to war with Iraq in 2003, it was clear that Iran and North Korea were serious threats. They had made real strides in developing weapons of mass destruction and would have the capability to deliver these weapons in a matter of time. But rather than take on either of these countries, we went after Saddam Hussein. Why? We are told the decision was based on reliable intelligence information. Reliable? Furnished to us by the Central Intelligence Agency—the same people who failed to bring us the plot to take down the World Trade Towers.

Today, we are faced with serious problems coming from Iran, North Korea, and elsewhere. As for Iraq, well, are things better because we went in? I, for one, don't really know, but I am hard pressed to think so.

At the time, we were told that Iraq had weapons of mass destruction and that going to war in Iraq would help to preserve American freedom. That sounded good. After the war was underway, and after we discovered that there were no weapons of mass destruction, the sales pitch changed. We were reminded that we were there to preserve "Iraqi freedom." Sounds like a bait-and-switch tactic, and not even a sophisticated one.

The problem is, the Iraqi people weren't really free to begin with, not with Saddam in business; but now we are to believe it is the American taxpayers' responsibility to pay for a war, put the nation trillions of dollars in debt, and waste thousands of American lives and the lives of others to save "Iraqi freedom." What happened to *our* freedom?

After the job we did on Hussein in 1990, it is difficult to believe that he could have amassed the materials and means to become a nuclear threat in the world without our detection via the massive intelligence-gathering apparatus we have spent jillions to support. And, I might remind the reader that this was after we gave the intelligence agencies unlimited power and increased funding. So, perhaps more money and more power does not equal more security for Americans.

However, six weeks after 9/11, the Patriot Act was passed. As previously mentioned, this document basically boils down to the Anti-Constitution of the United States of America, and in this 342-page document that was not read by most members of Congress before they signed it, our rights guaranteed in the U.S. Constitution have been effectively nullified. And, worse yet, a third of this document is about money, not terrorists—but your money.

Under the guise of anti-money-laundering, the government has devised a way to criminalize anyone they feel like pursuing, complete with extreme criminal and civil penalties if convicted. The legislation that was incorporated into the Patriot Act can be used effectively against the average citizen. But, even before you go to jail—and to add insult to injury, as they say—without the necessity for due process of law on your side, all your assets can be confiscated. Before you get to court, you could be penniless and unable to afford a lawyer, because all your worldly wealth has been taken away from you. Does this sound like America, or like another country from the pages of history? And what happened to personal sovereignty?

This is not my personal crusade. An awareness of these issues is now growing with vigor in the United States. Urgent countermeasures are required to meet the challenges presented today if we are to prevent the further decline and possibly the fall of the United States of America, or minimally, the loss of our own personal, individual sovereignty. Outspoken and undaunted people such as former Congressman Robert E. Bauman, JD, author of some straightforward books on these topics, are contributing to the awareness and the truth about what is really taking place in the United States today. Mr. Bauman is also legal counsel to a worthy effort known as the Sovereign Society, chaired by investment advisor and author John Pugsley. And, as a former Congressman, Bauman knows firsthand about the machinations of Washington.

The fight not only seems to be external—real threats and manufactured ones—but also is attacking from within—insidious attempts to strip us of our personal rights. It has come from all directions recently and we are bombarded on a regular basis—the effects of which promise to leave us with nothing.

Our situation is reminiscent of the Roman Empire on the verge of collapse. As great a civilization as it proved to be, it could not overcome the external and internal pressures that began to work on it daily during its evolution. The events today threaten to undermine our entire society, too, and may contribute to the collapse of global civilization. It wouldn't be the first time it has happened on this planet.

Not only are we faced with change due to adverse negative effects from foreign enemies, but worse, we are confronted with our own complacency.

We have empowered the bureaucrats with our tax money and our willingness to give them unbridled control over us at the federal level, rather than take responsibility into our own hands, at the local level, where true democracy lives. The politicians are telling us what we want to hear to appease the savage beasts, that is to say "we the people . . ." We have always possessed the power to keep government in check and accountable. Instead we seem poised to accept the big lies.

The Roman Empire collapsed under its own weight of ineptness and corrupt leadership—that and a presumptuous society. The once vibrant Roman economy was destroyed, law and order had disintegrated, and many of the educational institutions had vanished. And, with a little effort from its enemies, the barbarians stood at the gates to Rome and banged their way in. There wasn't much to stop them when the final days came. It was the collapse of a great civilization and it took humankind a thousand years to recover from the event. In the end, their demise was swift.

The *U.S. Government Guide to Surviving Terrorism* (New York: Barnes & Noble, 2003) is a compilation of official U.S. government documents addressing the subject. It is essentially a survival guide for Americans on how to live through and cope with the effects of terrorism. In the introduction to the manual by H. Keith Melton from the Center for Counterterrorism Studies, he closes with the following paragraph:

> *Is the terrorist threat "real enough" that extraordinary measures for survival may be necessary? The answer is an unqualified* "yes!" *Communication intercepts about impending terrorist attacks against the United States and her allies are received daily. The question is not* if *future attacks will occur, but rather when and where the next attack will happen. If you don't take precautions, you may become a victim! You've been wise enough to purchase this manual. Now, use it thoughtfully and deliberately to prepare each member of your family with the information they will need to survive.*

It appears that the U.S. government recognizes that the barbarians are near, which brings us to the proverbial crossroads. Whether there is time to make a difference, or whether we have the inclination to try to change the course of our country, there is one thing we must do immediately. We must decide, while we still have the semblance of personal sovereignty, what action we will take into our own hands.

As citizens, we have an obligation to preserve our national sovereignty. And how, you ask, can this be accomplished? By starting with the problem. We must downsize the bureaucratic machine that has taken over our lives. I hope that this book will give you some inspiration.

Meanwhile, as free people, we also have the inherent right to protect ourselves from the ravages of time and the prevailing winds of change that threaten our personal existence. And, as a sovereign individual, first and foremost, your right and obligation is to yourself and your family, and that right is the greater right, and more important than that of national sovereignty. Maybe that is why 250,000 patriotic Americans are choosing to leave the country every year—because they still can, and they know they *must.* Only free people can make a choice like that.

So, let's set sail, and together explore the blue seas of your offshore options.

PART TWO

Building a Solid Offshore Financial Fortress

Presented here are some of the best strategies available today to benefit people in the offshore financial and investment arena, and all deserve a closer examination. With these tools in hand, you can tailor your own strategy for building a solid offshore financial fortress. The following chapters will provide clear and motivating reasons for banking and investing offshore today.

9

THE BENEFITS OF GOING OFFSHORE

- Opportunity to diversify investments
- Strategies to defer taxes
- Strong asset protection
- Tax-free compound investment earnings
- Greater privacy and flexibility in banking offshore
- Higher investment returns and interest rates
- Reduced taxation
- Avoidance of currency restrictions
- Increased business opportunities
- Currency diversification
- Greater safety and security in banking and investments
- Maximization of financial and personal privacy
- Avoidance of the possibility of U.S. securities markets closing due to an unforeseen national emergency (e.g., terrorism)
- Circumvention of potential failure of U.S. financial institutions, and U.S. guarantee agencies—again!
- Immediate and long-term asset protection
- In some cases, avoidance of U.S. reporting requirements to the IRS and U.S. Treasury
- Greater convenience when traveling
- Exercising of your rights and freedoms to do the things that are still legal to increase your financial position and security
- Avoidance of disclosing your nationality or political alliance with others
- Keeping your physical location secret
- Easy access to your offshore funds no matter where you are
- Reduced estate taxes and security for your family's economic future through offshore estate planning

The list could run for pages!

Many of these benefits will give immediate relief and peace of mind from problems we face or potentially face in the United States, including potential collapse of the economy and financial institutions, overt government oppression, evaporating civil liberties, rapidly dwindling financial and personal privacy, discrimination, excessive government; domestic lawsuits, exposed business and personal assets, and the threat of crime.

With this book to guide you in your quest to avoid unnecessary personal hardship in any of its many forms, you can begin to gain the benefits of going offshore. You will effectively become your own best champion, waging your own defense against the erosion that threatens your prosperity, security, and very existence.

Not all the ideas, concepts, and possibilities presented here, however beneficial, will interest everyone, or apply to everyone's specific circumstances.

Among the many personal and financial strategies presented in these pages, however, numerous good matches and choices are available for virtually each person and each set of goals. Much of what follows includes little-known but effective strategies of particular interest to U.S. citizens in most circumstances.

10

BEST STRATEGIES FOR GOING OFFSHORE: PERSONAL AND FINANCIAL LIFESTYLE CHANGES

How, exactly, does an individual "go offshore?" Essentially, most people who do so are taking the step of moving part or all of their finances, investments, and assets offshore while still maintaining their lifestyle in their country of citizenship, such as the United States. This is the most common and simplest method, and this alone will provide the benefits that most people seek in going offshore.

A further option exists that a growing number of people, including 250,000 Americans each year, are choosing: They take, not just their assets and investments offshore, but their families, too, by leaving their home country and creating a lifestyle elsewhere as a happy expatriate (expat).

Whether you wish only to protect a few assets and reduce your tax burden, or are interested in the big leap as an expat or something in between, a detailed view of all the options follows here.

The ultimate goal is to reduce taxes, protect your assets, secure your investments, plan for retirement, and preserve your personal privacy and sovereignty. Sounds like a lot to accomplish, but, if you have the desire and use this book as a road map, you can get offshore today—safely and legally.

The choices you make in this process will be determined by what you are hoping to achieve. Nearly anyone can benefit from having an offshore bank account, which provides a fast and simple means for getting at least part of your finances and assets offshore without time-consuming planning. And in the right banking haven, your money will receive ironclad protection from lawsuits, creditors, angry spouses, or unexpected surprises from your own government. Think of reasons *you* want to protect your money. With the simple act of, say, opening an offshore bank account by mail, you have made a significant move to financially protecting yourself and your family. With this account in place, you will have tremendous banking and investment resources at your fingertips and utmost confidentiality. You can even seek out non-U.S. investments not normally accessible to U.S. investors and keep your money in a foreign currency like the solid Swiss franc, or multiple foreign currencies, thereby hedging against the declining U.S. dollar. The difference is your gain.

Without leaving your armchair, you can take numerous and relatively simple steps to go offshore and instantly avail yourself of exciting new opportunities. Aside from opening an offshore bank account, even the smallest investor can benefit from many safe and lucrative investments not found in the United States. These can provide a secure offshore nest egg that will grow while you sleep, with a high degree of asset protection and without complicated and expensive financial planning. In the pages that follow, I describe a wide range of offshore opportunities, most of which are available to you without leaving the comfort of your living room.

Part Two of this book is aptly named "Building a Solid Offshore Financial Fortress." You have already taken the first step by recognizing that reading the information explored here may provide solutions to your concerns. Now is your chance to take the next steps to securing a better future, and getting started takes little effort.

Be prudent: Keep your plans to yourself. Don't advertise your intentions. Share only what is necessary to accomplish your goals for your personal life and business affairs, whether it be with family, friends, neighbors, business associates, or the professionals whom you engage. Some things will be necessary to share to get the expertise you need, but stick to the point. The old adage "loose lips sink ships" applies here. Insulate your affairs like a submarine, compartmentalizing your activities for better protection, and keep the details to yourself. In this arena, like most of life, you never know what might turn up to haunt you later. Going offshore, financially and physically, involves major steps for accomplishment, as we shall explore, but in no way would acting less than prudent be wise. *Au contraire.*

11

EXPATRIATING

Arranging secure offshore banking and investments, as we shall see, are the first steps, and perhaps the only steps a person may want or need to take. But for those who are interested or later may become interested in the next phase, let's look at the concept of expatriating. Some may want to consider it in anticipation of potential future national problems that could affect their lives; others may have personal goals related to offshore benefits that may be augmented by taking the big leap; and some simply have a desire to retire overseas. If any of this sounds good, you need to think ahead to more advanced ideas on going offshore. These strategies require altering your current lifestyle to maximize the benefits and opportunities, but when you consider the numbers who are choosing to expatriate, you might guess that for many, the change is worth the effort.

Becoming an expatriate? Wow. How would you begin? Well, this course of action will simply pick up where your initial steps left off. Once your banking and investments are safely offshore, the next step is to physically move offshore, taking yourself, your family, and your personal effects, and claiming your new life. This phase may require considerable time and planning to implement, so if at some point you determine that this is a real option, then you must look at the alternatives.

What should you consider doing? Well, you might begin by moving part or all of your earning capacity offshore. That may be a challenge depending on your job or the career you are in, but many Americans today have ideal income-producing activities that are highly adaptable to going offshore. This process should begin before permanently leaving the country.

Many jobs can easily be converted into your own business, or you can develop your talents into a small business. In the United States today, many people have expanded their entrepreneurial talents and have done very well. These skills in starting a small business are perfect for moving your income offshore. With today's state-of-the-art communications and computers, there are very few moneymaking activities that can't become virtual, or be adapted to operate from virtually anywhere. You can take your talents and become a consultant in any field and perform the same services from afar. Maybe your current employer would be willing to retain your services as a consultant-at-large rather than as an employee so you could perform your job function from anywhere. This service could be rendered through your offshore corporation.

In Chapter 24, I discuss starting an offshore business that can be coupled with e-commerce, the ideal combination for your future career or business. These activities can easily be conducted using a tax haven like Belize as your business base, while living virtually anywhere. When your business is established, your cash flow and personal income can funnel offshore through a no-tax or low-tax haven like Nevis or Belize, as an example, and on further into your bank and investment accounts, securely salted away in a money haven like Switzerland, Liechtenstein, Austria, or Andorra. This arrangement will minimize your financial exposure to potential problems in the United States.

You may even wish to purchase a second home in another country as a vacation home. Should the opportunity or need arise sometime in the future, you may want it to be your permanent residence, at which time you can receive tax credits for your housing expenses. You may want to set up your retirement plan offshore, too, and structure it to be judgment-free so that your retirement income never reaches the United States.

At this point, your lifelines to the United States are all but free, and you are probably feeling a sense of personal achievement and firm control over your life. There is one exception: You are still a U.S. taxpayer. You have achieved financial diversification and asset protection, yes, and possibly a freer and improved lifestyle with lower living expenses, but you are still obligated to pay income tax on your worldwide income.

But wait, there is good news! By the sheer act of leaving the United States, you have set in motion an important tax strategy.

12

THE $80,000 ANNUAL LOOPHOLE

That's right! If you are living overseas, you can earn up to $80,000 a year tax-free and so can your spouse, for a total of $160,000 per year in the case of a couple. This income can be derived from overseas employment or from your own foreign-based business. Two simple qualification requirements must be met to exercise the $80,000 annual offshore tax-free loophole provided under Internal Revenue Code 6:

1. A bona fide residency test—if you are a legal resident of a foreign country and have lived there for at least a full year; or,
2. A physical presence test—if you have spent at least 330 days in a foreign country or countries, out of 365 days in any 12-month period.

The burden is on you to prove that you have a new "tax home" in another country, no matter whether that situation will actually subject you to taxes in your new country of residence. Naturally, an IRS form is required to be filed annually. It is Form 2555 and should be sent with your U.S. tax return.

To prove that you have established a tax home in a foreign country, you will need to pass one of the two preceding tests, and there are certain measures that you can take to prove that you meet one of these two criteria to qualify for the $80,000 loophole. Here they are.

BONA FIDE RESIDENCY TEST

Where do you live when you are overseas? A property lease could help prove your stay. Did you take personal belongings typical for your intended stay? You could document your move, thus showing you physically moved to the new tax home. Some countries will give you a one-time tax break for importing personal belongings. The status of your U.S. property sends a signal to the IRS. If you left your home vacant and did not rent or sell it, it appears as though you are not leaving the country for long, in which case, you are not establishing a tax home overseas. Any type of personal and business documentation—obtaining a local driver's license, local property lease, or purchase; paying utility bills in your name; meeting local requirements of various kinds, establishing a foreign business, securing a job—any and all will help support your move and claim to the $80,000 exemption. Even proving your local involvement in social matters can help.

As for taxes in your new tax home country, if you choose a country with no or low taxes, you are really bucks up after you qualify for the $80k loophole. But don't claim that you are not a local resident with the foreign government for tax purposes or you will immediately send up a red flag to the IRS. Better yet, you may want to consider the alternative test.

PHYSICAL PRESENCE TEST

Here you have a better chance, in fact, the ideal situation, short of renouncing your U.S. citizenship, to eliminate U.S. taxes, by qualifying for the $80,000 exemption *and* avoiding foreign national income taxes. In this scenario, you satisfy the physical residence test for the IRS's sake, by living outside the United States for at least 330 days a year.

To avoid being a taxable resident in your new tax home country, should it have significant taxes that you wish to avoid, you may want to spend part of your 330 days in a second foreign country, or on a boat, or enjoy the entire time in Andorra. If you choose two countries that don't tax residents on national income taxes until a person has lived there for at least six months, you can split the 330-day stay so you don't overextend yourself in either, subjecting yourself to their taxes. You would claim, of course, not to be a resident, and therefore not subject to be taxed as one. This would be especially important if local taxes are high. On the other hand, most foreign countries tax residents only on income earned within the country. If you are using a tax haven for business purposes, once again, preferably a no-tax haven or low-tax haven, then you can circumvent the tax home country's income taxes because your income will be derived from outside the country.

Further, you would need to document the preceding to satisfy the physical presence test. You could start by opening a local bank account in the country that you claim as your tax home. An employment contract covering the period of stay outside the United States would show your need and intent to be overseas. Your own offshore business activities could require you to be in these other countries and would be easy for you to substantiate. Document your foreign residence with a rental or lease agreement for a period matching your intended stay. The nice thing about this test is that you are only required to stay away 330 days of the year—the rest of the time you can visit the United States and still qualify for the exemption. Needless to say, you would not want to do anything to disrupt your well-established and documented foreign existence while on your return U.S. trips.

You also may travel to other foreign countries while maintaining your tax home, but take care not to do anything that would jeopardize your status.

The $80,000 loophole is a significant tax incentive to expatriate if you do it correctly, and this should not be difficult. You have a big financial motive for restructuring your personal and financial affairs by using this tax break to your advantage as long as possible. This move, coupled with the strategies outlined here for going offshore, can increase your cash position and give you greater personal financial liquidity while potentially opening up new opportunities for investment.

13

NEW CITIZENSHIP AND RENOUNCING YOUR U.S. CITIZENSHIP

Renouncing your U.S. citizenship is the only true way to get out of paying U.S. taxes, and with the exception of a few possible strings attached, the process is very much achievable. For anyone who faces significant income taxes and a desire to leave the United States, this is a viable option.

Depending on how you structure your post-U.S. life, it is quite possible to avoid personal income taxes entirely. Find a nice no-tax alternative country for securing *new* citizenship, like Dominica or Saint Kitts and Nevis, keep your offshore business in the same one, or better yet for further diversity, use yet another no-tax haven like Belize for business purposes, and keep your personal banking and investments in Switzerland, Liechtenstein, Austria, Panama, or even Andorra. As with the other strategies presented here for going offshore, the sooner the better, while the opportunities still exist. All good things are subject to change.

The Internal Revenue Service could perceive people in a high tax bracket who want to renounce their citizenship as wanting to avoid taxes. The government has developed some posturing to discourage and limit this practice. A person with over $100,000-a-year income at the time of renouncing U.S. citizenship might still be required to pay income taxes for 10 consecutive years thereafter. There is also the rather unlikely possibility that should your reason for leaving the United States be "tax motivated," that you could be permanently exiled, that is, unable to ever return to the United States. It remains to be seen if this tactic is constitutional and this has yet to be tested.

But *not* returning to the United States may not be a problem either. Your children and grandchildren may like coming to visit you during the holidays in sunny Corfu in the Greek Islands, where the government will not tax your retirement income. Or, they may enjoy speaking Spanish with the locals when they find you have taken up painting in San Miguel de Allende, Mexico. Probably they'll want to join you on that leisurely sailing trip through the Caribbean while you country-shop for your next retreat. After years of paying high taxes and working hard to legally avoid them, not being able to go back to the United States may be a nonissue. It could be just what the doctor would order.

Even if you wish to renounce your U.S. citizenship after you have expatriated your personal and financial affairs offshore, you must first obtain new citizenship in a favorable country, preferably with no income tax and other taxes. There are many possibilities, but Dominica and Saint Kitts and Nevis can give you citizenship as fast as within 60 to 90 days—and with it comes their passport, which in both cases is good for visa-free travel to 90 countries. Other citizenship opportunities exist, but without guarantees, unlike these two countries, which promote their Economic Citizenship Programs aggressively. Both of these countries, at the time of this writing, are excellent for this purpose. Neither of them imposes personal income tax, and both of them permit dual citizenship; nor will they report your activities or status back to the U.S. government.

Once you obtain your new citizenship and your life is now entirely offshore, you can renounce your U.S. citizenship whenever you wish (see Part Four: "Offshore Citizenship and Retirement Opportunities").

This is the final step in expatriating, and to get there, you should take it in steps, as outlined here. Prior to renouncing your U.S. citizenship, you should seek professional advisors with specific expertise in this area.

14

EIGHT WAYS TO SUNDAY

Citizens worldwide all face taxation from their own countries, but unlike most other countries, the U.S. taxes the worldwide income of U.S. citizens and resident aliens. This is the single biggest obstacle when implementing tax strategies. You can avoid this problem if you successfully renounce your U.S. citizenship. In any event, your objective is to beat the tax octopus to minimize your tax obligations and responsibilities regardless of where you are a citizen. The challenge is to avoid the following eight ways in which you could find yourself subject to taxes in other countries:

1. Residence
2. Domicile
3. Citizenship
4. Marital status
5. Income source
6. Location of assets
7. Timing
8. Status of beneficiaries

RESIDENCE

Many countries permit you to stay up to 182 days of the year without being subject to their national income tax. At some point, every country defines how many days constitute your being a resident for tax purposes. When switching citizenships, it would be advantageous to select a country like Dominica or Saint Kitts and Nevis where no income tax is imposed on new citizens. You can still travel and live elsewhere as desired, at which time you will want to consider the residence criteria.

DOMICILE

Your domicile of origin is the country where you became a citizen at your birth, as opposed to your residence, which is where you live. The latter can fluctuate frequently, and for tax reasons is usually redetermined annually. For tax purposes, the definition for domicile can vary greatly between countries and affect your tax situation. Know before you go what to expect in your intended country of arrival so you can plan your tax strategy.

CITIZENSHIP

It is important to remember that as a U.S. citizen, it does not matter where your residence is—you are subject to U.S. taxes on money earned anywhere in the world. The only way out of this would be to renounce your U.S. citizenship. But first, you had best have an alternative citizenship in place or you will find yourself without a country and in a strange and difficult legal quagmire. This happened to Garry Davis in 1948, founder of World Service Authority, in Washington, DC, and author of *My Country Is the World* (New York: G. P. Putnam's Sons, 1961). An American citizen can legally obtain dual citizenship and a second passport. At one time, this act alone would automatically cause you to lose your U.S. citizenship, but not any longer. Your tax dollars are too important!

MARITAL STATUS

This can affect your tax situation and your ability to be a tax exile. Likely, you and your spouse will need to be on the same page if you want to successfully expatriate and implement some of these tax-reduction strategies. And, further, if your marriage took place in a community property state or a foreign jurisdiction with community property laws, or if you had a marital home in one of these places, then your efforts to avoid taxes as an expatriate may be hindered and require professional planning.

INCOME SOURCE

When considering living in another country, you should know how that government taxes earned income. Governments usually levy taxes based on the source of income, so there must be a source test to determine what is taxable. One method is to tax all sources of income from within the country no matter where the earner resides at the time. If the recipient is a nonresident, then the government requires the payor to withhold taxes and remit them directly to the tax-revenue folks. Other countries determine whether the income was earned within the country, and if so, tax accordingly, and then exempt foreign-source income. This territorial method is common in tax haven countries.

LOCATION OF ASSETS

Assets can be taxed by virtue of their physical location rather than where the owner resides or is a citizen. Be sure to locate assets in friendly no-tax or low-tax jurisdictions. Often it is best to keep assets in a favorable venue outside your own country of citizenship or residence to avoid more than just taxation—such as lawsuits, creditors, or confiscation. Sometimes it is wise to hold assets in a corporation or trust and not in your own name. Certain assets such as real estate and physical business operations are difficult or impossible to relocate, but these can be owned by an offshore entity if everything makes sense. Even so, these assets can still be easier to attack legally as they pose a physical challenge to relocate. Assets such as securities, precious metals, and personal effects are easily movable and can be relocated at will. Ownership can be structured to your advantage and valuables can be stored in secure bank vaults or private vaults in foreign countries, or other safe places out of the grasp of others.

TIMING

As in the United States, taxes in virtually every venue worldwide are based on established periods for which taxes are due and payable. It may be that you can postpone receiving income until you make your next move and thus are no longer subject to the tax. It is better still if you can stay in no-tax haven countries and avoid taxes altogether.

Also, it can work to your advantage if you have several taxable foreign entities with different tax deadlines. This could give you some flexibility among these countries. You may even deliberately divert more income into one source than another, or from sources you control to yourself, because of tax deadlines or a tax rate that is more advantageous in one country over another.

STATUS OF BENEFICIARIES

At the time of death or when assets are distributed to your designated beneficiaries, they will likely be subject to taxation regardless of whether you expatriated or renounced your U.S. citizenship. This is true if your beneficiaries are U.S. citizens, or the citizens of other high-tax countries, because they will still be exposed to the taxes of their own country. You can avoid this if family members renounced their citizenship at the same time you did and thus are no longer taxpayers of that country. Advance offshore estate planning can also reduce or eliminate your heirs' tax liability. Consult a competent professional in this area as you execute your expatriating plans.

If you seek expert advise in areas such as legal, tax, investment, and expatriating, many competent professionals can be found throughout the pages of this book and by referring to the Offshore Evaluation Service (OES) in Part Four and the Appendix.

15

T-7 TAX HAVENS: THE GREEN LIST OF THE WORLD'S BEST OFFSHORE HAVENS

The collective countries known as the *G-7*—the industrialized nations of Canada, France, Germany, Italy, Japan, the United Kingdom, and the United States—are also some of the highest tax nations in the world. These seven giants are not the only tax-happy zealots. Australia and other nations, and organizations such as the European Union (EU), the Organisation for Economic Co-operation and Development (OECD), the Financial Action Tax Force (FATF), and the United Nations (UN), are all working to thwart or even crush the offshore opportunities of tax-haven nations. The UN also wants to be the new Global Internal Revenue Service, and if that's not enough, they also want to infringe on your Bill of Rights and the Second Amendment of your Constitution and take your gun away.

Well, if that's how they feel, it seems only appropriate to have some counterbalance by providing a convenient reference for readers and others about the most advantageous havens to bank, invest from, and put your money for profit, privacy, and protection. If only we could take away the *taxman's* guns.

The OECD has its blacklist, so here is my "Green List" of the world's best offshore tax havens, which I call the *T-7.* This exclusive list of seven excellent countries includes tax havens, money havens, asset havens, and offshore banking centers. I have evaluated them using factors that I explain later in this book including the all-important issues of confidentiality and safety, and I will revise the list annually.

In order of preference, here are my favorite money havens:

1. Switzerland
2. Liechtenstein

3. Austria
4. Panama
5. Saint Kitts and Nevis
6. Belize
7. Hong Kong

The top four are my favorite offshore banking centers, and the bottom four are my favorite tax havens and venues from which to conduct offshore business. Panama overlaps and is excellent in both areas. All seven can be considered money and asset havens. None of the T-7 countries have signed a Tax Information Exchange Agreement (TIEA) with the United States. This is favorable (see Part Three: Today's Tax Havens).

Here, then are some of the highlights and characteristics of each of the T-7 countries.

SWITZERLAND

This Alpine haven is one of the most politically and economically stable countries in the world.

Unlike the United States, which went off the gold standard in 1971, the Swiss government has mandated that the Swiss National Bank, under the Swiss Constitution, *must* back the Swiss franc, the country's solid currency, with accumulated reserves including gold. The value of the gold alone far exceeds the currency in circulation. This, coupled with a low growth in the money supply, contributes to economic stability, minimizing threats of inflation and deflation. This is a currency to hold, like gold and other precious metals, as a hedge against inflation and economic uncertainty.

The dollar has lost 300 percent value against the Swiss franc over the past 35 years. And, it stands to lose more. The Swiss franc has been the strongest currency in the world for decades, even rivaling the Japanese yen and the former German mark.

The Swiss system of government places emphasis on self-government and democracy, as it should, and it begins at the local level. Citizens meet and have a hand in important local government decisions. And they control their government, not the other way around, through a national referendum and initiatives. The central government has traditionally been weak, as it has not been empowered to be otherwise. The Swiss system could be considered a model for democracy, rather than what is being touted on the world today as democracy. The trend toward globalization is threatening to compromise even Switzerland, which may one day find its local Swiss democracy and economy undermined by the economic developments of the "new world order"—basically the attempted evolution into a centralized global economy, in direct contradiction to what democracy is all about.

As an aside: This trend directly contradicts the tenets of democracy. The question is, what form of government will preside over the new world order, as the political apparatus will need to catch up with the new global economy. Will it be a central global government? Frightening indeed.

Swiss banking is unparalleled. The country remains politically neutral and defends its 1934 Bank Secrecy Act with strict penalties. There is also the Swiss insurance secrecy law, which covers policyholders. They have staunchly opposed the outside forces coming from the G-7, the OECD, and the EU. In recent years and under tighter legislation, bankers are now required by law to report "suspicious" transactions. This may make sense on the face of it, but involves a subjective decision with the potential to erode Swiss secrecy on a case-by-case basis. But, although the opposition continues to push hard to change Swiss ways, the Swiss can be stubborn when it comes to changing their traditions. Financial safety for their customers is the cornerstone of their success. That is why, today, over one third of the world's assets are managed from Switzerland. Swiss bankers are the highly trusted money managers to the world.

LIECHTENSTEIN

This principality is in good company, lying between two other T-7 offshore havens (Switzerland and Austria) and is politically and economically stable. Liechtenstein is the world's oldest tax haven; it passed asset protection legislation as early as the 1920s. Liechtenstein has strict bank secrecy and only in the case of criminal prosecution will it be penetrated. The Swiss franc is the national currency.

Although the country boasts only 16 banks, it is an important international financial center. No companies domiciled in Liechtenstein are subject to income tax on foreign-source income. This little nation is a popular venue for holding and domiciliary companies and is home to some unique corporate and trust structures. One is the *Anstalt,* commonly known as the "Establishment," which has the option to be a stock company and the *Stiftungs,* a private foundation. These structures and others are described in greater detail later in this section of the book. Blacklisted by the OECD for refusal to cooperate, Liechtenstein adamantly refuses to succumb to outside pressures. As 37-year-old Crown Prince Alois said with a smile, "Bank secrecy is very firmly anchored in the population."

AUSTRIA

This is another attractive European haven with a long tradition of bank secrecy. In recent years at the behest of EU pressures, sadly, Austria eliminated two unique accounts, the anonymous *Sparbuch,* a bearer type passbook account, and the anonymous *Wertpapierbuch,* a bearer type passbook account coupled with a securities and commodities trading account. Regardless, Austria still prevails as an important money haven with strict bank secrecy. Austria is also an excellent expatriate haven. You can enjoy Austria's many charms and stay close to your money and your gold Philharmonics (see Part Four: "Profiles of Retirement Havens and Foreign Residency").

PANAMA

A stable democracy with Latin-style politics and a free economy, Panama is the Latin version of Switzerland or Hong Kong. This narrow country connecting Central and South America is one of the oldest tax havens in the world, dating back to the 1920s. Today, it is a modern international financial center with as strict bank secrecy legislation as can be found anywhere. There is a tight fraternity among Panamanian bankers. Panama is a superior tax haven, with no corporate or personal tax on income from foreign sources, and it is growing in popularity with expatriates who find the country friendly and the cost of living reasonable. Panama is home to the Panama Canal and is a favorable flag-of-convenience country for yachtsmen and shipping companies. The Panama corporation has armadillo-like qualities and is useful in international business where strong insulation is desired.

NEVIS

This is a pure no-tax haven in the spirit of what a tax haven was originally meant to be. A little two-island nation, known formally as Saint Christopher-Nevis (Saint Kitts and Nevis), it is completely independent, having no ties with Britain or any other imperial nation and makes its laws according to its whims. Nevis is a proactive tax haven with modern corporate and trust legislation. Nevis strongly supports its offshore industry and staunchly protects the offshore trade. The strict bank secrecy in Nevis is close to impenetrable. There are no detracting treaties or agreements with the United States or any international organization. There are good legal, financial, and business support services, including services for offshore e-commerce business. Nevis, Belize, and the Cook Islands are three of the best jurisdictions for establishing an asset protection trust. Bearer shares are permitted to be issued by Nevis International Business Companies (IBCs) and beneficial owners can enjoy complete anonymity. This haven is an excellent choice for the quick redomiciliation of a foreign company. For a swift second citizenship, Nevis and Dominica both have first-rate Economic Citizenship Programs. Although offshore banking services are limited in Nevis, the Ministry of Finance has been working to establish good relations with Swiss bankers for the benefit of Nevis companies.

BELIZE

Like Nevis, Belize is an attractive no-tax haven with progressive corporate legislation. Once a British colony, Belize gained its independence in 1981. This tropical Central American country has been aggressively promoting itself as an international financial center, and the future looks promising. There is strict bank secrecy and there are no treaties or agreements with the United States or other international organizations. The OECD had blacklisted Belize for a while in 2000 until the country made a few concessions, but nothing dramatic. However, your IBC will not be able to issue bearer shares and Belize no longer has an Economic Citizenship Program. Still, the Supreme Court defends their laws and protects depositors against outside attacks. This business-friendly haven offers a wide variety of offshore financial services, and some forthcoming offshore legislation will allow Belize to expand into a completely independent offshore financial center providing many more services. Belize is an excellent offshore e-commerce base, and has one of the strongest asset protection trust laws anywhere.

HONG KONG

This world-class banking center and tax haven provides strict bank secrecy and is an excellent location for conducting international business in the Far East and elsewhere. Even with Beijing's potential influence, China has done a pretty fair job at keeping its hands out of this successful capitalist enclave, as was agreed in their 99-year lease with Britain. It was also agreed that Hong Kong would continue to operate under the status quo for 50 years beyond the expiration of the lease, which ended in 1997, without interference from China. If this situation should change, two Asian alternatives to Hong Kong would be Singapore and Malaysia. Hong Kong is a major shipping port. It is also the Western gateway to China.

More information on the T-7 tax havens can be found in Part Three: "Today's Tax Havens," under the individual country profiles, complete with offshore business contacts.

16

SELECTING THE BEST TAX HAVEN FOR YOUR PLANS

Here are 12 important factors for gauging a tax haven's suitability for your purposes and the criteria for determining the T-7 tax havens. When researching potential tax havens, have your foreign contacts provide you with current information on their jurisdiction's status; changes frequently occur and often go unnoticed. An offshore professional will gladly provide you with what you need to make an intelligent decision. The countries profiled in Part Three cover 40 tax havens, all worth further discussion. Less notable venues have been eliminated to save you time and unnecessary deliberation. All tax havens in this book are still viable and open to consideration or, in the case of certain once-strong havens that have recently experienced significant changes such as the Bahamas, they must be addressed even though they are no longer recommended for use.

Your object should be to secure the most advantages from the tax haven you have selected while satisfying your primary objective. These are the most important criteria to consider in choosing your haven:

1. Tax structure
2. Political and economic stability
3. Exchange controls
4. Treaties
5. Government attitude
6. Modern corporation laws
7. Communication and transportation
8. Banking, professional, and support services
9. Legal system
10. Secrecy and confidentiality

11. Investment incentives and opportunities
12. Location

The country profiles in this book give a reasonable amount of information to help you narrow down your selection. The fastest way may be to start with the T-7 list of the world's best offshore havens; if none of them seem to fit your plans, you can take a more thorough look into the many other tax havens and their unique characteristics.

TAX STRUCTURE

This is probably the single most important factor in considering a tax haven, although several others should be seriously considered as well. Tax havens commonly have two tax systems, one for local business and one for those to whom they cater in their offshore trade. As an offshore client, you need to know what taxes, if any, will affect your banking or what taxes, if any, might be imposed on the corporation you establish for business purposes. There are no-tax havens, foreign-sourced income havens, tax treaty countries, and special use tax havens.

POLITICAL AND ECONOMIC STABILITY

Stability is a serious consideration in choosing any tax haven. However nice Montserrat might have seemed, you wouldn't have wanted your offshore business located there when the lid blew off the volcano, taking much of the island with it. Nor do you want to be in Liberia, a tax haven that was dumped from my list due to endless murder and mayhem. Almost all the tax havens here are very stable, with the exception of Cyprus. But although the Turks and the Greeks apparently would rather not stop fighting, Cyprus has managed to hold its own as a tax haven, unlike a venue such as Nauru in the Central Pacific, which was yanked from international banking after it was discovered that their banking system was mostly a laundromat for the Russian mob.

EXCHANGE CONTROLS

Restricting the free flow of funds between countries is a form of governmental control and annoying to anyone having to conduct international business within these countries. "Flight capital" occurs frequently when people are restricted from freely moving their money in and out of their country. Let's hope we don't experience it in the United States anytime soon. However, it is possible. That is why you want to consider the potential negative repercussions of geopolitics on your finances, investments, and assets. Going offshore is the best way to avert these troubles. In recent history, many people have employed the same methods and then followed their money out of their country as well. Most serious banking centers and tax havens do not have exchange controls that would affect offshore business.

TREATIES

Know where your prospective tax havens stand on tax treaties, particularly ones signed with your own country. They are important when doing tax planning. Many tax havens impose a low or no tax on foreign earned income and have no tax treaties. Where there are tax treaties, your offshore business might be ideally suited to reap significant tax benefits. An ordinary tax treaty usually helps you escape double taxation. Another type of treaty is called a Tax Information Exchange Agreement (TIEA), but it is not really a tax treaty. The sole purpose of the TIEA is to permit the U.S. Internal Revenue Service (IRS) to obtain otherwise secret or highly confidential financial and other information from foreign financial institutions and from lawyers, for tax investigations against U.S. tax payers. The TIEA is being used to crack down on alleged offshore tax evasion, and many tax havens are expected to agree that it is in their interest to sign such an agreement. But it is not in your best interest.

The Mutual Legal Assistance Treaties (MLAT) are bilateral agreements used in criminal investigations to obtain information and evidence. Although many tax havens are party to this agreement, it does not cover tax evasion. A list of countries that have signed this type of treaty is included in Chapter 30. Consult a U.S. attorney who is well versed in these matters, or an offshore legal professional knowledgeable on how existing treaties with the United States would affect your offshore plans.

GOVERNMENT ATTITUDE

Political parties holding office can have a positive or negative effect on their offshore industry. Go with a tax haven that promotes the offshore field and the benefits of doing business from their venue. If an election process exists, transitions between administrations may go smoothly, and you won't have to run for cover. But, should you ever need to quickly redomicile an offshore corporation to another venue (which could be necessary for a variety of reasons), Nevis is an excellent choice, and the government will honor the original incorporation date of the company from the country from whence it came.

MODERN CORPORATION LAWS

Today, most tax havens have modernized their corporation laws and incorporation procedures to keep up with the stiff competition. Tax haven corporation laws often have features not found in U.S. corporations, and these usually afford more advantages and flexibility. The offshore corporate vehicle of choice is the international business corporation (IBC), which is specifically designed for offshore use by nonresidents, and is generally exempt from taxes. As for incorporation and annual maintenance costs, the fees are usually competitive to get into one, and reasonable to keep it alive. There are exceptions, such as in Bermuda and Switzerland where these costs are relatively hefty.

COMMUNICATION AND TRANSPORTATION

Unless you plan to retire or immigrate to your chosen tax haven country, or your business warrants shipping, chances are you won't be staying there for long, if at all, so transportation isn't too important. Most tax havens today have upgraded to state-of-the-art facilities so that conducting international business without being present should not be a problem. If you are doubtful, ask your tax haven contact.

BANKING, PROFESSIONAL, AND SUPPORT SERVICES

Top-notch banking, professional, and support services will make your life easier, especially if you are operating from long distance. Most of the tax havens have reliable experts in the field. If a recommendation or personal introduction is desired, for further information, refer to "Offshore Evaluation Service" in Part Four.

Banking offshore has been affected by outside influences, as well as by the internal changes the offshore venues may have experienced. Familiarize yourself with these developments and assess where your tax haven stands and may be headed tomorrow. The Bahamas and the Caymans were touted as ironclad tax havens, but both tanked quickly under pressure, giving in to outside influences.

LEGAL SYSTEM

Half of all tax havens are based on English common law, which is generally a good thing. The concept of confidentiality in financial transactions is customary, and even without secrecy laws, they will generally provide greater confidentiality than you experience in the United States. That is because many were former British protectorates or Crown Colonies, some of whose external affairs are still handled and protected by England. English common law has a long tradition and case law history from which to draw. In countries like Panama, Mexico, France, and elsewhere, civil law is the prevailing system, and is based on Napoleonic law, or "guilty until proven innocent."

Confidentiality is being eroded even in certain common law countries and some attacks on banking privacy are succeeding. In Great Britain, thanks to a special ruling recently passed, the U.K. Revenue (the British IRS equivalent), and Customs can now force banks and other financial institutions to turn over all financial records held in their databanks on their customers, all in the name of tax evasion prevention, even though there is little proof to substantiate the claims against individual depositors. This tactic is similar to the one used by the IRS against offshore debit and credit card holders. English Revenue and Customs wasted no time in exercising their new power, and for starters, have gone after Barclays Bank account holders, including their offshore accounts held in tax havens like Guernsey, Jersey, and the Isle of Man. These high-handed measures have become a trend and will get even worse as the G-7, the European Union, and other nations try to reduce mounting deficits as a result of pension crises, escalating health and welfare costs, and all-around poor fiscal management by many governments. Talk of "harmonizing taxes" and "creation of a level playing field" and "unfair tax competition" are all lines directed at eliminating the tax competition offered by lower-taxing countries. Only if these offshore avenues are significantly reduced or plugged can the high tax bodies of the world jack up taxes further to support their missions. Otherwise, they fear that even further revenues will be lost to tax havens and other lower taxing countries.

SECRECY AND CONFIDENTIALITY

Panama is a good example of a tax haven that is attractive for bank secrecy. There are statutory guarantees protecting financial privacy and providing a very high level of confidentiality. Stiff civil and criminal penalties help keep lips sealed. A handful of money havens stand out as having possibly the strictest secrecy laws anywhere. Many tax havens and banking centers, however, have succumbed to the pressures of the OECD and the United States, and have abandoned their secrecy policies, as with those tax havens that signed a Tax Information Exchange Agreement (TIEA).

The best money havens for maximum secrecy are the countries on my T-7 list, and, concerning this topic, I must also add Andorra. Although in terms of confidentiality these eight are my favorites, still others (such as Luxembourg, Vanuatu, and even Denmark) have secrecy laws and could be useful. Although all are subject to change, as with the T-7, they are likely to remain strong for some time.

Let the buyer beware. Even tax havens peddling secrecy do not want criminal elements. Secrecy can be penetrated under circumstances where criminal activity is involved.

INVESTMENT INCENTIVES AND OPPORTUNITIES

Tax havens have many attractive financial benefits and unique characteristics that draw business to these islands, enclaves, and legislative wonders. Some of these countries encourage onshore investment to develop industries in the hopes of creating new jobs and stimulating their own economies. These incentive programs frequently come in the form of tax holidays, grants, and loans.

LOCATION

Today's state-of-the-art communications have transcended the importance of where a tax haven might be located. The time zone will make a difference if you are far away, in which case, you will want to adjust your calling times to reach people during business hours. At times, I have found myself awake at all hours of the night to talk to people in certain parts of the world. Certain investors tend to stay close to home. The English use the Channel Islands; Americans like the Caribbean; Asians and Australians use the South Pacific and Asian tax havens; Africans might use Madagascar or the Seychelles. The Italians like Switzerland and Monaco, or so the story goes. The answer to which will be your best tax haven is to minimize your concern with location in favor of the most important factor—solving your financial objectives, wherever that may take you. You needn't limit your options because of your proximity to a tax haven. Language is occasionally a barrier, but professionals in most sophisticated banking centers and tax havens speak fluent English, the business language of the world.

17

ESTABLISHING AN OFFSHORE PRESENCE WITHOUT LEAVING HOME

THE OVERSEAS MAIL DROP

To go offshore implies action. You can initiate that quickly by implementing any of the ideas presented herein. Opening an offshore or foreign bank account is a proactive, fast, and easy means to get started. And, various offshore investments offer quick and safe solutions to getting all or part of your financial life offshore.

Regardless of your decision on which methods to employ, two thoughts are worth your immediate consideration. First, for the sake of enhanced privacy, especially if you are still living in the United States or another country you call home, you should maintain a mailing address in another country for sensitive mail such as bank and financial statements from foreign banks and other financial institutions, and confidential correspondence of all kinds. Mail postmarked from Zurich might provide a hint to the onlooker that you could have a bank account there, or at least raise some snoopy thoughts. In fact, snooping on mail is an old custom used by government people and others to discover some of your secrets. The CIA even has published a manual entitled *CIA Flaps and Seals Manual* that teaches agents how to spy on people's mail. The more oppressive a government is, the more likely it is to resort to these tactics, all of which can and do compromise your privacy. An inexpensive solution providing a higher degree of security, is to simply engage a mail-drop service in a foreign country. For Americans, Canada is an ideal location. The service can hold your mail for further instructions or automatically forward it per your advance instructions. A good mail-drop service will carefully follow your directions, and when forwarding mail to you, enclose it in another mailing envelope or box, and secure it well. Expect to pay a few hundred dollars a year for the service, plus the cost of postage. Most services will require a postage deposit. Provide as little personal information as required to engage the service.

Eden Press in Fountain Valley, California markets two directories that list hundreds of such services worldwide. They are *The Eden Directory of Private Mail Drops in the United States and 90 Foreign Countries* and the *Worldwide Mail-Drop Guide.* Both are excellent sources, giving full names, addresses, telephone and fax numbers, and good advice on how to best use your mail-drop for maximum privacy. These directories and online sources for additional overseas mail-drops and serviced offices worldwide are listed in Part Four on pages 280–281.

Your foreign bank or other financial institution may be willing to hold your mail until further instructed. This would be best, and then when needed, or on occasion, you can have them forward it to you at your mail-drop address. This also applies to other confidential correspondence. You can give the mail-drop service instructions to forward any received mail on to you immediately on receipt so that it is not sitting around. Discourage anyone from writing you or sending mail without first informing you that it is being sent, so you are aware of it and can have it forwarded without delay.

CREATING A LEGAL BUSINESS ENTITY

Another approach for establishing an offshore presence is to incorporate an offshore company in a tax haven, preferably a no-tax haven or a low-tax haven with an income tax treaty. In most tax havens, this type of company will be an international business company (IBC). The IBC is an ideal corporate vehicle providing a versatile corporate form for conducting international business.

As in the United States, the IBC is a legal entity, making it basically a citizen of that jurisdiction, whether it is a state or a foreign country, and subject to their laws. An IBC will provide you with an offshore presence from which you can conduct business or from which you can also conduct your investments. There are benefits to using an offshore or foreign corporation for investing, aside from whatever tax benefits that may be derived, including more privacy. This application of your IBC also opens up new opportunities for you, including the ability to make foreign investments that were previously unavailable.

18

OFFSHORE BUSINESS STRUCTURES

THE INTERNATIONAL BUSINESS COMPANY

International business companies (IBCs) are common in most tax havens, particularly in the Caribbean. They are easy to form, easy to operate, and they are ideal for e-commerce business. A local attorney or bank in the desired tax haven can perform the function of incorporating the IBC for you and providing additional, valuable services to the beneficiaries, meaning you, the owners. Many reliable onshore professionals (in the United Kingdom, the United States, or Canada) can also provide these incorporation services. Refer to the contacts in the Appendix, or contact Barber Financial Advisors (BFA) in Vancouver, BC, Canada, to establish an IBC quickly. Although BFA can provide these services anywhere, they specialize in Nevis, Belize, and Panama, three preferred no-tax havens.

The IBC is like a domestic corporation, providing many of the same features for the same reasons you would incorporate in the United States. They resemble Delaware, Wyoming, and Nevada corporations in having more attractive features and benefits than corporations of other states, but an IBC is even more flexible. These benefits can vary by country of incorporation, but generally are characterized as follows:

- Personal liability is limited to the amount of money paid into the corporation by its shareholders.
- A corporation is more attractive to potential investors than other business forms.
- A corporation has many more tax options than do other forms of business, such as proprietorships or partnerships.

- Favorable pension plans, profit-sharing, and stock option plans may be adopted for shareholders, directors, officers, and employees.
- In the event of the owner's death, a corporation can continue to operate without interruption.
- Shares can be readily distributed to family members.
- Ownership interest can be transferred without the corporation having to be dissolved.
- Management is centralized.
- Additional shares of stock may be issued to raise more capital.
- Shares of stock may be used for estate and family planning.
- Earnings may be accumulated by the corporation to ease the tax burden.
- A corporation may own shares of stock in another corporation and receive dividends.
- Life insurance and health programs are available to shareholders, directors, and officers at reduced group rates.
- Corporate owners receive greater benefits than self-employed individuals.
- Shareholders may borrow money from the corporation and pay it back at their convenience and at a preferred interest rate.

There are many other advantages and creative uses for the corporate form of doing business.

Some of the typical advantages of an IBC are as follows, where permissible. In addition, the benefits will also vary with the individual tax haven. Check with your expert prior to choosing the jurisdiction for your new corporation. There are often these advantages:

- A minimum of one shareholder is allowed.
- A minimum of one director is allowed and is not required to be a shareholder. A corporation, trust, or partnership may act as director.
- Telephonic board and shareholder meetings are acceptable; also attendance by proxy. Actions can be ratified after the fact.
- Bearer shares are frequently acceptable.
- Registered and bearer shares may be issued with or without par value, unnumbered, and issued in any currency.
- Names of shareholders and directors are not public record; or if so, nominee shareholders and nominee directors can be substituted.

- No filing of annual statements or financial returns is required.
- No taxes are levied on corporate income, and in most cases, no other taxes, either, on any business derived outside the host country.
- Sometimes the tax haven will provide a written guarantee of no taxes for a fixed period, such as 20 years or 50 years.
- No ultra versa rule—the corporation may be established for any purpose.
- The corporation may transfer its domicile, or an existing company from another country may transfer in as an IBC.
- The corporation may transfer its assets to a trust.
- It may be owned by a trust, such as an Asset Protection Trust (APT).
- Government regulations and fees are low.
- The corporation is an ideal structure for offshore e-commerce business.
- Third-party obligations may be guaranteed.
- Shares are not subject to seizure by a foreign government under nationalization schemes or to satisfy claims based on tax legislation.
- The corporation is not subject to exchange controls, if there are any in the country of incorporation.
- The Memorandum of Association and Articles of Association can be altered by the company without restriction. These documents are the Articles and Bylaws of the company.
- There are no limitations on nationality, citizenship, or residency of shareholders and directors.
- Nominee shareholders and directors are permissible.
- Company books may be maintained in another jurisdiction. Also, a trustee of an APT, for example, could be the sole director of an IBC owned by the trust.

As with domestic corporations, there are many uses and advantages to the IBC. The ability to redomicile quickly to another favorable jurisdiction and with minimal formalities gives the IBC tremendous mobility and flexibility for the beneficiaries and can help you avert unexpected problems due to changes in a jurisdiction or legal matters developing elsewhere.

International business companies and other types of offshore companies are commonly used for doing business worldwide: for trading purposes, such as the import-export business, drop shipping of merchandise, offshore sales distributor, offshore purchasing agent; for holding companies, investment companies, mutual funds, avoidance of probate, personal privacy reasons; for hotel operations, professional service companies, shipping companies, as a flag of convenience; for intellectual property companies for holding copyrights, patents, and trademarks; for receipt of royalties; for licensing arrangements, banking and trust companies, insurance, captive and reinsurance companies, income saving through invoicing (aka reinvoicing), international contracting and consulting, marketing, leasing, administration, and management of other companies; for personal investment purposes and e-commerce business; in short, for almost any type of business that can be legally established anywhere. In the case of finance-related enterprises, such as banking or insurance, special licensing requirements within the venue will have to be satisfied by the beneficial owners.

As with almost everything, there are usually a few pitfalls. Since U.S. citizens and resident aliens are taxed on their worldwide income, Congress has passed measures to control its more far-reaching subjects. There are complex regulations for imputing income to U.S. shareholders. These statutory provisions include the Foreign Controlled Corporation (FCC), the Foreign Personal Holding Company (FPHC), the Passive Foreign Investment Company (PFIC), the foreign investment company, and other provisions addressed by thousands of pages in the Internal Revenue Code (IRC). Avoidance of these measures requires professional advice and assistance, and the cost and trouble may not be worth it. However, if there is much to gain, it is worth seeking professional advice. Unless you can legally circumvent these tax rules, expect, as a shareholder, to pay tax on income generated by the offshore corporation currently or eventually.

Your IBC will have a local registered office and registered agent who are required in the event of service of legal process, to provide a legal address within the incorporating jurisdiction, and to keep statutory records. This function will usually be performed by a local attorney or bank, and is typically included in the cost of incorporation. In most tax havens, expect to pay between $2,000 and $3,000 in incorporation costs, and more for any additional services your offshore company may require. On an annual basis, there will be the registered office/registered agent service in the range of a few hundred dollars, and the nominal annual government fees to maintain the corporation, so you can typically expect your total annual costs to be in the neighborhood of $1,000.

In addition to incorporating your company, the incorporator can provide other services and functions on a prearranged basis. These may include appointing nominee shareholders and directors for your offshore company, usually under a confidential written agreement; providing a base of communications for the company, including telephone, mail receiving and forwarding, fax, telex, and cable services; conducting the organization meeting, special meetings, and annual meetings as required; consulting with you on tax and legal matters if the incorporator is a legal or accounting professional; giving advice on international tax planning if qualified; acting on the company's behalf as a director, professional, or attorney-in-fact under a power of attorney granted by the shareholders or directors as so engaged; opening bank and securities accounts as directed; and finally, arranging for bookkeeping services, secretarial services, investment advice, and other services relevant to operating your company. These services will vary by the offshore service provider.

When you receive your initial corporate documents for your new IBC, the local attorney or bank will likely retain copies, but you will also receive documents depending on what you paid for and where you were incorporating. In general, you can expect to receive the Memorandum of Association, commonly called Articles of Incorporation in the United States; the Articles of Association or the bylaws of the company; the original share certificates (aka stock certificates), which will either be registered or bearer, if available, and per your instructions, and representing 100 percent of the outstanding stock; the organization minutes, minutes appointing the respective directors and/or nominees, and any other relevant corporate records; a general power of attorney from the board for the beneficial owner to transact business on behalf of the company (this would usually have to be requested, would likely be an additional expense, and its benefits and drawbacks would need to be weighed). A Certificate of Good Standing may or may not be included, but can be obtained, a full certified English translation of the Memorandum and Association in the event of a Latin corporation or other non-English-dominated jurisdiction, such as a Panama corporation. A corporate seal, and a minute book might also be thrown in.

As a result of pressure from outside, many tax havens, in their effort to comply, have passed local anti-money-laundering legislation and require greater transparency in financial matters. Some have eliminated bearer shares, or they do not permit nominee shareholders and directors. Many offshore service providers, including offshore advisors, attorneys, or banks are now required to "know your customer" under regulations commonly called "KYC" regulations. They generally will want to know whom they are dealing with, which may require the provision of identification, the source of any funds being transferred to an account, and the type of business activity you are involved in or your proposed business plans. This information is maintained in strict confidence and is subject to the secrecy or confidentiality laws of a given jurisdiction. In the offshore world, aside from the letter of the law, confidentiality has been the cornerstone and general practice.

For specific benefits of an individual tax haven, Part Three: "Today's Tax Havens" provides detailed profiles on over 40 offshore havens. For the author's favorite offshore havens, refer to the T-7 tax havens discussed in Chapter 15.

OTHER TYPES OF COMPANIES

The Exempt Company

This is a company given an exemption on the basis that all business will be conducted outside the tax haven of incorporation; in return, the government provides a guarantee not to tax the company for a given number of years—20, 30, 50, and so on, typically on income, inheritance, estate, or capital gains.

The Nonresident Company

A company incorporated outside a tax haven where it has a presence is a nonresident company. An example is Monaco, where an offshore company can create a base for legal, accounting, banking, and communication purposes without registering, but cannot conduct business within Monaco, and whose shareholders are all nonresidents of Monaco.

The Hybrid Company

This type of company can be found in the Isle of Man, Gibraltar, and the British Virgin Islands and is commonly used as a charitable organization. This company is limited by guarantee and is also referred to as a quasi-trust or incorporated trust. It may consist of shareholding and nonshareholding members. Control is stipulated in Articles and either or both groups of members can retain control. The annual return does not disclose the identity of any member. The hybrid company provides greater flexibility and fewer restrictions for rich investors than a regular trust. Owners can rest assured that their estate will be properly dispersed according their wishes. A good contact in the Isle of Man is Charles Cain (see the contact listing in the Isle of Man profile in Part Three).

The Liechtenstein Anstalt (Establishment)

This entity is unique to English common law, and because it cannot be accurately characterized as either a company or a trust, it could be a problem for U.S. tax purposes. There are no withholding taxes on distribution until such time as shares are issued, and until then, the founder retains control of the Anstalt. A Liechtenstein attorney or a trust company often acts as the founder. The shares may be transferred at any time by the founder. All rights are transferred to a successor through a deed of transfer, and if the successor is left unnamed, the document is essentially in bearer form. The successor is usually the offshore investor, the real beneficial owner. Further, the deed of transfer can be held in a Swiss or Austrian safe-deposit box, providing another level of security. This structure provides excellent confidentiality.

Limited Liability Company (LLC)

This is a nice combination of advantages of the corporate form, having limited liability and the flexibility of a partnership where tax advantages pass through to the owners in the same way as in a U.S. incorporated S corporation or partnership. Management is conducted by members/owners and a manager as opposed to directors and officers. Members and owners can be individuals or other legal entities. A definite advantage of the LLC over the IBC is that there is no U.S. reporting requirement for U.S. residents under Subpart F of the Internal Revenue Code, and it is a tax-neutral entity like the limited partnership.

Offshore Partnerships

Offshore jurisdictions have a variety of partnerships, each with their own advantages, but this book does not cover partnerships. Part Three indicates by country profile if partnerships are encouraged. Refer to an offshore professional for further information on offshore partnerships.

Other company forms are offered in the different tax havens and other countries. The hybrid company and the Anstalt have distinctive personalities, and others like the exempt company, the nonresident company, or limited liability company are frequently found in tax havens. Other types of companies used for international purposes are mentioned Part Three. Specific interest in a certain type of company should be addressed to a local professional for a full description and review of the benefits and uses.

THE OFFSHORE BANK

Many people have liked the idea of owning their own offshore bank, and have done so. And, many of these people subsequently found themselves in trouble with the law, basically for two reasons. Either these folks were using the bank fraudulently, or were suspected of doing so, or they were just not qualified to run a bank. Easy qualification requirements in the past made it simple to get a banking license. That has since changed drastically as there has been much pressure from law enforcement worldwide to stop this practice. Today, few jurisdictions want to attract this type of business, but it is still possible to secure a banking license. The imposed requirements are typically much tighter on capitalization, qualification of management and owners, the bank's operations, and annual disclosures.

A Class A banking license permits the bank to conduct both local (onshore) business and international business. A Class B banking license limits the bank's operations to outside the host country where the bank was chartered, commonly known as an "offshore bank." Another license, sometimes called a *restricted license,* will limit the bank from operating with anyone not named on the bank's license.

There are certain potential U.S. tax benefits to owning an offshore licensed bank. Income derived from owning your own foreign bank is not considered subpart F income. Normally in an offshore corporation, this income would pass through to the shareholders in the same way as with an S corporation or a partnership. The bank would have to be really operating as a bank to qualify on this point, but if it does, you can defer paying income tax, can accumulate profits, have money to invest or operate the bank with, and receive tax-free compounded interest.

Tax havens granting bank licenses today are included in Part Three under the individual country profiles. Local tax haven professionals can advise you on their country's licensing practices and attitude. A U.S. tax advisor can give you full particulars on the tax benefits for U.S. citizens considering such a move.

SHIP AND YACHT REGISTRATION: FLAGS OF CONVENIENCE

Numerous tax havens have legislation addressing the registration of ships and yachts. Usually an offshore corporation is established to own the vessel and then it is registered in the name of the company. The company would be managed and owned the same as any offshore company and would have the same attractive company benefits. The ship or yacht will then fly the flag of the country of which it is a subject. That is why these countries are referred to as a *flags of convenience.* They are registered in these countries because of their advantageous maritime laws and flexibility for the owners. Of course, the tax benefits are an important reason, too. When it comes time to sell the boat, the owner merely transfers the outstanding stock in the company to the buyer, and the vessel remains registered to the company. Naturally, any other assets or liabilities would go with it unless agreed otherwise, but generally speaking, there shouldn't be any, or they would have been kept minimal. The company would buy an insurance policy to cover the vessel in the event of loss.

Panama is an attractive flag of convenience and has an exchange-of-note agreement with the United States. This arrangement permits Panamanian-registered vessels to enter U.S. ports. The Panama corporation that owns the vessel can also establish a representative office in New York or Los Angeles without being subject to U.S. taxes. And, Panama is a T-7 tax haven.

OTHER OFFSHORE VEHICLES—INVESTMENT FUNDS, INSURANCE COMPANIES, OFFSHORE INTERNET CASINOS, AND MORE

There are many specialty companies, some of which require special licensing. Each tax haven tends to favor certain types of activities, which is why you will find ships registered in Panama, asset protection trusts in the Cook Islands, and insurance companies in Bermuda. A few of the many types of companies and their areas of specialized activity are investment funds, mutual funds, insurance companies, and Internet casinos. By reviewing the individual country profiles in Part Three, you will quickly deduce which tax havens attract the various activities and issue licenses for specific activities where required. Also, countries promoting e-commerce are identified, like Belize and Nevis, two of the T-7 countries. A local tax haven professional can provide more details on the advantages of their country for specific company activities.

19

SECRETS OF OFFSHORE BANKING

OFFSHORE BANK ACCOUNTS: PERSONAL AND CORPORATE

Having an offshore bank account can be the core of your offshore financial life. With it, you avail yourself of the many banking, financial, and investment services that your bank has to offer. Simply having an account like this can be significant, depending on which bank you are with, and in which country it is located. And, of course, an offshore bank account is legal. In Part Four, you will find several good sources for locating banks anywhere in the world. To determine the financial standing of any bank, visit www.fitchratings.com.

It is said that history repeats itself. For tens of thousands of people in the past 50 years alone, establishing an offshore or foreign bank account has been a way to ease their tax burden and protect assets, if not actually to survive and escape the clutches of totalitarian governments. It is a simple means to provide financial security during times of warfare and economic and political instability. With such an account in place, you can move funds offshore anytime, in advance of what might become your sole nest egg and financial life jacket in a state of uncertainty or even emergency.

Having money invested outside your own country is also a way to avoid the unforeseen possibility of currency exchange controls, a means governments use to keep your money from leaving the country. This is a virtual act of oppression and could become a first in a series of steps designed to gain more control of citizens, including their free, physical movement. If your country has imposed currency exchange controls, you should hope that your money, assets, and income are already outside your country. This is an important reason to go offshore before such restrictions are imposed. A government that is intent on such measures is not likely to make an advance announcement, so you need to recognize the signs. If travel becomes more restrictive, new identification methods are imposed, financial reporting requirements are tightened up, then your liberties are diminishing and exchange controls may be on the horizon. Once your money is safely outside the country, you will achieve financial peace of mind. And, should you wish in the future, you are only one step away from being able to leave altogether.

There is a tendency to believe that the closer you are to your bank, the more secure is your money. This is a fallacy. Aspects that make your money safer are the strength of your bank, the currency held, and the stability of the jurisdiction in which the bank is located.

The strength of the bank is not how much it has in assets, but how liquid it is—how much cash is on hand, or cash equivalents that can be converted into cash quickly to meet demands. If the bank can pay off its immediate demands, including depositors and debts and still be in a cash position, then the bank is liquid. Banks in the United States are notorious for being far from liquid, and this is why many had to close when there was a run on the banks in the Great Depression. The banks were not up to the demand when a significant number of the depositors wanted their money. The banks were not liquid, and who was the loser?

Not much has changed in the United States since then. And, don't count on any government's "guaranteeing" agency to bail the banks out. In the early 1980s, we saw the Federal Deposit Insurance Corporation (FDIC) go under and it didn't take too many shaky banks to cause that problem.

On the contrary, many banks in Switzerland, Liechtenstein, and other bank havens are very liquid, sometimes by hundreds of percent. Liquidity of 100 percent or better is ideal. And, these are some of the most stable countries in the world. A government's policy on the reserves that a bank is required to maintain, and the country's own fiscal practices, including reserves backing their currency, are what help to make a country economically stable. It is no wonder then that the Swiss franc has been by far the most stable currency in the world, even surpassing the Japanese yen, and the former German mark. When shopping for a bank or a country to bank in, these are important factors to consider. In the case of Switzerland, its neutrality has contributed to its political stability.

Many types of accounts are available in a variety of currencies. You may want to open one account first, then open additional accounts as needed. The basic account in a foreign country is a current account, which is a *demand account,* like a checking account in the United States. The *multicurrency account* is a demand account also, likely with checks written in any of the currencies offered. Then, there is the interest-bearing *deposit account,* similar to a savings account. A combination of these two types of account would be a *twin account,* incorporating features of both. A *fiduciary account* is useful if you would like to invest anonymously, as the bank will keep assets in their name; also in this case, the bank can establish accounts in foreign countries for investing on your behalf. By doing this in Switzerland, you would avoid the 35 percent withholding tax referred to elsewhere. For higher interest rates, you can purchase *Certificates of Deposit* (CDs) that can be denominated in many different currencies, are usually in bearer form, and are easily transferable. Foreign currency CDs are also available for different lengths of time up to five years. Usually there is no withholding tax on CDs, and you can be earning interest payments tax-free. A *precious metals account* can be set up to buy gold, silver, platinum, and other precious metals on your behalf, and the bank will store them for a small fee in their vault, or you can place them in your safe-deposit box. Larger banks can provide an *investment account* to invest in mutual funds or commodities in your name. *Managed accounts* are popular with high net worth individuals. The bank can invest on your behalf, in their name, and will act on your investment instructions by letter, phone, or fax. The minimum to open this type of account is $250,000, but in Switzerland, more typically it is $1,000,000. The bank will hold securities and other valuables in a *custodial account* or *safekeeping account,* which is segregated from the bank's assets, and the bank will manage the assets on the customer's behalf.

The bank will offer many other services as well, such as commercial loans, real estate loans, consumer credit loans, foreign currency exchange, letters of credit, money transfers, bank drafts, traveler's checks, debit cards, credit cards, safe-deposit boxes, and more.

Then there is the corporate bank account. If you have an offshore or foreign corporation—in particular, an operating company—you will likely need a bank account. Basically, the same features regarding bank accounts apply to corporations with a few variations, and also with some advantages. The opening of the account will require additional paperwork, a few more questions, and a corporate resolution or two. The advantages of a corporate account include that the company is an independent entity and so are its accounts. As the account is under the name of the corporation, bank records will reflect this, and your name will not be readily identifiable by account names. Should you wish to change signers, you merely advise the bank, provide them with the usual required documents on the signer(s), and answer the usual questions, and there should be no problem in making the switch. The account continues in the same company name. If coordinated properly, there should be no interruption of banking service.

Many banks are listed in Part Three. Due to the restrictions imposed on U.S. taxpayers and pressures from the U.S. government, some foreign banks and financial institutions do not care to do business with U.S. citizens. This is unfortunate, but there are still many who are willing to do business.

As for minimum opening deposits, these have gone up considerably in recent years, and in some of the more attractive banking havens like Switzerland, they are generally high, as in the neighborhood of $50,000. There are still some where an initial deposit of $25,000 will open an account, such as the Union Bank of Switzerland (UBS), but you should think twice about banking with this bank or any other bank that maintains an office or branch in your home country. In the case of UBS, the U.S. government put pressure on them, and because they had a presence in the United States and were doing business there, the bank agreed to provide what the government wanted regarding U.S. depositors with accounts in Switzerland.

That said, the cantonal banks, which are more like community banks and are chartered in individual cantons in Switzerland, require much smaller opening deposits; you can probably open an account with as little as $5,000. Barber Financial Advisors can open a Swiss account for clients with no minimum initial deposit required if no credit or debit card is needed. There are banks in other T-7 tax havens where you can open an account for as little as $1,000, such as in Belize. If you have trouble finding the right bank for your requirements, visit www.barberfinancialadvisors.com for more information.

Most banks today are complying with the "know your customer" practice. Expect to be required to prove your identity with professional references, a copy of a certified passport and other photo identification, a copy of a utility bill, and explanation of where the funds to open the account originated, how you earn your money, and where future funds will be coming from.

Other than supplying this information, you will need to complete, sign, and submit the usual banking forms. These will vary by bank, but may include a signature card, a customer information questionnaire, verification of account agreement, an agreement regarding the operation of the account, a fax authorization form, and so forth.

When the bank informs you that your account is open, they will give you the account number and you can arrange to transfer at least the minimum opening amount required. This can be in the form of a bank wire transfer to the new account, or you may send a negotiable instrument for deposit, such as a check or draft. However, the bank will put a hold on the funds until they clear or are collected, whichever the case may be.

As a result of these beefed-up requirements, the time to open the account may take longer than expected, so work on opening your account in advance of needing it. Once you are established with the bank, opening subsequent accounts will be easier and faster. It is good to establish a personal relationship with a contact at the bank on whom you can rely for assistance when needed.

There are many ways to communicate with your new bank—by telephone, mail, fax, or online. If by telephone, you will come up with an identifying password that only you and the bank will know. This, coupled with other information about you or the account, will identify who you are. Then, if you have a personal banker who knows you and your voice, verbal telephone instructions are possible. Fax instructions are generally accepted, but you must sign a hold harmless agreement. Some banks have a clever system providing you with a series of codes in advance. Each time you send faxed correspondence you change the code.

Remember, there are U.S. reporting requirements of foreign bank and financial accounts by U.S. taxpayers (see Chapter 25 for a review of the various requirements).

It is perfectly legal to maintain multiple bank accounts, each with less than $10,000, and avoid the requirement to file U.S. Treasury Form 90-20.1, Report of Foreign Bank and Financial Accounts. This is not considered structuring as defined by the Anti-Money Laundering Act of 1986, as this reporting requirement came into effect with the Bank Secrecy Act of 1970, and no provisions with regard to structuring were incorporated into that act.

Keep in mind that currency exchange rates, which fluctuate daily, could throw you over the $10,000 reporting threshold if your currency holdings appreciate. Official exchange rates are required to determine the value of the currency you have on deposit. You may want to lower the maximum amount you maintain in the account(s), so you don't exceed the $10,000 limit unknowingly.

OFFSHORE CREDIT CARDS AND DEBIT CARDS

Credit cards are available from many banks in the T-7 havens and other tax havens. Debit cards are also available on existing accounts. Offshore credit and debit cards can be issued to you personally or to your offshore corporation. There is an additional level of privacy with the corporate version, if just the company name is embossed on the card. But both are plastic, and regardless of the issuing bank or the bank's location, if they happen to be Visa, MasterCard, or American Express, they are American companies. In extraordinary cases, as described in Part One, they can be subject to access by the Internal Revenue Service. Also, you may have a difficult time in some circumstances with a company card due to personal identification requirements. When that is not required, particularly in the case of debit cards that typically only require knowing the pin number, the cards will work fine. These cards make it convenient to access your offshore accounts for cash and through purchases and are quite useful for those reasons.

However, use of the cards can be a red flag. The offshore debit card is attached to an underlying offshore bank account, and if this account has not been reported, as required, you could end up with a major problem (see Chapter 25). As previously mentioned, there are severe civil and criminal penalties in certain circumstances for not reporting an offshore bank account.

With offshore credit or debit cards, remember, if nothing else, your privacy is compromised when they are processed by those American credit card brands.

There are also offshore prepaid Visa "credit cards" that you can purchase from certain offshore banks for a fee and can use worldwide just like a debit card at ATM machines or for purchases wherever you see the Visa symbol. It is not a traveler's check or an actual credit card. Your entire financial transactions are available online. The amount charged is withdrawn from the cash balance up to the card's limit. These cards are available for as little as $500, and in $500 increments, up to $10,000. You have the same asset protection with a card like this as you would with an offshore bank account from the bank of that country. By far, this surpasses any prepaid card or bank account available in the United States for gaining asset protection for your cash while still having easy access to it.

For further information on offshore credit, debit, or prepaid cards, visit www.barberfinancialadvisors.com.

TAX-FREE COMPOUNDED INTEREST

The best way to maximize your investment earnings is through compounding your earnings, tax-free.

This brings to mind my great-grandfather, Herbert Lee ("H.L.") Barber of Chicago, an economist and investment writer, among his many other successful roles in life. H.L. was a great advocate of compound interest, before and after the passage of the 1913 U.S. income tax. He espoused his investment and economic philosophies in two of the three books he wrote. These were *Making Money Make Money* in 1912, and *Investing for Profit* in 1917, both published by Munson Press, Chicago, Illinois.

H.L. liked Benjamin Franklin's quote, "Money makes money, and the money that money makes, makes more money." But it is difficult for this principle to be terribly effective when you are paying astronomical taxes. Aside from the transfer of wealth that takes place, as in the case of inflation, this is also a way to keep the populace from getting ahead.

It has been said that Howard Robard Hughes, the famed billionaire and aviator, could have put his original inheritance in a savings bank and made as much or more money than he did through all his many ventures over the years. In other words, his original inheritance would have grown into a couple billion dollars, over the course of his lifetime, just from the interest compounding from about 1924 when he inherited, to his death in 1976, particularly if it had been compounding tax-free. According to his accountant, Noah Dietrich, the value placed on his inheritance at the time of his father's death was based on the net worth of his acquired interest in Hughes Tool Company, which had a market value for estate purposes of $660,000. Of course, had he chosen this path, humankind would have missed out on thousands of important advancements that were a direct or indirect result of his personal interests, efforts, passions, and business pursuits. And, I daresay, he would have had far less fun!

To name another luminary, Albert Einstein once said, "The greatest principle in the universe is the power of compound interest." Need I say more?

So, what is the point of all this? Well, the concept of compounding interest is one of the great advantages to going offshore, while it is not the primary reason most people do so. However, by using some of the financial vehicles and strategies put forth in this book, you, too, can be building a fortune offshore, if you truly wish to, even in today's adverse economic climate. Compounding, preferably tax-free or at least tax-deferred, is a fundamental principle often overlooked by many. Debt, and its cost, also compounds quickly, and it can put you in the poorhouse. This is why the general public needs to better understand the underlying principles of their actions and choose the course that will keep them in the positive column, and not the negative. Bad choices have put not just the public, but also the government of the United States into serious debt. Fortunately, you still have a chance to take your money and assets offshore, even if only some of it, where it will be protected from creditors and confiscation, and have a chance to build into something worthwhile.

BACK-TO-BACK LOANS

This a good way to bring some of your money home when needed while maintaining your principal securely in your offshore account. You simply negotiate with your offshore banker to arrange the loan, which is fully collateralized by funds on deposit. The interest rate on the loan will be the "spread," a rate between the maximum and minimum going interest rates at the time of borrowing. This is a tax-neutral private transaction. Back-to-back loans can also be arranged for your offshore corporation and used for business purposes, or loaned to the beneficial owners, either directly from the bank where the funds are held on deposit, or made through a correspondent of the bank, adding another degree of confidentiality. And, the beauty is you are not going to pay taxes on the borrowed money. The low cost to get your money onshore is worth the expense. In fact, the cost could be utilized as a business expense. This method is perfectly legal, but it is always wise to use discretion in all offshore financial matters.

PERSONAL ASSET MANAGEMENT

Chapter 22 describes how personal asset management is addressed in Switzerland. Basically, the same plan can be administered through other stable tax havens, but, this would require studying the advantages and disadvantages among the various jurisdictions. You would then choose a capable bank, keeping in mind the individual merits of the bank and its experience with international investment management. Most banks that provide this service require a minimum of $250,000 to begin. The asset portfolio can be placed in a trust structure or insurance wrapper like an offshore life insurance policy. You will still need to satisfy appropriate U.S. reporting requirements.

20

OFFSHORE FINANCIAL AND INVESTMENT STRATEGIES

OFFSHORE MANAGED COMMODITY ACCOUNT

This is another way to invest in a diversified portfolio of commodities not available in the United States. Through your offshore corporation or trust, which can provide additional asset protection, you can establish an offshore managed commodities account and be making excellent returns in precious metals, foreign currencies, financial futures, and commodities markets worldwide, including the United States. These can be investment pools offered by offshore specialists who have developed such programs. In the current economic climate, commodities are worth investigating. You will want to carefully review any investment proposals and their tax implications. For a personal introduction to an excellent offshore brokerage firm, e-mail me your contact particulars, and I will place you in touch immediately and free of charge.

OFFSHORE INVESTMENT FUNDS

There are thousands of investment funds worldwide, many of which exclude U.S. citizens and residents for a couple of reasons. The funds do not want to spend time and money complying with U.S. securities laws to gain the additional business, and even if they did so, their operations would become subject to the all-imposing U.S. government and its myriad laws. They would also be exposed to the predatory whims of the U.S. litigation industry, which constitutes 94 percent of all lawsuits filed worldwide, thanks partly to mentality and partly to the ease of suing on a contingency basis in the United States.

Even if these funds avoid doing business in the United States, the long arm of the Internal Revenue Service still has a far-flung reach into its own taxpayers' affairs including whoever they might be doing business with. Having U.S. customers can be plain troublesome.

On the flip side of this sad tale, the U.S. government has created investment protectionism through laws and policies designed to discourage average investors from venturing abroad with their money. These policies are designed to keep the money on Wall Street, and in American banks.

As a result, investment choices are limited for Americans, but the news is not all bad. Many top-performing offshore funds exist, all producing greater returns than their domestic counterparts. Although it is illegal for Americans to purchase them directly, you can still get into these productive investments indirectly and gain all the benefits.

By using the offshore strategies illustrated here, you can invest for better returns worldwide, and legally, just as the rich and powerful always have. While gaining valuable investment diversification, American investors also can achieve asset protection and engage some real tax reduction strategies.

Investing in international funds, like the mutual fund, is an easy way to participate without buying into foreign companies directly. But, that would be too simple, and the IRS has other ideas about what they want to do, which is to subject you to the unfavorable Passive Foreign Investment Corporation (PFIC) rules. These regulations constitute a penalty and a means to curtail investing overseas. In this way over time, the IRS can hit you with a punitive interest charge that can ultimately wipe out all your gains, and in some cases, even your principal. You want to avoid this at all costs.

Instead, you can invest in funds that are not corporations, but tax-neutral limited partnerships or limited liability companies, thereby allowing you to pay your taxes on your prorated portion of the income or profit, and not break the law.

Other options are presented in this book, such as investing through a tax-protected offshore retirement plan, variable annuity, or portfolio bond. Other offshore vehicles could be structured for the same purpose, allowing you to legally invest in the offshore investment funds of your choosing.

International fund sources such as Standard & Poor's and Fund-Insite are listed in Part Four on page 268, "Financial Information and Business Opportunities," along with competent financial advisors located in the Appendix who can give you straight-up advice on proceeding legally and avoiding the pitfalls. Take a close look at some of the offshore funds and compare them with your experience and knowledge of investing domestically.

Another option for investing in international funds, and for that matter, back into U.S. markets, is through your offshore or Swiss bank. But, a word of caution here: So convinced is the IRS that every taxpayer with a foreign bank account is trying to cheat on taxes, they have implemented the *qualified intermediary* (QI) regulation, under the Administrative Procedures Act, in hopes of capturing more tax dollars. In an effort to stop Americans from investing back into the states anonymously from offshore, they have imposed far-reaching requirements on foreign institutions, expecting them to disclose the identity of any U.S. account holders.

The idea is to prevent "U.S. persons," as the IRS defines them, from investing back into the U.S. markets through an intermediary such as a foreign bank or financial institution without disclosing their identity to the IRS. The penalty for not complying is a 30 percent withholding tax on foreign-source earned income, including the entire investment and its cash flow. And, how is the IRS going to enforce these actions and collect this money? Sadly, this would only work through the "qualified intermediaries," who will receive compensation to act as auditors and agents on behalf of the U.S. government. Fortunately, not all banks are going to jump on this bandwagon to play pseudo tax cop and risk their image and reputation.

You can get around this problem, but get solid professional advice before starting, so that legally you are completely in the clear.

Offshore investments funds are an easy way to diversify your investments, and invest in equities overseas, typically with a nominal initial investment. Minimum requirements to open an account can be as low as $5,000.

PRECIOUS METAL CERTIFICATES

An excellent program for acquiring and safely storing precious metals is known as the *Perth Mint Certificate Program* (PMCP).

The PMCP is a Western Australia (S&P AAA investment rated) government-guaranteed program where you can invest in gold, silver, or platinum, in either coin or bullion, with your holdings represented by ownership certificates. The certificates are easy to both purchase and liquidate. The precious metals in question are safely stored in the Perth Mint, and have been since 1899, located in politically and economically stable Western Australia, and are fully insured by Lloyds of London at the expense of the mint. The certificates may be in increments of as little as $50 each and can even be held by an Individual Retirement Account (IRA), a foreign trust, or an offshore corporation. The ownership relationship of the precious metals is with a government vault, not a foreign bank. The certificates are issued in the name of the purchaser and each certificate has a number. They are nonnegotiable and transferable. The certificate fee is low. The mint uses a system of code numbers to ensure client confidentiality and security. The Perth Mint is accredited by the London Bullion Market Association, the New York Commodities Exchange, and the Tokyo Commodities Exchange. As an additional benefit to U.S. and Canadian taxpayers, the mint does not maintain any corporate presence in either the United States or Canada. Minimum investment of U.S. $10,000 required.

For complete information, refer to Asset Strategies International, Inc. in part Four, "Financial and Investment Services."

GOLD-BACKED ELECTRONIC CURRENCY

There is an alternative payment system to the federal banking system that deserves discussion and lends itself nicely to asset diversification, providing asset protection and consideration of the geopolitical aspects with regard to your banking and investments.

Banking provides a wide variety of services; one that we all use daily without thinking twice is the ability to make and receive payments. Banks are also where we store our money for short and long periods, believing it is safe. Unfortunately, security is as much perception as reality.

With the advent of high technology and computers, a new era has emerged. The digital age has posed new opportunities and also new threats to previous ideas and methods. The government and the banking system are working hard to rid us of cash, a commodity that empowers us as individuals by allowing us anonymity and sovereignty, and replace it with a digital system that can record all financial transactions. Right now, "they" are even considering eliminating the U.S. $50 and $100 bills. This overt pressure has given way to some excellent options.

Gold-backed electronic currencies are an interesting alternative to traditional banking. They allow the customer to make and receive payments online. And the funds on account are backed 100 percent by gold or other precious metals of the customer's choice. In the United States, we were taken off the gold standard by the U.S. government in 1971, so that our U.S. dollars are backed by nothing more than the "good faith and credit of the United States government." Basically, this promise is a big IOU, and only as strong as the issuer. Money printed today under this system is essentially fiat money that has no value backing it. In countries where fiat currencies have been issued, there have been tremendous cases of runaway inflation. And, to compound the matter, the promisor in this instance, the U.S. government, is trillions of dollars in debt already.

The gold-backed electronic currency provides the user with a cash-payment system backed up by gold, silver, and other precious metals, at the choosing of the customer. The value of the account fluctuates with the value of the precious metals being held. In today's economic climate, it is a favorable environment to be holding gold and other precious metals. They are the best hedges against what we have today, a declining U.S. dollar, inflation that promises to rise dramatically in the near future, a shaky national real estate market, rising interest rates, the depletion of worldwide oil reserves, rising gas prices, war with no end in sight, terrorism, and huge private and public national debt. Independently of each other, these influences put positive upward pressure on precious metals. Combined, they have sent gold and other commodities soaring in the recent past, and it could just be the beginning. And, even if precious metals were to drop, the truth is, you still have a real asset with real value, whereas the person holding printed currency has something of no hard value but really just a promise.

This new payment system works internationally, 24/7, and protects you from your cash being stolen. It allows you to move money across borders instantly without red tape and eliminates the usual collection problems and costs associated with other forms of payment like checks, cashier's checks, drafts, credit card processing, and so on. Plus, it circumvents fraud.

The initial step to establishing an account can be completed online within minutes, and an account number will be assigned and ready for use. Many conveniences, cost savings, and security measures are built into this system. It is also one of the simplest and fastest means to buy and hold gold and other precious metals. Now you can join the many individuals and businesses worldwide that are benefiting from a secure payment system and alternative to the traditional banking system and the weakening U.S. dollar.

For additional information on the gold-backed electronic currency and how to sign up free within minutes, visit www.barberfinancialadvisors.com.

EURODOLLAR BONDS

Eurodollar bonds are a secure means to invest offshore. Eurodollars are simply U.S. dollars on deposit by American banks with a foreign counterpart or one of their foreign branches in Europe. As these deposited U.S. dollars are held overseas, they are not regulated by the Federal Reserve Board or the Securities and Exchange Commission (SEC), and thus they are a popular investment. Eurodollars are issued in the Netherlands and Delaware by international finance subsidiaries of giant transnational corporations. Both the principal and interest are fully and unconditionally guaranteed by the issuer and are not subject to U.S. withholding taxes. Often, they can be exchanged for common stock in the parent company, and the stock can be sold tax-free. Similarly, U.S. dollars that are held by foreign banks in Asia are known as Asiadollars.

For more information on Eurodollar bonds, contact Mr. Thomas P. Azzara in Nassau, Bahamas (see Part Four: "Financial and Investment Service Contacts").

OFFSHORE PHYSICAL STORAGE; OFFSHORE SAFE DEPOSIT BOX

The best place to store physical items of value is outside your own country, such as the United States. It is a bit inconvenient, but it is also a great deal safer. It would be challenging, depending on the country and the bank or vault where the valuables are stored, to get a court order forcing the bank or other vault to open up.

A safe-deposit box is not reportable, as would be a safekeeping or custodial account with a bank, which will hold assets in their care per your instructions, including in sealed packages. These accounts are only reportable if their value, like a foreign bank account, exceeds an aggregate value of $10,000 in a year. But, by using a safe-deposit box for this purpose, you would avoid the necessity of filing Treasury Form TD F 90-22.1 and acknowledging it on Schedule B of your U.S. tax return no matter how high the value of the contents.

Smaller items like stock certificates, bonds, any negotiable instruments, bearer bonds, bearer share certificates, jewelry, precious metals, cash, important documents, collector items, hard-to-replace items, copies of trust papers, wills, and evidence of asset holdings (e.g., gold certificates) are best placed in an offshore safe-deposit box of a reputable bank. Banks in Switzerland, Liechtenstein, and Austria are ideal. But, as a first step, or for items not so sensitive, or on a temporary basis, an American may want to hold some items in a safe-deposit box in Canada for convenience.

Although the degree of security and privacy is not the same, say, as in Switzerland, it would still be outside the United States and better than your local bank. If travel is a problem, you could give an entrusted family member, friend, or associate a limited power of attorney authorizing their access to the box for the purpose of putting things in it and removing them per your instructions. Naturally, trust is the key factor here, and it raises the risk level.

This is also important in the event of your death, as the bank would be required by law to seal the box, and it would become part of your estate. Your beneficiaries may not be allowed to access the box in such event, until the Internal Revenue Service gets a chance to look inside. They might try to seize anything that appears not to have been reported as required by law, including going after the contents of any hidden accounts, anywhere. Keeping the safe-deposit box outside the United States keeps its contents out of their reach. At least easy reach. This move could also allow rightful beneficiaries the time to gain legal access to the box through the foreign jurisdiction rather than under the authority of U.S. laws.

This also applies to offshore physical storage facilities, often as secure as a bank's vault, which could be used for similar items or maybe more voluminous records and possessions (see Via Mat Management AG, in Kloten, Switzerland, and Safes Fidelity, S.A. in Geneva, Switzerland, in Part Four: "Financial and Investment Service Contacts").

A better way to allow beneficiaries access to a safe-deposit box or other secure facility on your death, would be to have the box rented by your offshore corporation. Since the corporation is usually for perpetuity, and regardless of a shareholder's death, it will continue, and the status of the safe-deposit box will remain the same. Access to it could be secured by a director or officer, or the major shareholders. So, a beneficiary could already be in such a position, or a director or officer could authorize a beneficiary to have the right to access the box. A corporate resolution could be furnished to the bank, and it would be required to comply. Of course, this authorization could be withdrawn or changed at any time. The corporate approach also removes it a step from creditor claims. This can be done in the United States as well, but it wouldn't be as airtight.

FOREIGN REAL ESTATE

There are some excellent real estate investment opportunities in foreign countries, including tax havens and other locales that would make attractive retirement havens. Property could be purchased in advance of wanting to move, and can provide rental income in the meantime. Part Four provides detailed information on two countries offering Economic Citizenship Programs and over 30 other countries for possible residency and citizenship. Most of these countries permit foreigners to purchase real estate. Tremendous real estate opportunities exist worldwide, and real estate prices are often lower, even much lower, compared with U.S. prices. Many of these countries are experiencing good appreciation in the area of real estate. You could easily establish a comfortable lifestyle while lowering or totally avoiding personal income tax by exercising the $80,000 annual loophole discussed earlier. Review the real estate related contacts listed in Part Four and you can be on the road to discovering your own quaint hideaway. There are no U.S. reporting requirements in the case of foreign real estate ownership; keep in mind, however, that foreign public ownership records are likely. Often, a piece of real estate, like a private island, will be owned by a local or offshore corporation, and ownership can be changed simply by transferring the stock. With this structuring, the stockholder would not be a part of the property records.

I suggest a visit to www.InternationalLiving.com for foreign real estate opportunities and information of interest to prospective expatriates. Their contact information can be found later in this section under "Real Estate."

21

OFFSHORE ESTATE PLANNING

OFFSHORE VARIABLE ANNUITIES

The threatening posture and complex nature of U.S. laws and the far-reaching attempts of the U.S. government to control U.S. taxpayers, and influence foreign governments, financial institutions, and others to cooperate with their whims has left many offshore services and professionals hesitating to conduct business with U.S. taxpayers. This problem, coupled with regulations forbidding U.S. taxpayers from doing certain things offshore, including where they are not allowed to invest, has effectively shut U.S. investors off from many of the best foreign investment opportunities.

To avail themselves of these forbidden opportunities, many well-off U.S. investors are purchasing offshore variable insurance annuities from offshore insurance companies that are not restricted by U.S. laws. This is perfectly legal. Not only can investors thus diversify their foreign investments, but they are also actively engaging asset protection and accumulating faster and greater wealth. Since this is not a life insurance policy, there is no requirement for a medical exam. The biggest drawback is the entrance fee, which can begin at $250,000. But, for many Americans, that is within reach. If you wish, you can borrow against the annuity immediately, and if this occurs before any accumulation occurs, there is no tax on the distribution of money. Otherwise it would be taxable.

The offshore variable annuity can act as a savings or a retirement plan, but in actuality it is a contract with an insurance company, and you get to choose where the money will be invested. The annuity is acquired with a single payment, but as the underlying investments appreciate, the money compounds, tax-deferred. You decide when to withdraw money and only then are you taxed on it as ordinary income. There is no limit to how much you can withdraw. However, if you leave it to accumulate tax-free, you are getting the added benefits of a large sum compounding, thereby earning you more the longer you don't touch it, or until the annuity matures. If it matures at some given age, then it would either be surrendered or converted to a life annuity.

Most investors are attracted to this type of annuity to defer taxes on their investments and for asset protection. They also can get money when they need it. Many offshore jurisdictions specializing in the offshore insurance industry have laws that protect annuities from foreign creditors or from foreign estate proceedings. Even if the insurance company has problems (and this is not likely if you pick the right one from the start), the individual policies are held as separate assets, not as part of the insurance company, and therefore are not subject to their creditor claims. Switzerland, for one, has a strong insurance industry and no companies have failed. In some cases, annuities cannot be included in a bankruptcy procedure. If you die, the cash value of the annuity is paid to the designated beneficiaries. Of course, the accumulated deferred tax and any estate taxes will be due.

There are other possibilities for structuring the offshore variable annuity, including having a trust take out the annuity, and at the time of your death, its value will be excluded from your estate. Consult with your tax advisor or insurance specialist, and as always, stay with a reputable insurance company in a good offshore jurisdiction, have a professional review, and translate the policy so you understand what you are committing to. Insurance policies are generally nonreporting. Expect to invest a minimum of $50,000.

Part Three: "Today's Tax Havens" reviews the unique characteristics and areas of specialization of the different countries, including local contacts. Reputable advisors who can assist with offshore variable annuities can be found in Part Four: "Financial and Investment Service Contacts."

TRUSTS, ASSET PROTECTION TRUSTS, CHARITABLE TRUSTS, THE LIECHTENSTEIN FOUNDATION, AND THE ANGLO-SAXON FOUNDATION

Trusts are formed under English common law in countries such as England, the United States, Canada, and a few others where the concept of equity is understood. Otherwise, trusts are formed under civil legal systems of countries such as Panama, Liechtenstein, and France, and thus are based on a code of express provisions. Most European and Latin American countries are civil law countries. Also, a few civil law countries have adopted legislation recognizing the common law trust.

In the United States, parties to a trust and the underlying assets being held for the beneficiary are all subject to the whims of the Americans, a litigious bunch of people who sometimes act as if winning a lawsuit is the same as winning the state lottery. This prevailing attitude spills over into the legal system, including the lawyers, who often fuel the fire. With this backdrop, clever foreign jurisdictions, often English common law based countries, have drafted their own legislation to better clarify their position on trusts and the special advantages that they offer foreigners, like those savvy Americans who need protection from their litigious fellow citizens. In response to this hostile environment and the potential to attract business to their offshore jurisdiction, the foreign asset protection trust was born.

The *asset protection trust* (APT) is the favored offshore trust designed to substantially reduce the rights of creditors by placing the situs of the trust in a foreign land. If set up properly, it affords maximum protection and preservation of assets, but it must be irrevocable to be considered a separate entity from the trustor. This means that you cannot have control of the trust.

Trust laws are well developed in many offshore jurisdictions including Nevis, Belize, and the Cook Islands, the three strongest APT jurisdictions. Among the trustees of the APT, there will need to be at least one foreign trustee, usually a local professional, and, in case of an attack on the trust by a U.S. court, all U.S. trustees would immediately resign, leaving only the foreign trustee, whom the United States would have no jurisdiction over. This would leave the attacker the option of an action de novo in the courts of the offshore jurisdiction, which, once creditors learn the potential difficulty and expense, they are unlikely to pursue. Creditors must prove their claim beyond a reasonable doubt and the statute of limitations on such claims in the offshore jurisdiction is likely to be short.

Assets are generally secure in the hands of a foreign trustee who is a professional, but as an added precaution, a protector can be inserted into the trust by the trustor—a person or committee—to keep tabs on the trustee for the sake of the beneficiaries. An important issue is whether the trustor or grantor (the creator of the trust) had the capacity to establish the trust and subsequently transfer assets to it. Therefore, besides selecting an offshore haven with strong trust laws, also be certain that there are clear laws on capacity.

The APT can have flexible trust provisions for the trustor, such as to add or remove a beneficiary, to change the share of beneficiaries on occasion, and to change the trustee powers. Investment advisors and custodians can be appointed to assist the trustee as needed. The trustor can draft a letter of wishes for the trustee to follow as a guideline, but the trustee is not legally bound to do so, particularly if the trustor's wishes do not correspond with the purpose of the trust. The time to establish the APT is before creditor problems or lawsuits arise. If these pop up after the trust is set up, the trust assets will be completely protected. Otherwise, a transfer of assets under such conditions could be fraudulent. The APT is tax-neutral and not established to save on taxes. For tax purposes, it is considered a grantor trust, not a foreign trust. This is an ideal device for U.S. professionals to protect assets against malpractice suits. There are numerous advantages to the foreign asset protection trust and a local professional or qualified estate planner can answer any questions you may have. The cost will likely be more than the cost to establish a trust in the United States.

A *charitable trust* can be employed for personal tax planning by a well-heeled person for perfectly charitable reasons. Foreign charitable entities include foundations, trusts, and certain types of companies, but these are complicated for U.S. citizens to use, and the benefits may run out quicker than hoped, requiring further tax planning alternatives. A few charitable vehicles worth looking into are the Austrian private foundation known as the "Privatstiftung," the Bermuda international charitable trust, the Cayman Island Special Alternative Regime, the Gibraltar company limited by guarantee, the Isle of Man hybrid company, possibly the Gibraltar hybrid company limited by guarantee, the Liechtenstein foundation known as the *Stiftungen,* the Panama foundation, and the Swiss tax-exempt foundation.

Foundations are generally organized in civil law countries as legal entities created under statutes and basically they serve the same purpose as the trusts found in common law countries. Foundations are established by a founder for wealth management either for the beneficiary or for a specified purpose. There are no shareholders. Administration is by a corporation or individual members.

This applies to Liechtenstein and Panama, where you will find favorable civil law foundations.

The *Liechtenstein Foundation,* or Stiftungen, is not taxed by Liechtenstein if it qualifies as an offshore corporation, and any beneficiaries who are outside the country and receiving monies from the foundation are also not subject to tax. The founder may be a corporation or an individual of any nationality and may reside anywhere in the world. The Liechtenstein foundation is a cross between a corporation and a trust, similar in that way to the Anstalt described previously. A certified foundation deed must be filed with the Public Register; however, no information is available to the public.

From a tax perspective, it might be advisable for U.S. citizens to avoid using a foundation in a civil law country as the Internal Revenue Service may categorize it as a trust or alter ego of the founder's right. That is to say, they might perceive that the founder, maybe a local lawyer, has established the foundation on behalf of an offshore investor that the IRS has a particular interest in, causing them to look closely. This could also possibly apply to the Liechtenstein Anstalt. In both cases, there are no associates, which the IRS requires to clearly define such an entity for tax purposes as a corporation; otherwise, it may be that it will be taxed as a trust. A Liechtenstein domiciliary or holding company might work better. Part Three provides more information on the Liechtenstein and Panama types of legal entity for international use.

Either of these entities, if for the benefit of a nonresident alien, should avoid investment in real estate, securities, or other assets within the United States, so as not to be taxed on its income and also to avoid the Anstalt or foundation from being taxed on its U.S. assets at the time of the nonresident alien's death.

The *Anglo-Saxon foundation* is the English common law answer to the Liechtenstein foundation. A guarantee company would be organized by the founder in an attractive offshore jurisdiction, and it would be structured in a way to mimic a Liechtenstein foundation, although it will be a more sophisticated and flexible version. Once established, the founder appoints two classes of directors, the founder directors, constituting the founder and his family who have control of the financial benefits of the foundation, and the general directors who would be professional advisors to run the daily affairs. The founding directors can elect new members, such as themselves, who are the recipients of the benefits of this structure. As for the general directors, they are paid for their services and have no control over the founding directors, who may be elected, or what benefits the members are to receive. The Anglo-Saxon foundation would be treated as a corporation for tax purposes.

OFFSHORE LIFE INSURANCE

Beneficiaries of an offshore life insurance policy are not taxed on receipt of the death benefit when the policyholder dies, avoiding estate taxes and taxes known as "generation-skipping" taxes. With income taxes and estate taxes gobbling up as much as 50 percent and more of the value of an estate, offshore life insurance looks very attractive. It is also possible to borrow nearly the full value of the policy with no requirement to service the loan. Policy loans are tax free. Good asset protection is afforded in jurisdictions that legislate protection of the death benefit and underlying investments, making it more challenging to contest the estate. In a tax haven with secrecy or strong confidentiality laws, privacy is maximized. Formerly blacked-out foreign investment opportunities are available, and the asset manager you appoint can make any type of investment at your discretion. Purchase of an offshore life insurance policy is nonreportable, and the tax-free income and profits it earns are also nonreportable.

The best type of offshore life insurance policy is known as a Private Placement Variable Universal Life Insurance (PPVUL). This policy can be held by a foreign trust, and at the time of the grantor's death, the beneficiaries could effectively avoid estate tax. You would want to consult with a reliable advisor. Although not expensive to establish and administer annually, it would require a significant estate of at least $500,000 to be worth pursuing.

THE OFFSHORE WILL

A will is to an investor what a safety net is to a high-wire circus performer. If he should fall, the safety net is in place to catch him. It would be of little use to construct the net after he is falling. The same goes for your will. Fate does not give advance notice.

Most likely, you do not want to leave your estate, no matter how large or how small, to the state. Even if you don't have or don't wish to allow family members to benefit from your hard efforts and financial accomplishments, there is always someone or a charitable cause that would be worthy of a financial infusion.

To die without a will is to die intestate, and it is a sure way to help the government coffers. If nothing else, someone is going to have to attend to the details of your death, including costs related to burial. We all want someone to see to those details, so it is best to decide in advance who that is likely to be. If no one else is on your list as a beneficiary, this person might be a likely choice for that privilege.

Offshore assets will complicate the settlement of your estate if not planned for in advance. Your beneficiaries may suffer longer delays and greater expense in settling the estate. If the bulk of your estate is held in offshore assets, you should consider having a will that covers them, and possibly a foreign trust, too, like an asset protection trust. In fact, you could have one trust for covering U.S. holdings and another for foreign assets. What doesn't get covered by the trust(s) will be covered by the will.

The cleanest and most common method for holding foreign assets is to place them in an offshore corporation and then have the shares of the corporation be owned by the trust. That way you can have good control over the assets and manage them better.

It is wise to have a reputable foreign attorney who is versed in estate planning review the status of your estate as early as possible. Besides getting it in order, you may discover, as presented in this book, the many financial benefits you could be gaining while alive, including tax-deferred and tax-free earnings, asset protection, and diversified investment strategies that can increase your wealth.

With foreign assets comes the need for the executor of the estate to appoint legal representatives in each country where they are located. This effort can be coordinated on behalf of the executor by your offshore attorney, making the task much easier. You will also have a greater level of privacy by having your personal affairs attended to offshore because the foreign attorney, even though bound by attorney-client privilege, is not licensed in the United States or whatever your country of origin may be, and thus is not directly subject to the laws of your government.

It is fairly easy *not* to leave your estate intestate as Howard Hughes did, which is pretty amazing, since he managed to build an empire.

22

THE SWISS ANGLE

Switzerland has a host of banking and investment services that are exceptional, unique, and often more advantageous than other offshore havens. A few of the financial products and services worth reviewing include Swiss bank accounts, personal portfolio management, Swiss annuities, tax-deferred gold accumulation, premium deposit accounts, and the Swiss company.

Additional features of Switzerland are reviewed in Part Three. It expounds many banking, legal, and business professionals who are either in Switzerland or specialize in Switzerland, and who will gladly provide in-depth information and advice.

The many engrossing aspects and unique benefits of Switzerland and Swiss banking can only be adequately shared with readers by devoting a book solely to this subject. Therefore, my next forthcoming book, *Secrets of Swiss Banking: An Owner's Manual to Quietly Building a Fortune,* will be published in 2007, with a vaultful of Swiss banking and investing treasures.

The famous Swiss bank account may just offer the offshore investor access to the widest banking and investment services to be found anywhere, so extra coverage is offered here, providing a glimpse into Switzerland's many tempting avenues and secrets.

Switzerland is a T-7 tax haven because of its status as a low-tax haven and banking haven, and its success speaks for itself. Switzerland and her professionals and institutions have earned their reputation as "bankers to the world." Fully *one-third* of the world's assets are managed from this Alpine money haven.

Swiss banks are unsurpassed. The reasons include Switzerland's long history in banking, the country's neutrality and political and economic stability, and the array of financial services available, some of which extend beyond our concepts of traditional banking. They include such financial and investment areas as stocks, bonds, precious metals, currency trading, margin accounts, forward contracts, asset management, and more. Swiss banking is famous for its secrecy, an important historic element and the cornerstone of the business, which has attracted untold numbers of clients, some among the mysterious and infamous, since the later half of the nineteenth century. Even today, the customers of banks are beneficiaries of this tradition, as Switzerland continues its ironclad defense of its secrecy and its practices.

But, Swiss banking comprises more than just banking . . . it is a world of financial services and products reflecting the whole investment community and frankly addresses the investors' overall financial health and their big-picture goals. This is beyond the magnitude and scope of your local banker.

Swiss banking is not finite in its approach, merely seeking to promote the deposit-taking and lending and borrowing capabilities that most banks are limited to offering. Individual investors have a powerful resource at their disposal, and it all begins with the simple act of having a Swiss bank account.

The Swiss bank account is the door that opens the Swiss vault containing financial freedom. This includes everything already said about offshore bank accounts in Chapter 19, the previous discussion of Switzerland in Chapter 15, and the further information to be found in Part Three under the Switzerland profile.

Several things happen immediately on opening a Swiss bank account. You have just internationally diversified your financial holdings and engaged asset protection for cash, investments, and other valuables.

Of course, a bank account must be denominated in a currency, which is in fact an investment in its own right. Here, you may decide which of the world's many currencies you would rather hold. Has the news of the U.S. dollar got you down? As it drops, so does your buying power, taking more dollars to buy the same goods and services. No wonder you begin to feel poorer and poorer as time goes on. Add inflation to the scenario and the story gets worse. Prices inflate upward, and again it takes more dollars to make purchases and to pay off car loans, mortgages, and even taxes.

Instead, why not keep your money in a currency that is increasing in value over time, or at least holding its own, against many other currencies. Although currencies can fluctuate up and down like any commodity, one currency has withstood the test of time. This is the Swiss franc. Most likely, you will keep a local U.S. account in U.S. dollars, so that you can receive and make payments on a daily basis for your local needs and obligations. If you have funds on deposit in Switzerland, your intent is probably to keep these funds secure offshore while investing from offshore. This makes sense and further facilitates your ability to make important payments. You may want to implement various other Swiss services such as having a Swiss annuity, accumulating gold, setting up a premium deposit account with a Swiss insurance company, and more. These services can be paid for in Swiss francs, and by having a Swiss bank account, making these payments is easy while staying invested in Swiss francs. That way, as the U.S. dollar is dropping, a trend likely to continue for the unforeseeable future, you will have peace of mind knowing your Swiss bank account is held in a strong currency. And typically, the best is the Swiss franc.

As the dollar continues its slide, you are likely making money if you are holding Swiss francs because the difference between the value of the dollar and the Swiss currency is profit. And, as the dollar drops, there will also be further upward pressure on the Swiss franc, a commodity nearly as good as gold that can be a hedge against all kinds of economic crises. Then the upward increase in your Swiss francs will translate to even greater gains between the U.S. dollar and the Swiss franc, and that goes in your pocket, or rather, is accumulating in your Swiss franc denominated Swiss bank account in the form of a more valuable asset, a stronger Swiss franc with more purchasing power. Now you are getting ahead. And, you are proactively countering the negative effects that may have undermined your individual sovereignty, personal well-being, and financial health.

This little Alpine haven has managed customer's investments for eons, but in recent times, Switzerland has been grooming itself further in the role of premier asset manager, deliberately attracting the well-heeled, high net worth individuals of the world.

Personal portfolio management is also known as "personal asset management," which I like to call the "Swiss Millionaire's Club." The reason is simple: The banks that specialize in catering to elite customers, the crème de la crème of the world's investors, generally require a minimum of one million dollars to begin. This is the ultimate place to keep your cachet secure and working for you while you enjoy retirement, or even better, while you move on to making your next fortune.

There are over five hundred banks in Switzerland, but a good example to consider for managing your personal portfolio is the private bank, Bank Julius Baer, in Zurich. It has a fine reputation and extensive experience with international investment management. Bank

Julius Baer has been one of the preeminent banks of Europe since 1890, maintaining offices in major financial centers.

Preservation and enhancement of capital is this bank's main area of expertise. Their conservative philosophy assures clients of superior returns and reduced risk by diversifying the portfolio to include a basket of multicurrencies and multiasset strategies. Only high quality, highly liquid investments are entertained, further reducing risk.

At Bank Julius Baer, your personal portfolio manager will tailor a custom investment strategy designed to fit your investment goals, and is personally responsible for executing investment decisions on your behalf. This same bank representative is also at your disposal to introduce you to the bank's other financial services.

On an individual basis, Bank Julius Baer will accept management authorization over investment accounts starting at U.S. $1,000,000. If you wish to manage the account and provide investment instructions to the bank, the minimum to establish the account is U.S. $500,000.

For further information, or to engage Bank Julius Baer as your investment advisor and portfolio manager, please refer to their listing in Part Four: "Financial and Investment Service Contacts."

Many other Swiss banks provide similar services, and in some cases, the initial requirement to open a personal portfolio management account is as low as U.S. $200,000, as in the case of Anker Bank Lausanne, but this bank is an exception to the rule.

The Swiss insurance business, like the Swiss banks, also has a sterling reputation in the financial world, and provides some valuable and unique products and services. The fact that Swiss insurance companies are not banks gives them certain decisive advantages over Swiss banks in some strategies. The insurance industry is conservative and strong, and concentrated among only 20 insurance providers. The industry is strictly regulated by the Swiss Federal Bureau of Private Insurance, and never has one failed.

The Swiss annuity offers many benefits similar to the offshore variable annuity discussed earlier. It is a great way to create retirement income and receive tax-free withdrawals. And, you can borrow up to 90 percent of the value of the annuity. (Note: Beware of provisions allowing borrowing.) This can be helpful on one hand, but on the other, it is a means for a court or government confiscation (i.e., through exchange controls or other means) to force you to repatriate the funds even if you have to borrow to get them. This would defeat the asset protection features. However, this government action would be an extreme-case scenario.

The principal amount is invested with the Swiss insurance company, and a contract is created between you and the insurance company and is known as an annuity. This money accumulates as tax-deferred savings, so that tax-free compounded interest can really be effective. It is legal for U.S. citizens to have a Swiss annuity.

The Swiss annuity is benefited by interest, profit sharing and the appreciation of the Swiss franc. In the past 30 years, money held in a Swiss annuity would have multiplied by a factor of more than 15 times. Aside from the financial rewards, the Swiss annuity is a simple way to invest and get armadillo-quality asset protection because the owners and beneficiaries, under Swiss laws, are expressly protected from outside creditors or government confiscation. The Swiss annuity can also be placed in an offshore trust, like an asset protection trust, and gain even greater asset protection. A Swiss annuity can be custom tailored to your individual requirements and there are no U.S. reporting requirements.

A beneficiary can be named, so if the purchaser of the annuity dies before the annuity distributes, it will bypass probate. The full value of the annuity will go directly to your loved ones. A beneficiary can also be someone other than family.

As mentioned, the United States could implement exchange controls, a real possibility. Besides restricting the free flow of funds in and out of the United States, they could force investors with known overseas bank and investment accounts to repatriate funds back to the states. This would be counterproductive to what you are trying to accomplish; in fact, it could be devastating. The offshore investment selection process is then critical to meeting your requirements, especially if you have an eye toward avoiding future exchange controls. The annuity would escape these controls. *A Swiss bank account and other types of investments, including offshore trusts, may be in jeopardy under this scenario, especially financial accounts and investments that are required to be reported by U.S. law.*

The best way to purchase a Swiss annuity is to consult with a financial advisor in Switzerland who specializes in them. This specialist will gladly provide you with in-depth information and will assist with the arrangements. Several reputable firms are listed in Part Four. The minimum investment is $20,000. Also, a Liechtenstein insurance investment is an excellent alternative to Switzerland.

Here's a thought on how to make those Swiss annuity payments, and also a way to have a Swiss bank account without actually having one. And, it won't be subject to U.S. reporting requirements, providing a high level of confidentiality. The *Premium Deposit Account* is an interest-bearing account in Swiss francs, established with an insurance company, usually for making insurance premiums on Swiss annuities and other insurance products. The deposits are considered "premium deposits," and you can deposit as much as you like. Your policy number is used as reference instead of a bank account number. Interest payments received from the account are all tax-free. The insurance company will issue an annual statement. Your insurance premiums will be automatically deducted from the account.

The Portfolio Bond, or Offshore Insurance Bond, combines the benefits of offshore banking and offshore insurance to create a unique holding structure. The best jurisdiction for this is Switzerland. This device affords excellent asset protection and strong confidentiality. The customer establishes a relationship by buying a Portfolio Bond with a Swiss insurance company, essentially a contract like the annuity, and in turn, the insurance company issues a policy, and then invests the money at the direction of the customer. You may direct them to purchase shares of stock, unit trusts, bonds, cash deposits, mutual funds, and in fact, any investment where value can be established. To facilitate these financial transactions and insulate the client further, the insurance company sets up a bank account with a bank chosen by the customer, and then the funds are deposited with the bank, all of this being orchestrated by the insurance company on behalf of the client. Talk about effective! The money grows, tax-free, giving the principal the maximum ability to compound and increase. Life insurance coverage can also be purchased through this structure. A nice feature of the Portfolio Bond is the ability to separate distributions from the estate and designate a beneficiary directly. On your death, the money would be quickly dispersed by the insurance company to the named beneficiaries, usually within a few days of proof of death. The biggest drawback to the Portfolio Bond may be that some insurance companies require a minimum of around U.S. $160,000 to purchase one. It may be that you can find an insurance company, as in the case of Swiss banks, that will allow you to begin with less. Try starting with the names of the Swiss investment advisors in Part Four who can provide Swiss annuities.

The *tax-deferred gold accumulation plan* is a means to acquire gold for investment and to inflation-proof yourself without the physical problems of handling, storage, shipping, and theft. This plan allows for a single purchase, multiple purchases over time, or monthly accumulation. For small investors who want to diversify into gold, the monthly accumulation plan makes it easy and the minimum monthly amount required to be in the program is $250. You may also stop the program at anytime. You can also make purchases anytime, and the additional gold purchases will be added to the gold already being held. The plan can be tailored to your requirements so it is very flexible to the investor's needs.

Purchases are whole or fractional because they are based on the dollar amount purchased, not on the ounce. Orders are combined daily by the bank executing the purchase; therefore the customer is the beneficiary of the lowest purchase price, giving them more gold for their money, because the bank buys and sells on the wholesale bullion dealer market, and the commission rates are heavily discounted. And, there are not the usual small order surcharges. This is an economical way to invest in gold, and there are no storage charges.

The best part of the plan may be relief from worry about your gold being stolen from your home, personal safe, or other vulnerable place. The gold can be stored in banks in Switzerland, Canada, or the United States, and is insured. But, if you want the numerous benefits that go with Swiss banking and Switzerland, there is only one real choice. The account is a fiduciary account, and although the gold is held on the client's behalf in the name of the bank, it is segregated on the bank's books and not subject to creditors or other bank obligations. It is the property of the bank's customer—you. The investor receives regular statements of activity and gold holdings (see Part Four: "Financial and Investment Service Contacts").

The *tax-free money market account* offers higher interest rates, and the best part is that your earnings accumulate tax free. Funds may be deposited and withdrawn at anytime without restriction. This is a really good choice and alternative to a conventional Swiss bank account as earnings are not subject to the 35 percent Swiss withholding tax. It is a convenient way for making all types of Swiss and foreign investments, and also for holding Swiss francs. Several other currencies are offered including the U.S. dollar and the Euro. The denomination of the account can change anytime you choose. The minimum to establish the account is $10,000. The tax-free money market account is offered by a strong, liquid Swiss investment bank founded in 1965. They can also provide Swiss securities trading accounts.

The Swiss Company has a certain appeal. Switzerland is a low-tax haven, therefore a Swiss company could have tax benefits as found in other tax havens. The choice of corporate vehicles would include the holding company whose income is generated only from passive sources; it may completely avoid federal income taxes if it is considered a pure holding company. Otherwise, as with the domiciliary company, a non-Swiss company with its home base in Switzerland but its business conducted elsewhere, would pay around 10 percent in federal taxes, and there would be low cantonal taxes, too. The Swiss tax law is complex and it may require extra work and expense to gain the benefits. Swiss companies are also expensive to incorporate (see Part Three for a profile of Switzerland and Swiss contacts). Also review the profile for Campione (Italy), an excellent alternative to Switzerland or Liechtenstein. If you're interested in doing business in Switzerland, look at the Canton of Zug first.

For more information on the financial and investment services mentioned here, refer to Part Four and the Appendix for company contacts, and visit www.barberfinancialadvisors.com.

23

PLACING YOUR ASSETS OFFSHORE AND AVOIDING FRAUDULENT TRANSFERS

There are several types of fraudulent transfers, none of which you want to get caught doing, even unknowingly. Laws against fraudulent transfers intend to protect the creditor under civil law, "the people" under criminal law, and a trustee under bankruptcy law. It may not be easy for any of them to pursue a person who has fraudulently transferred assets; in fact, it would have to be financially motivating to make it economically worthwhile. The cost of pursuit could easily outweigh the benefits. Assets taken out of your home country are difficult to attach, especially once put into a corporate, trust, or other structure. But, there could be severe civil and criminal penalties if transfers were determined to be fraudulent. And, individuals fraudulently transferring assets could be undermining their own plans to securely place assets offshore.

Therefore, a person's reason for transferring assets must have a proper motive, such as legal tax planning, estate planning, legitimate business plans, or other logically perceived reasons. This will create a better argument for why assets were taken offshore if ever challenged. But the hope should be that no creditors or bankruptcy court are looking in the first place. Your solvency is the pivotal test of whether a transfer was fraudulent.

Under two civil law systems, the Uniform Fraudulent Conveyances Act (UFCA) and the Uniform Fraudulent Transfers Act (UFTA), creditors have certain remedies and protections. To prove fraud, one must prove intent to defraud. This is not so easy, but case law and the UFTA provide the option of proving fraud by showing a badge of fraud. There are 11 badges of fraud, and an indication of just one would raise a red flag and the possibility of fraudulent intent. A badge of fraud is easier to determine than intent to defraud.

In *constructive fraud,* there is lack of fair value or consideration in exchange for the asset being transferred. And unlike actual fraud, there is no requirement to prove intent to defraud nor is a badge of fraud required.

You should carefully determine your situation with potential creditors, including spouses, and understand the structure and laws of the country where you propose to transfer assets. These laws will vary by country, including statutes of limitations. Get advice from a professional if you have any doubts.

24

OFFSHORE BUSINESS

Starting and operating a business offshore is much like doing the same domestically, except that if you are not leaving your country to accomplish the task, you will be doing it through long distance or electronic communications. More than anything, this will require personal confidence in yourself, and trust in your chosen offshore professionals.

The discussion and mechanics of establishing a business presence were covered in Chapters 17 and 18. With the legal requirements accomplished, such as incorporating in the best jurisdiction for your intended purpose and selecting the offshore professional management who can handle the necessary tasks, opening the financial accounts as needed with stable institutions will be the next critical step.

Once these are properly established and the company can function on a day-to-day basis per your instructions, then when ready, you can consider your options on establishing a physical presence, if necessary. Some business, such as for investment purposes, or e-commerce activity, may not require a physical office. This is particularly true if most of the business activity is purely financial transactions of some kind.

Today, establishing a physical presence anywhere in the world has become relatively easy. Executive office services abound. For example, HQ Business Centers is a network of over 750 office services worldwide, where you can arrange anything from a business presence of the most basic kind with an answered telephone and fax numbers, to the leasing of a small office or even an entire suite. If creating a permanent presence is the object, a lease would be wise. Sometimes with even the simplest of services, as in the case of an accommodation relationship with one of these companies, they will provide you with, or require, a minimal lease. With these serviced offices, you can become a transnational corporation overnight, albeit, maybe one of the world's smallest.

Almost any business, even those that seem typically domestic, can be operated from offshore, thereby availing you of its benefits. Offshore business is conducive for international activities and even for conducting business with your home country.

Services are easy to provide through an offshore business structure. Where goods and manufacturing are concerned and a physical warehouse or plant would generally be required to operate the business, there are tax-free trade zones to locate such operations. Often, services can be contracted in these favorable tax locales that specialize in providing the necessary facilities without having to staff them. They can also be located in jurisdictions other than where the company is incorporated, but in any case, it would be best to situate this activity in a tax-free economic zone.

Perhaps the most ideal business to take offshore is a cyberbusiness. It is the perfect marriage between e-commerce and offshore business, a natural means to conduct business 24/7 worldwide. Location is the least important aspect. Any entirely virtual business operating domestically can just as easily operate offshore.

Aside from the previously discussed legal, financial, and tax aspects of any offshore-operated enterprise, a cyberbusiness also brings special tax aspects into consideration. The business entity is always subject to the taxes of the jurisdiction where it is incorporated, but in the case of a cyberbusiness, if a significant part of the business is conducted through a server, it is likely that the server's location will be considered a permanent establishment (PE) of the business, and subject the business to the tax structure of the country where the server is located.

Thus, if you are considering operating an offshore cyberbusiness, the jurisdiction where you incorporated and the location of your business's Internet server will both have a potentially direct effect on taxes it will have to pay. A local offshore professional can give you guidance in pinpointing their jurisdiction.

Guidelines known as the Framework Conditions have been established by the Organisation for Economic Co-operation and Development (OECD) and are being widely accepted by member and nonmember countries for determining taxation of e-commerce business.

Should you incorporate in a tax haven for the tax benefits, however, and in one that promotes e-commerce business, you are likely to get around this problem. Many offshore jurisdictions have adopted e-commerce legislation and have the technological support to service these businesses. In other words, the server could be located in the same tax-advantaged jurisdiction where you incorporate the company, so that the tax implications as a result of the location of the server make it a neutral issue. By having the server and your e-commerce business outside your home country, and particularly in a tax haven, you will gain privacy from domestic government snoops from back home, and others. An example of the availability of this dynamic combination would be Belize.

25

INTERNATIONAL TAX PLANNING

Here are some important highlights affecting international tax planning decisions.

THE PENTAPUS

The term *Pentapus,* as well as other expressions, has been coined for five challenging areas of the Internal Revenue Code that international tax planners face on behalf of their American clients. Their assignment for helping U.S. taxpayers with these potential tax liabilities is to work around them legally when both possible and advantageous for reducing or deterring taxes.

These are the five stumbling blocks:

1. Controlled foreign corporation
2. Foreign personal holding company
3. Personal holding company
4. Passive foreign investment company
5. Accumulated earnings

These complex IRS codes are only briefly described here.

CONTROLLED FOREIGN CORPORATION

Subpart F of the Internal Revenue Code was enacted to tax U.S. shareholders on undistributed profits of foreign corporations regardless of whether a dividend is paid. This measure prevents majority owners of foreign corporations from accumulating profits and delaying payment of taxes until they choose to declare a dividend.

The IRC defines a controlled foreign corporation (CFC), IRC 951–64, as a corporation having more than 50 percent of its outstanding voting shares owned by a maximum of five U.S. shareholders. A U.S. stockholder is defined as an American who directly or indirectly owns 10 percent or more of the voting stock.

It is difficult, but not impossible, for a U.S. majority shareholder in a foreign corporation to circumvent the CFC tax, but if direct control can be relinquished, taxes can be deferred indefinitely or until the corporation is sold or liquidated.

For example, the U.S. shareholder is permitted to own up to and including 50 percent of the voting stock of the corporation. Although this is not majority control, it still amounts to considerable interest. The U.S. shareholder brings in another shareholder, an unrelated foreign person or corporation, to take possession of the remaining 50 percent of the voting shares. The bylaws of the offshore corporation call for the shareholders to elect two directors who will sit on the board and manage the corporation's affairs. The articles also stipulate that an additional, nonelected director may be appointed by the U.S. director, although the U.S. director-shareholder cannot influence the third director's decisions or appoint another one. This strategy amounts to indirect control and ultimately gives the U.S. director-shareholder the upper hand.

There are two other methods for a U.S. shareholder to own shares in a foreign corporation. They fall under the Attribution of Ownership Rules: Chain of Ownership, IRC 958(a); and, the Constructive Ownership rule IRC 958(b). Explore these avenues with your chosen international tax planning expert.

FOREIGN PERSONAL HOLDING COMPANY

The foreign personal holding company (FPHC), IRC 551–58, derives its income from passive sources, such as dividends, interest, royalties, annuities, profits from stock sales, certain commodity profits, rents, income from the sale of an estate or trust, certain personal service contract monies, and a few other sources.

A U.S. shareholder is taxed on a proportionate share of the undistributed income if a maximum of the five U.S. citizens own 50 percent or more of the value of the outstanding stock and if at least 60 percent of the gross income is FPHC income. As with the CFC, the FPHC tax can be circumvented by not directly controlling the corporation or by attribution.

PERSONAL HOLDING COMPANY

Another tax is the personal holding company (PHC), IRC 542(a), which is similar to the foreign personal holding company (FPHC). The PHC tax is not levied against U.S. shareholders but a tax against the company.

PASSIVE FOREIGN INVESTMENT COMPANY

Regardless of the number of shares held by Americans, if 75 percent of a foreign corporation's income is from passive sources or more than half its assets contribute to the creation of that income, the U.S. citizen owning shares will pay taxes on the proportionate amount along with interest when profits are no longer deferred, as defined by IRC 904(d)(2)(A). The passive foreign investment company (PFIC), IRC 1291–1297, effectively replaced the foreign investment company provisions.

ACCUMULATED EARNINGS

The accumulated earnings (AE) tax, IRC 532(a) is intended to discourage accumulated earnings so that funds will be reinvested or distributed and/or taxed. Both U.S. and foreign corporations are subject to the AE tax, but it only applies on U.S. income. The IRS computes the tax rate at 39.8 percent.

Effective 2003, there are exemptions from the AE income tax with respect to its shareholders, regardless of the number of shareholders, which include:

- PHC—a personal holding company, IRC 542
- FPHC—a foreign personal holding company, IRC 552
- Subpart F—a tax-exempt corporation, IRC 501
- PFIC—a passive foreign investment company, IRC 1297

For a more comprehensive review of these Internal Revenue Codes, how they can affect your offshore activities, and possible strategies for avoiding them, readers and their tax planners will benefit by reviewing

Tax Havens of the World by Thomas P. Azzara (see Appendix A: "Offshore Reading") and *Offshore Planning* by Mary Simon, LLM, JD (see Part Four: "Offshore Reference Works" for further information).

REPORTING REQUIREMENTS OF U.S. CITIZENS

Special requirements are imposed on U.S. taxpayers to report certain international financial transactions including income, profit, transfers, ownership, and other purposes. Here are some of the more frequently used IRS forms that you should be aware of:

Form 5471—Information Return with Respect to a Foreign Corporation—This form is used when acquiring or disposing of an interest in a foreign corporation, when a controlled foreign corporation conducts certain transactions, and when declaring income received from a foreign corporation.

Form 5472—Information Return of a 25 percent Foreign-Owned U.S. Corporation or a Foreign Corporation Engaged in a U.S. Trade or Business—It is used when an American company has substantial foreign ownership or a foreign company is doing business in the United States.

Form 3520—Annual Return to Report Transactions with Foreign Trusts and Receipt of Certain Foreign Gifts—Use it when establishing or transferring assets to a foreign trust.

Form 926—Return by U.S. Transferor of Property to a Foreign Corporation—This is used when transferring property to a foreign entity.

Form 3520A—It is used to declare income of a foreign trust when a U.S. taxpayer holds an interest.

Forms 1042 and 1042S—Use this form when payments are made to a foreign person.

Forms 1020NR (corporation) and 1040NR (individual)—This form is used for receipt of U.S. income or foreign effectively connected-with income by a resident or nonresident alien, respectively.

Form 4789—Currency Transaction Report (CTR)—It is used by financial institutions to report cash deposits or transactions of $10,000. or more. (These same financial institutions are also required to keep records of all transactions of $3,000 or more.)

Form 4790—Report of International Transportation of Currency or Monetary Instruments—This form is to be filed with the Bureau of Customs if $10,000 or more in cash or monetary instrument equivalent is being carried in or out of the United States.

Form 8300—The form that is used to report business transactions involving $10,000 cash or more.

Form 8362—Currency Transaction Report by Casinos (CTRC)—It is the same as a CTR but is used by casinos to report transactions exceeding $10,000.

Form 8621—Return by a Shareholder of a Passive Foreign Investment Company or Qualified Electing Fund.

Treasury Form TD F 90-22.1—Report of Foreign Bank and Financial Accounts (FBAR)—A U.S. taxpayer must file this form annually disclosing any financial interest in or signing power over a foreign bank or other financial account if the aggregate value of the account exceeded $10,000. Multiple accounts can now be reported on the same form.

The FBAR reads, in part:

> *F. Bank, Financial Account. The term "bank account" means a savings, demand, checking, deposit, loan, or other account maintained with a financial institution or other person engaged in the business of banking. It includes certificates of deposit. The term "securities account" means an account maintained with a financial institution or other person who buys, sells, holds, or trades stock or other securities for the benefit of another. The term "other financial account" means any other account maintained with a financial institution or other person who accepts deposits, exchanges, or transmits funds, or acts as a broker or dealer for future transactions in any commodity on (or subject to the rules of) a commodity exchange or association.*

SUSPICIOUS ACTIVITY REPORTS

This is the ultimate requirement. A Suspicious Activity Report (SAR) gets filed anytime anyone thinks you are doing something wrong. Actually, all it takes is for you to look suspicious. The eagle eye is usually a financial institution. The SAR is required to be filed with FINCEN, a division of the U.S. Treasury, in the case of "any suspicious transaction relevant to a possible violation of law or regulation." So far, they are fairly ineffective, as very few lead to prosecution. What they do is create a lot of paperwork and more bureaucratic expense.

STRUCTURING

Under a 1991 amendment to the Bank Secrecy Act of 1970, the Financial Record Keeping, Currency and Foreign Transactions Reporting Act, *structuring* is basically the act of avoiding the system set up to detect money laundering, and this is illegal. This includes structuring deposits to avoid the $10,000 currency transaction reporting required by the government of banks. This form is a red flag that a suspicious transaction may have taken place. In an effort to get around this detection, a method of structuring transactions is executed in hopes of avoiding attention. This is also known as *smurfing*.

If you take a lump sum of whatever amount, and break it down into amounts smaller than $10,000 each, and deposit these in various accounts rather than depositing the single sum as originally received in a single account (requiring the receiving bank to file Form 4790), or if you delay depositing such lesser amounts into one or more accounts, spreading them over time to avoid the $10,000 threshold at which the bank must file their report, then you are structuring, and this in itself is illegal. It can be an individual acting independently or any number of others assisting in the process. The penalties are stiff, so it's worth avoiding.

TAX TREATIES

There are numerous income tax treaties between the United States and foreign countries, including tax havens. These are also referred to as double-taxation agreements and provide the U.S. taxpayer living in the United States with a foreign tax credit, not a deduction, for all foreign taxes that qualify.

Frequently, these treaties include exchange-of-information clauses that allow several possibilities for exchanging information between countries, such as routine or automatic transmittal of information, requests for specific information, and spontaneous information requests. More disconcerting than having this type of clause incorporated into an income tax treaty is the Tax Information Exchange Agreement (TIEA), which is not a tax treaty at all, but a way for the

IRS to obtain from another country that is party to such an agreement, confidential information that would otherwise be protected by the tax haven's secrecy and confidentiality laws. Chapter 28 provides more information on TIEAs.

These treaties are important in countries like Switzerland where there is a 35 percent withholding tax on investment earnings and will save the taxpayer from paying twice as much tax, once to Switzerland and again to the IRS. The amount of the withholding tax is deducted right off the amount you would be owing the IRS that year. You can also get a refund direct from the Swiss.

26

OFFSHORE PRIVACY

Simply put, unless you go offshore, you have no privacy—at least not in America. By taking your money and investments offshore, you immediately gain considerable privacy. And, you are then outside your own country's jurisdiction, making it very difficult for the government to get information or your assets. The next action that you may choose to take is to physically leave, avoiding the potential of future forced travel restrictions or a court's ability to conveniently serve you. Any assets within the United States, regardless of ownership claim, are potentially subject to attachment or forfeiture.

As for asset protection, the same applies. In most foreign countries, frivolous lawsuits are not going to fly, especially on a contingency basis. If some folks want to pursue you internationally, either personally or in business matters, they will have to put up their money, retain local legal counsel, and go through the machinations of due process in a foreign country. And then, they are likely to discover that they cannot succeed. They would have to have a real financial motive to continue their pursuit, and when their new foreign lawyer gives them his opinion, they may quit immediately. The offshore structure being attacked will be a deterrent. Litigation-happy hunters may discover the hard way what chances they *don't* have of winning a lawsuit, thanks to the hunted thinking ahead and realizing that a good offshore structure would be smart and arranging it long before being pursued. This gave the hunted, and the hunted's assets, a great deal of privacy.

Most discussion regarding offshore includes the topic of privacy. This has everything to do with personal sovereignty—your right to keep your affairs to yourself, and others out of them, especially your own government. This is why there has been so much pressure to destroy it. Privacy contributes to giving individuals sovereign power over their lives. The more power each individual possesses, the less power their government has to wield over them. Privacy has been the cornerstone of Switzerland's banking success since the nineteenth century. Why? Because it has afforded their banking customers the financial privacy they seek from outside intrusion, specifically, the Swiss government and nosey neighbors. Only truly free people have true personal privacy.

27

OFFSHORE CAVEAT

Plenty of pitfalls exist in life and the same applies to going offshore. It would be impractical to itemize them all here. But, many of the major obstacles and troublesome areas have been addressed in this book so you know what to expect and can deal with them intelligently and with the help of qualified professionals. For starters, you should avoid breaking laws, stay clear of offshore predators, and travel wisely.

The best I can do is to point you in the right direction. Part Four and the Appendix of this book are loaded with good resources and sources of information. It would be well worth your time to explore many of the ideas and personal contacts to increase your knowledge of the subjects contained herein, and expand your horizons in the direction of new opportunities and alternatives to preserving your wealth, keeping your privacy, and generally living a better life.

The world is rapidly changing, and as you read this, the war in Iraq is likely to still be going on, inflation or recession will still be threatening to become a significant problem, dwindling world oil production and high gas prices will not be going away, the real estate market will be in decline, precious metals and other commodities will be headed upward, and so will the national private and public debt, at an astronomical rate, and with no end in sight.

These are some solid reasons to be considering a new game plan in life—and these are the real pitfalls and threats if you *don't* go offshore. To help lessen the risks, use this book as your guide and consult qualified professionals to answer your questions and provide the services you require. I highly recommend not to resort to the Internet to get your advice, but instead to seek out reliable sources, preferably with a referral from a trusted source. I have tried to provide some of the best and most reputable contacts in the offshore field and in the financial and investment arena where you can obtain further information and get reliable advice and professional guidance. If you would like assistance in this process, please refer to "Offshore Evaluation Service" in Part Four. Now you, too, can get offshore quickly, and without a lot of cash. It is important to take the initial steps early, such as getting certain offshore accounts in place in advance of needing them. With minimal capital, you can even start an offshore e-commerce business that can generate an offshore cash flow, possibly your future lifeblood, and all from your armchair. Not only would this be useful, especially if exchange controls are passed in the United States, but it could be lucrative.

Dwindling personal sovereignty and vanishing liberties should be your most urgent concern in today's volatile world. Exercising your rights helps ensure their continued existence. Going offshore is still perfectly legal for Americans, but the opportunity is being attacked with regular frequency. The biggest pitfall may be to do nothing at all. So, what are you waiting for? *Carpe diem*—"Seize the day."

PART THREE

Today's Tax Havens

INTRODUCTION

Part Three serves as an introduction to most of the countries that are considered tax havens, and in some instances, countries such as Austria that are not tax havens in the pure sense, but that deserve introduction as they have something exceptionally beneficial to offer the investor going offshore. In Austria, the benefits include superb bank facilities and strong bank secrecy laws, making this country an attractive banking, money, and asset haven, although one not notable for tax benefits. Aspects of banking and banking services such as asset management make these countries important to consider for personal asset protection.

You could, for example, bank in Switzerland or Austria, and then for business purposes and international tax strategies, you could engage another of the T-7 tax havens like Belize, Nevis, or Panama to be your tax haven jurisdiction of choice. Together, these choices would create a powerful combination to shelter your personal and business assets, investments, and financial activities. You should consider other asset protection strategies, too, such as an asset protection trust (APT) in a favorable asset venue like Nevis, Belize, or the Cook Islands; and of course, you should also explore the many excellent offshore investment products available.

There are other tax havens not profiled in Part Three because, as they stand today, they either are, or have become insignificant for serious consideration. In some cases, they have lost their former stature among tax havens. A few glaring examples are Nauru in the Central Pacific, Montserrat in the Caribbean, and Liberia in North Africa. Too many viable tax havens are available that simply rate higher; in fact, about 40 worthy tax havens are available in any given year. Indeed, in Chapter 30, you will find profiles for 40 offshore havens, but inclusion in itself is not a recommendation or endorsement. Some havens have fallen from prominence as their benefits have been greatly impaired by such devices as the Tax Information Exchange Agreement (TIEA). This agreement has severely hurt the Bahamas and the Cayman Islands as acceptable venues for U.S. citizens to place money or otherwise do business. However, because these tax havens still play an important role in the field, they must be included.

I have identified several favored tax havens as the T-7 or Green List of offshore tax havens, but the possibilities are certainly not limited to these countries. This list is merely a gauge based on my years of knowledge and experience with tax havens and a general consideration of the benefits in today's climate.

Choice of venue or multiple venues has much to do with customized decisions depending on each individual's general goals. Countries like Andorra, Luxembourg, and Denmark could be considered worthy countries to bank for secrecy purposes. Also, Andorra and Denmark would both provide a lower profile as they have minimal or no tax haven attributes. In fact, Denmark is not a tax haven whatsoever and Luxembourg is more of an investment haven with a highly developed global banking center.

Certain facts are presented in the profiles, including important aspects that would be pertinent in the selection process. But this information is merely an overview and, if interesting, may lead you to a further investigation of any given country. The profiles provide highlights, giving you a thumbnail point of reference. Here is the format used for each profile:

- *Affiliations*—Who this country is closely aligned with, such as an international organization or another country or group of countries. These affiliations are not complete because a country may have many possible affiliations, but these are some of the major ones.
- *Location*—The geographic proximity of the country to other countries and regions for quick reference.
- *Capital and Largest City.*
- *Government*—The type of government and its relationship, if any, to another government.
- *Legal System*—The basis of the country's laws—common law and civil law are the most frequently encountered.
- *Official Language.*
- *Stability*—An important factor in doing business, administering financial matters, and banking.
- *Currency.*
- *International Time*—Based on the country's location plus or minus the number of time zones from Greenwich Mean Time (GMT), which passes through Greenwich, England.
- *Country Code*—A specially designated number representing a country, similar to a city or area code. Access by telephone

requires this code to be dialed after the required access number for dialing in or out of a country, such as 01 or 011, and so forth; and the country code is followed by a city code, if any, and local number.

- *Embassy*—The appropriate U.S.-based embassy to contact for business, travel, and country information, including address and telephone number.
- *Type of Legal Entities*—Legal vehicles used for offshore business. Other types of legal entities are likely to exist, too. But the entities included here will be most pertinent to the reader and the topic at hand. Special purpose entities are mentioned as well, such as banks, trusts, investment funds, insurance companies, and shipping. The choice of business vehicle in most tax havens today is the International Business Company (IBC).
- *Unique Characteristics*—Helps determine the unique attributes of a tax haven that you may find attractive. It also covers unique situations presently affecting the haven that may make it more or less desirable. These pointers will help you narrow your choices in the selection process.
- *Taxation*—Brief explanation of any taxes affecting offshore business.
- *Exchange Controls*—Best if there are none.
- *Treaties with the United States*—Important considerations for U.S. citizens using a specific tax haven. Treaties can be advantageous, such as certain circumstances when an income tax treaty will be beneficial in avoiding double taxation, or disadvantageous, such as the Tax Information Exchange Agreement (TIEA), which is designed so that the U.S. government can get what would otherwise be confidential financial information on your activities from financial institutions, possibly defeating your reason for going offshore.
- *Useful Web Sites*—A government web site providing more information on the country.
- *Business Contacts*—Hundreds of hard-to-find business, financial, and professional contacts for the tax havens profiled. Some of these contacts have offices and affiliates in other tax havens as well.

The last profile is Western Samoa. Following that, you will find Part Four followed by the Appendix containing important business, financial, and professional contacts located in the United States, the United Kingdom, and Canada who can assist with many aspects of wealth protection and offshore activities.

28

TAX INFORMATION EXCHANGE AGREEMENTS

This type of treaty has had an understandably profound negative impact on tax havens that have elected to sign a Tax Information Exchange Agreement (TIEA) with the United States. This agreement has no redeeming value to U.S. citizens doing business in these particular tax havens. Information on TIEAs, as they are known, is being provided here in advance of the individual profiles of the tax havens, so that you are aware of them before you read on.

The TIEA was drafted simply to exchange domestic tax information between the United States Internal Revenue Service and the tax haven that chose to be a party to it. The TIEA has no benefit to a private third party like the offshore investor. In fact, the only beneficiary of such a treaty would appear to be the IRS. Secrecy laws in financial matters is the linchpin of success for tax havens, and the single most important reason for their popularity over the decades. But, a TIEA undermines this purpose. Knowing which countries have a TIEA in place with the United States is important, and if financial confidentiality is a concern, you should not do business with a TIEA tax haven. Forget "bank secrecy" or confidentiality if a tax haven or other country has signed a TIEA, and this warning pertains to lawyer relationships in these places, too. This device has undermined once good tax havens including the Bahamas and the Cayman Islands. The following 13 countries have signed TIEAs with the United States and they will surely pay the price for bowing to this outside pressure. (Other tax havens could concede in the future):

1. Antigua and Barbuda
2. Aruba
3. Bahamas
4. Barbados
5. Bermuda
6. British Virgin Islands (BVI)
7. Cayman Islands
8. Channel Islands (includes Guernsey and Jersey)
9. Costa Rica
10. Dominica
11. Grenada
12. Isle of Man
13. Marshall Islands

A total of 20 TIEAs are currently in existence. The other 7 are not tax haven jurisdictions:

1. Dominican Republic
2. Guyana
3. Honduras
4. Mexico
5. Peru
6. St. Lucia
7. Trinidad and Tobago

This leaves the following tax haven countries that have *not* signed a TIEA and should be considered first:

1. Andorra
2. Anguilla
3. Austria*
4. Bahrain
5. Belize*
6. Brunei Daraussalam
7. Cook Islands
8. Cyprus
9. Dubai (U.A.E.)
10. Gibraltar
11. Hong Kong*
12. Labuan (Malaysia)
13. Liechtenstein*
14. Luxembourg
15. Madeira
16. Malaysia
17. Malta
18. Mauritius
19. Monaco
20. Netherlands
21. Netherland Antilles
22. Panama*
23. Saint Kitts and Nevis*
24. Saint Vincent
25. Seychelles
26. Switzerland*
27. Turks and Caicos Islands
28. Vanuatu
29. Western Samoa

*The asterisk denotes a T-7 tax haven, one of my most favored money havens. Fortunately, a greater number of tax havens still have turned down the invitation to sign away their lucrative offshore business than have succumbed. Maybe the remaining countries have realized the harm they will cause themselves if they do sign a TIEA.

29

MUTUAL LEGAL ASSISTANCE TREATY

Here's another treaty that has no tax ramifications, but that, in some cases, allow assets to be seized even without a court order. The Mutual Legal Assistance Treaty (MLAT) was created to help law enforcement in criminal investigations, but is not used in tax evasion cases. This treaty lacks regard for due process of law, which requires "probable cause" under the Fourth Amendment, and substitutes it with "reasonable suspicion." Since its creation in 1973, forty-nine countries have signed the agreement between themselves and the United States, and together they split the booty—billions of dollars to date.

The following countries have signed an MLAT with the United States, effective as of January 1, 2002:

1. Anguilla
2. Antigua and Barbuda
3. Argentina
4. Australia
5. Austria*
6. Bahamas
7. Barbados
8. Belgium
9. Brazil
10. British Virgin Islands (BVI)
11. Canada
12. Cayman Islands
13. Czech Republic
14. Dominica
15. Egypt
16. Estonia
17. Greece
18. Grenada
19. Hong Kong*
20. Hungary
21. Israel
22. Italy (includes Campione)
23. Jamaica
24. Latvia
25. Lithuania
26. Luxembourg
27. Mexico

28. Montserrat
29. Morocco
30. Netherlands
31. Panama*
32. Philippines
33. Poland
34. Romania
35. Spain
36. Saint Kitts and Nevis*
37. Saint Lucia
38. Saint Vincent and the Grenadines
39. South Africa
40. South Korea
41. Thailand
42. Turkey
43. Turks and Caicos
44. Trinidad and Tobago
45. Ukraine
46. United Kingdom
47. Uruguay
48. Venezuela

The following tax havens are profiled in this book and *have not* signed an MLAT with the United States:

1. Andorra
2. Aruba
3. Bahrain
4. Belize*
5. Bermuda
6. Brunei
7. Cook Islands
8. Costa Rica
9. Cyprus
10. Dubai, U.A.E.
11. Labuan, Malaysia
12. Liechtenstein*
13. Madeira
14. Malta
15. Monaco
16. Mauritius
17. Seychelles
18. Switzerland*
19. Vanuatu
20. Western Samoa

For non-U.S. citizens who are reading this book, there may be more advantages for you in some of these tax havens as the treaties in place with your country of citizenship are likely to be different, and there is a good possibility that you are not subject to taxation on your worldwide income as are U.S. citizens. These factors will have a great bearing on which tax haven will work best for you.

* Again, the asterisks indicate T-7 countries.

30

PROFILES OF TAX HAVENS

Andorra

Affiliations: France and Spain; United Nations.

Location: Western Europe, between France and Spain in the Pyrenees Mountains.

Capital and Largest City: Andorra la Vella.

Government: Parliamentary Co-Principality of France and Spain, but remains autonomous.

Legal System: Civil law system.

Official Language: Catalan. Also speak French, Castilian Spanish, and Portuguese.

Stability: Stable.

Currency: Euro.

International Time: +1 hr. GMT.

Country Code: 33 628.

Embassy: Embassy of Andorra/Permanent Mission to the UN, 2 United Nations Plaza, 25th Floor, New York, NY10017. Telephone: (212) 750-8064.

Type of Legal Entities: SC-Societate de responsibilitat limitada is a private limited company; International Business Company (IBC).

Unique Characteristics: Strict bank secrecy. Numbered accounts. Good expatriate haven. Not cooperating with the OECD. A blacklisted country. No extradition treaties or diplomatic relations with the United States.

Taxation: There are no direct taxes.

Exchange Controls: None.

Treaties with the United States: No income tax treaties. No Tax Information Exchange Agreement (TIEA). No Mutual Legal Assistance Treaty (MLAT).

Useful Web Site: http://www.andorra.ad

Business Contacts:

Barber Financial Advisors
355 Burrard Street, Suite 1000
Vancouver, BC, V6C 2G8, Canada
Telephone: (604) 608-6177
Fax: (604) 608-2984
Web site: www.BarberFinancialAdvisors.com
Private Bank Accounts

Banc Agricol i Commercial d' Andorra S.A.
Center De Negoci, Av. Fiter i Rossell, 4-bis
Escalades-Engordany, Andorra
Telephone: (376) 873-333
Fax: (376) 863-905
Banking

Banc International/Banca Mora S.A.
Av. Meritxell 96
Andorra La Vella, Andorra
Telephone: (376) 820-607
Fax: (376) 829-980
Web site: www.bancamora.ad/entrada-fra.php
Banking

Banca Privada d' Andorra S.A.
Placa Rebes, 7
Andorra la Vella, Andorra
Telephone: (376) 808-400
Fax: (376) 867-729
Banking

Banca Reig, S.A.
Av. Meritxell 79
Andorra la Vella, Andorra
Telephone: (376) 872-872
Fax: (376) 872-875
Web site: www.andbanc.com
Banking

Caixabank, S.A.
Placa Rebes 3
Andorra la Vella, Andorra
Telephone: (376) 874-874

Fax: (376) 862-762
Web site: www.caixabank.ad
Banking

CPA Consultors, S.L.
Ctra. De L'Obac 12-14, PL 1, Porta 4
Andorra La Vella, Andorra
Telephone: (374) 822-081
Fax: (374) 860-978
E-mail: cpa@andorra.ad
Accounting

Servissim
Edifici Areny, Baixos, Carretera General, Arinsal, La Massana, Principat d'Andorra
Telephone: 33 (628) 837836
Fax: 33 (628) 837179
Business Services/Real Estate/other

Anguilla

Affiliation: Overseas Territory of the United Kingdom.
Location: Leeward Islands in the Caribbean.
Capital and Largest City: The Valley.
Government: Self-governed.
Legal System: English common law.
Official Language: English.
Stability: Stable.
Currency: Eastern Caribbean dollar; U.S. dollar.
International Time: –4 hrs. GMT.
Country Code: 809.
Embassy: British Embassy, 3100 Massachusetts Avenue, NW, Washington, DC 20008. Telephone: (202) 588-7800.
Type of Legal Entities: International Business Company (IBC); Limited Liability Company (LLC); Limited Partnership; private and public companies for onshore and offshore activities. Bearer shares are permitted.
Unique Characteristic: Bank secrecy under their Confidentiality Ordinance.
Taxation: No personal or corporate tax. No capital gains, gift, estate, inheritance, sales, or capital transfer.
Exchange Controls: None.
Treaties with the United States: No income tax treaty. No TIEA. There is an MLAT.
Useful Web Site: www.gov.ai

Business Contacts:

Caribbean Commercial Bank (Anguilla) Ltd.
PO Box 23, The Valley
Anguilla, British West Indies
Telephone: (264) 497-2571
Fax: (264) 497-3570
E-mail: ccbaxa@anguillanet.com
Personal and Corporate Banking

C.E.G. Limited
PO Box 294, Heywood House
Anguilla, British West Indies
Telephone: (264) 497-6468
Fax: (264) 497-6080
E-mail: info@ceg.ai
Incorporation/Management

HWR Services (Anguilla) Limited
PO Box 1026, The Valley
Anguilla, British West Indies
Telephone: (264) 497-5000
Fax: (264) 497-5001
E-mail: mail@harneys.com
Full-Service Law Firm

MeesPierson Intertrust (Anguilla) Limited
Intertrust Building, The Valley
Anguilla, British West Indies
Telephone: (264) 497-2189
Fax: (264) 497-5007
E-mail: anguilla@intertrustgroup.com
Professional/Financial/Trust Services

Sinel Trust Anguilla Limited
11 Fairplay Commercial Center
PO Box 147, The Valley
Anguilla, British West Indies
Telephone: (264) 497-2189
Fax: (264) 497-5007
E-mail: jbrice@sineltrust.com
Asset Protection Trusts/Incorporations

Antigua and Barbuda

Affiliation: Commonwealth of Nations.
Location: British West Indies—Caribbean.
Capital and Largest City: St. John's.
Government: Constitutional monarchy.
Legal System: English common law.
Official Language: English.
Stability: Stable.
Currency: Eastern Caribbean Dollar.
International Time: –4 hrs. GMT.
Country Code: 268.
Embassy: Embassy of Antigua and Barbuda, 3216 New Mexico Avenue, NW, Washington, DC 20016. Telephone: (202) 362-5122.
Type of Legal Entity: International Business Company (IBC).
Unique Characteristics: Flag of Convenience. A successful tax haven that became linked to money laundering, drug trafficking, and arms smuggling.
Taxation: A no-tax haven. Nonresidents are not taxed on income, capital gains, or inheritance. Companies are tax-exempt for 50 years.
Exchange Controls: None.
Treaties with the United States: No income tax treaty. There is a TIEA and an MLAT.
Useful Web Site: www.antigua-barbuda.com
Business Contacts:

Antigua Overseas Bank Ltd./ABI Trust Ltd./ABI Financial Group
High Street & Corn Alley
PO Box 1679
St. John's, Antigua, West Indies
Telephone: (268) 480-2734
Fax: (268) 480-2750
E-mail: adiaz@abifinancial.com
Web site: www.abifinancial.com
Offshore Banking/Incorporation/Management

Gary D. Collins & Company
36A St. Mary's Street, Suite No. 3
PO Box 1424
St. John's, Antigua, West Indies
Telephone: (268) 462-2115
Fax: (268) 462-2888
E-mail: garycollins@lawyer.com
Law Firm

Global Bank of Commerce
#4 Woods Center
PO Box W1803
St. John's, Antigua, West Indies
Telephone: (268) 480-2240
Fax: (268) 462-1831
E-mail: Customer.service@gbc.ag
Offshore Private Banking

Maritime International Ltd.
PO Box WC166
Bay View Place, Crosbies
St. John's, Antigua, West Indies
Telephone: (268) 461-2024
Fax: (268) 462-2718
Web site: www.milonline.com
E-mail: maritime@candw.ag
Offshore Banking/Incorporations/Financial Services

Pannel Kerr Forster
Redcliffe Street
PO Box 159
St. John's, Antigua, West Indies
Telephone: (268) 462-0827
Fax: (268) 462-4747
E-mail: pannellf@candw.ag
Onshore and Offshore Tax Services

Aruba

Affiliation: Separate entity within the United Kingdom of the Netherlands.
Location: 12 miles off the coast of Venezuela in the Caribbean.
Capital and Largest City: Oranjestad.
Government: Parliamentary democracy.
Legal System: Dutch legal system of civil and penal law.
Official Language: Dutch. Also speak Papiamento, English, and Spanish.
Stability: Stable.
Currency: Aruban guilder/florin.
International Time: –4 hrs. GMT.
Country Code: 2 978.
Embassy: Refer to the Netherlands.
Type of Legal Entity: Aruba Exempt Company (AEC) is limited by shares.

Unique Characteristic: Popular destination with beautiful beaches.
Taxation: No corporate income tax. No withholding taxes.
Exchange Controls: None.
Treaties with the United States: No income tax treaty. There is a TIEA. No MLAT.
Useful Web Site: www.aruba.com/home.htm
Business Contacts:

ABN AMRO Trust Company (Aruba) Limited
Caya G.F. Betico Croes 85
PO Box 1023
Oranjestad, Aruba, Dutch West Indies
Telephone: (297) 834-225
Fax: (297) 834-178
E-mail: aatrust@cura.net
Web site: www.equitytrust.com
Incorporation/Management

Alfaro, Ferrer & Ramirez (Aruba) N.V.
Zoutmanstraat 35
PO Box 1311
Oranjestad, Aruba, Dutch West Indies
Telephone: (297) 834-323
Fax: (297) 834-781
E-mail: lopezalfaro@afra.net
Incorporation/Management

Aruba Bank Ltd.
Caya G.F. Betico Croes 41
PO Box 192
Oranjestad, Aruba, Dutch West Indies
Telephone: (297) 822-261
Fax: (297) 829-152
E-mail: fsimon@ank.com
Commercial Banking

Aruban Investment Bank
Wilhelminastraat 36
PO Box 1011
Oranjestad, Aruba, Dutch West Indies
Telephone: (297) 827-327
Fax: (297) 827-461
E-mail: alb@setarnet.aw
Investment Banking Services

Century Trust Agencies N.V.
48 L.G. Smith Boulevard
PO Box 1061
Oranjestad, Aruba, Dutch West Indies
Telephone: (297) 583-3662
Fax: (297) 583-4018
E-mail: centrust@setarnet.aw
Incorporation/Management

Ernst & Young Aruba Tax Advisors
Vondellaan 31
PO Box 197
Oranjestad, Aruba, Dutch West Indies
Telephone: (297) 824-050
Fax: (297) 824-548
International Tax Planning

MCB Trust (Aruba) N.V.
Palm Beach 4B
Noord, Aruba, Dutch West Indies
Telephone: (297) 860-590
Fax: (297) 860-593
E-mail: trust@mcb-bank.com
Incorporation/Management

Austria

Affiliations: European Union; United Nations.
Location: At the heart of Western Europe. Bordered by Germany and Czech Republic, Italy, Yugoslavia, Switzerland, and Hungary.
Capital and Largest City: Vienna.
Government: Federal Republic.
Legal System: Based on the Federal Constitutional Act of 1920 providing for separate judicial and administrative functions.
Official Language: German.
Stability: Stable.
Currency: Euro.
International Time: +1 hr. GMT.
Country Code: 43.
Embassy: Embassy of Austria, 3524 International Court NW, Washington DC 20006-3027. Telephone: (202) 895-6700.

Type of Legal Entities: GesmbH—Gesellschaft mit beschrankter Haftung, a limited liability company; AG—Aktiengesellschaft, a stock corporation, the preferred vehicle for foreign companies operating in Austria. Bearer shares are permitted.

Unique Characteristics: Strict bank secrecy. Good expatriate haven. Member of the Financial Action Task Force (FATF).

Taxation: Although not a tax haven, it is a T-7 country for being an excellent money haven. No withholding tax on investment earnings by nonresidents as in Switzerland. The GesmbH and AG are both subject to unfavorable taxes. Best to use a no-tax haven for offshore business purposes.

Exchange Controls: None.

Treaties with the United States: No income tax treaty. No TIEA. There is an MLAT.

Useful Web Sites: www.austria.gv.at; www.austria.org

Business Contacts:

Barber Financial Advisors
355 Burrard Street, Suite 1000
Vancouver, B.C. V6C 2G8 Canada
Telephone: (604) 608-6177
Fax: (604) 608-2984
Web site: www.BarberFinancialAdvisors.com
E-mail: Info@BarberFinancialAdvisors.com
Personal and Corporate Bank Accounts

Law Offices Dr. F. Schwank
Stock Exchange Building
Wipplingerstasse 34
A-1010 Vienna, Austria
Telephone: 43 (1) 533-5704
Fax: 43 (1) 533-5706
E-mail: offices@schwank.com
Web site: www.schwank.com
International Tax Planning/Corporate Services/Wealth Planning

Peter Zipper
Anglo Irish—Austria
PO Box 306
Rathaustrasse 20
A1011 Vienna, Austria
Telephone: 43 (1) 406-6161
Fax: 43 (1) 405-8142
E-mail: welcome desk@angloirishbank.at
Personal Bank Accounts

The Bahamas

Affiliations: Commonwealth of Nations; United Nations.

Location: An archipelago of about 700 islands, rocks, and cays, just off the southeast coast of Florida and stretching into the Caribbean.

Capital and Largest City: Nassau.

Government: Parliamentary democracy.

Legal System: English common law and Bahamian statute law.

Official Language: English.

Stability: Stable.

Currency: Bahamian dollar (pegged to the U.S. dollar).

International Time: –5 hrs. GMT.

Country Code: 809.

Embassy: Embassy of the Commonwealth of the Bahamas, 2220 Massachusetts Avenue, NW, Washington, DC 20008. Telephone: (202) 319-2660.

Type of Legal Entities: International Business Company (IBC). Nonresident and restricted banking licenses. Bearer shares in IBCs can only be issued with the permission of the Central Bank.

Unique Characteristics: Good expatriate haven under the "Investment Promotion Program." Popular for holding, trading, banking, investment, insurance, mutual fund, and shipping companies. Flag of Convenience.

The Bahamas *was* an excellent tax haven before 2000 and is one to seriously avoid today if you are a U.S. citizen. But, the fishing is good!

Taxation: There are no corporate income taxes, profits, earnings, capital gains, distribution, estate, probate, or inheritance. There are no withholding taxes on dividends, interest, royalties, or payroll.

Exchange Controls: None.

Treaties with the United States: No income tax treaty. There is a TIEA and an MLAT.

Useful Web Sites: www.bahamas.gov.bs; www.bfsb-bahamas.com

Business Contacts:

Gavin D. Cassar
Cassar and CO
Norfolk House Annex II
Market and Frederick Streets
PO Box CB-13744
Nassau, Bahamas
Telephone: (242) 328-4695
Fax: (242) 328-4694
E-mail: cassar@batelnet.bs
Incorporation/Trusts/Immigration Law

Bahamas Realty Limited
East Bay Street
PO Box N-1132
Nassau, Bahamas
Telephone: (242) 393-8616
Fax: (242) 393-0326
E-mail: brealty@bahamasrealty.bs
Web site: www.bahamasrealty.bs
Real Estate Brokers

Bank Leu Limited, Nassau Branch
The Bahamas Financial Center
Shirley & Charlotte Streets
PO Box N-3926
Nassau, Bahamas
Telephone: (242) 326-5054
Fax: (242) 323-8828
Swiss Bank/Full Line of Services

Berkeley (Bahamas) Limited
2nd Floor, One Montague Place
East Bay Street
PO Box N-3927
Nassau, Bahamas
Telephone: (242) 502-5570
Fax: (242) 394-6841
E-mail: trader1@bahamas.net.bs
Web site: www.bbloffshore.com
Comprehensive Offshore Brokerage Services

Callenders & Co.
One Millars Court
PO Box N-7117
Nassau, Bahamas
Telephone: (242) 322-2511
Fax: (242) 322-2514
E-mail: callenders-law.com
Web site: www.callenders-law.com
Incorporation/Estate Planning/Real Estate

CIBC Trust Company (Bahamas) Limited
PO Box N-3933
Shirley Street
Nassau, Bahamas

Telephone: (242) 323-3314
Fax: (242) 328-2102
Offshore Trust Services/Management

Ernst & Young
One Montague Place
PO Box N-3231
Nassau, Bahamas
Telephone: (242) 502-6000
Fax: (242) 502-6090
E-mail: eynassau@bahamas.net.bs
International Tax Planning

Lennox Paton
Fort Nassau Center, Malborough Street
PO Box N-4875
Nassau, Bahamas
Telephone: (242) 502-5000
Fax: (242) 328-0566
E-mail: info@lennoxpaton.com
Web site: www.lennoxpaton.com
Law Firm/Incorporation/Management/Trusts/Real Estate

Montaque Securities International
Saffrey Square
Bay Street and Bank Lane, 1st Floor
PO Box N-7474
Nassau, Bahamas
Telephone: (242) 356-6133
Fax: (242) 356-6144
E-mail: montaque@batelnet.bs
International Investment and Financial Advice

The Winterbotham Trust Company Limited
Bolan House, 3rd Floor
King & George Streets
PO Box N-3026
Nassau, Bahamas
Telephone: (242) 356-5454
Fax: (242) 356-9432
Electronic Banking Services/Financial/Trust/Corporate

Bahrain

Affiliation: Arab League.
Location: This sheikdom is known as the "Pearl" in the Arabian Gulf off the coast of Saudi Arabia.
Capital and Largest City: Al-Manamah.
Government: Constitutional monarchy.
Legal System: Based on Islamic law and English common law.
Official Language: Arabic. Other languages spoken—English, Farsi, and Urdu.
Stability: Stable.
Currency: Baharain dinar.
International Time: +3 hrs. GMT.
Country Code: 973.
Embassy: Embassy of the Kingdom of Bahrain, 3502 International Drive, NW, Washington, DC 20008. Telephone: (202) 342-1111.
Type of Legal Entity: Unrestricted foreign company ownership.
Unique Characteristics: Bahrain is the financial hub of the Middle East and one of the world's most free economies with a skilled English-speaking labor force. Home to the Bahrain Stock Exchange.
Taxation: No personal, corporate, or withholding tax.
Exchange Controls: None.
Treaties with the United States: No income tax treaty. No TIEA. No MLAT.
Useful Web Site: www.bahrainembassy.org
Business Contact:

Arab Banking Corporation (B.S.C.) (ABC)
ABC Tower, Diplomatic Area
PO Box 5698
Manama, Bahrain
Telephone: (973) 543-000
Fax: (973) 533-163
Web site: www.arabbanking.com
International Commercial, Merchant, and Investment Bank

Barbados

Affiliations: Commonwealth of Nations; United Nations.
Location: In the Lesser Antilles of the Caribbean.
Capital and Largest City: Bridgetown.
Government: Parliamentary democracy.
Legal System: English common law.
Official Language: English.
Stability: Stable.

Currency: Barbados dollar.

International Time: –4 hrs. GMT.

Country Code: 809.

Embassy: Embassy of Barbados, 2144 Wyoming Avenue, NW, Washington, DC 20008. Telephone: (202) 939-9200.

Type of Legal Entity: International Business Company (IBC). Private and public companies are recognized.

Unique Characteristics: Flag of Convenience. A leading e-commerce center. Popular for banks, mutual funds, and insurance companies. Home of the Bermuda Stock Exchange. A tax haven with horse racing.

Taxation: A low-tax haven. Effective 2006, the corporate income tax rate has been reduced to 25 percent, and if properly structured, offshore business could escape much of the tax altogether.

Exchange Controls: None on companies.

Treaties with the United States: There is an income tax agreement and a TIEA and an MLAT.

Useful Web Site: www.barbados.gov.bb

Business Contacts:

Dr. Trevor A. Carmichael
Chancery Chambers
Attorneys-At-Law
Chancery House, High Street
Bridgetown, Barbados
Telephone: (246) 431-0070
Fax: (246) 431-0076
E-mail: chancery@caribsurf.com
Comprehensive Legal Services for International Business

Barclays Bank PLC (International Banking Center)
PO Box 180, Barclays House, 1st Floor
Rendezvous
Christ Church, Barbados, W.I.
Telephone: (246) 431-5294
Fax: (246) 429-4785
E-mail: barcbobc@sunbeach.net
International Bank

Citadel Bank & Trust
One Financial Place, Suite 100
Lower Collymore Rock
PO Box 118
Bridgetown, Barbados, W.I.
Telephone: (246) 430-5350

Fax: (246) 430-5353
E-mail: invest@citadelbt.com
Banking/Trust/Portfolio Management/Corporate

CLICO Mortgage and Finance Corporation
CL Duprey Financial Center
Walrond Street
Bridgetown, Barbados, W.I.
Telephone: (246) 431-4719
Fax: (246) 426-6168
E-mail: cmfc@sunbeach.net
Incorporation/Secretarial Services/Real Estate

Deloitte and Touche
PO Box 806E
Whitepark House, White Park Road
Bridgetown, Barbados, W.I.
Telephone: (246) 429-5257
Fax: (246) 436-7887
E-mail: rjbourque@deloitte.bb
Incorporation/Management/Accounting

Ernst & Young Trust Corporation
PO Box 261
Bush Hill, Bay Street,
St. Michael, Barbados, W.I.
Telephone: (246) 430-3900
Fax: (246) 429-6446
E-mail: eybic@caribsurf.com
Trust Services/International Tax Advise

Excelsior Bank
Tom Adams Financial Center
Bridgetown, Barbados, W.I.
Telephone: (246) 435-3155
Fax: (246) 435-3157
E-mail: excel@caribsurf.com
Full Range of Trustee Services

Garth Patterson, Attorney at Law
Dewsbury House, Aquatic Gap
St. Michael, Barbados, W.I.
Telephone: (246) 427-9551

Fax: (246) 427-7802
Incorporation/Commercial Transaction

PricewaterhouseCoopers
PO Box 111
St. Michael, Barbados, W.I.
Telephone: (246) 436-7000
Fax: (246) 436-7057
E-mail: pwcbb@sunbeach.net
Trustee Services/Professional Taxation/Accounting

Royal Bank of Canada (Caribbean) Corporation
2nd Floor, Building 2, Chelston Park, Collymore Rock
St. Michael, Barbados, W.I.
Telephone: (246) 429-4923
Fax: (246) 436-7057
E-mail: mike.moodie@RBC.com
Web site: www.rbc.com
Banking/Trust/Corporate

The Towner Management Group
Second Street, Holetown
St. James, Barbados, W.I.
Telephone: (246) 432-4000
Fax: (246) 432-4004
E-mail: mailbox@towner.bb
Web site: www.towner.bb
Management of All Types of Offshore Companies

Belize

Affiliations: Commonwealth of Nations; United Nations.
Location: Central America. Formerly British Honduras. On the Caribbean Sea between Mexico and Guatemala.
Capital and Largest City: Belize City.
Government: Parliamentary democracy.
Legal System: English common law.
Official Language: English. Also speak Spanish, Mayan, Garituna, and Creole.
Stability: Stable.
Currency: Belize dollar.
International Time: –6 hrs. GMT.

Country Code: 501.

Embassy: Embassy of Belize, 2535 Massachusetts Avenue, NW, Washington, DC 20008. Telephone: (202) 332-9636.

Type of Legal Entity: International Business Company (IBC).

Unique Characteristics: An excellent tax haven for offshore business operations, offshore e-commerce, and trusts. Bank secrecy. A T-7 tax haven. A potential expatriate haven under the Qualified Persons Program. Very strong asset protection trust laws.

Taxation: A no-tax haven.

Exchange Controls: None.

Treaties with the United States: No income tax treaty. No TIEA. No MLAT.

Useful Web Site: www.belize.gov.bz

Business Contact:

Barber Financial Advisors
355 Burrard Street, Suite 1000
Vancouver, BC V6C 2G8 Canada
Telephone: (604) 608-6177
Fax: (604) 608-2984
E-mail: info@BarberFinancialAdvisors.com
Web site: www.BarberFinancialAdvisors.com
Incorporation/Management/Personal & Corporate Bank Accounts/Credit & Debit Cards/Pre-Paid VISA Card/Offshore E-Commerce/Ready-made Companies

Bermuda

Affiliation: Overseas Territory of the United Kingdom.

Location: Situated 650 miles east of North Carolina in the Atlantic Ocean.

Capital and Largest City: Hamilton.

Government: Parliamentary democracy.

Legal System: English common law.

Official Language: English. Also speak Portuguese.

Stability: Stable.

Currency: Bermuda dollar.

International Time: –4 hrs. GMT.

Country Code: 809.

Embassy: British Embassy, 3100 Massachusetts Avenue, NW, Washington, DC 20008. Telephone: (202) 588-7800.

Type of Legal Entities: Exempted company; exempted partnership; unit trusts, overseas company by permit. Segregated accounts companies.

Flag of convenience. Ship, aircraft, and intellectual property registrations. Many types of partnerships; trusts; a popular wealth management haven.

Unique Characteristics: In recent years, Bermuda has attracted large private and U.S. corporations for redomiciliation. Also known for captive insurance companies. Home of the Bermuda Stock Exchange.

Taxation: A no-tax haven. No taxes on corporate income, profit sales, value added, withholding, or capital gains.

Exchange Controls: None.

Treaties with the United States: There is an income tax treaty and a TIEA. No MLAT.

Useful Web Sites: www.gov.bm; www.bermuda-inc.com; www.Bermuda-Online.com

Business Contacts:

John Harper
Managing Director
Harrington Trust Limited
Windsor Place, 4th Floor
22 Queen Street
PO Box HM 1179
Hamilton, HM EX, Bermuda
Telephone: (441) 298-7878
Fax: (441) 296-9825
E-mail: jharper@htl.bm
Wide Range of Trustee Services

Graham Wood
Appleby Spurling & Kempe
Cedar House, 41 Cedar Avenue
PO Box HM 1179
Hamilton, HM JX, Bermuda
Telephone: (441) 295-2244
Fax: (441) 292-8666
E-mail: askcorp@ask.bm
Web site: www.ask.bm
Full Service Law Firm/Trusts/E-Commerce

The Bank of Bermuda Limited
6 Front Street
Hamilton, HM 11, Bermuda
Telephone: (441) 295-4000
Fax: (441) 299-6559
Web site: www.bankofbermuda.com
Personal and Corporate International Investment Management

The Bank of N.T. Butterfield & Son Limited
65 Front Street
PO Box HM 195
Hamilton, HM AX, Bermuda
Telephone: (441) 295-1111
Fax: (441) 292-4365
E-mail: contact@bntb.bm
Personal & Corporate Banking/Investment Management/Securities

Deloitte & Touche
"Corner House," Church & Parliament Streets
Hamilton, HM 12, Bermuda
Telephone: (441) 292-1500
Fax: (441) 292-0961
E-mail: contact@deloitte.bm
Web site: www.deloitte.bm
Accounting/Incorporation/Management

Ernst & Young
Reid Hall, 3 Reid Street
PO Box HM463
Hamilton, HM BX, Bermuda
Telephone: (441) 295-7000
Fax: (441) 295-4680
E-mail: info.bm@ey.cm
Web site: www.ey.com/bermuda
Accounting/Legal/U.S. Tax

International Trust Company of Bermuda Limited
PO Box 1255
Bermuda Commercial Bank Building
43 Victoria Street
Hamilton, HM 12, Bermuda
Telephone: (441) 299-2875
Fax: (441) 292-6128
E-mail: ptucker@bcb.bm
Web site: www.bcb.com
Personal and Corporate Trusts/Investment Accounts

KPMG
PO Box HM 906
Hamilton, HM DX, Bermuda
Telephone: (441) 295-5063

Fax: (441) 295-9132
E-mail: kpmg@kpmg.bm
Web site: www.kpmg.com
Accounting/Management

LOM Securities (Bermuda) Ltd.
The LOM Building, 27 Reid Street
Hamilton, HM 11, Bermuda
Telephone: (441) 292-5000
Fax: (441) 292-3343
E-mail: info@lom.bm
Web site: www.lom.com
Securities Brokerage/Discretionary Asset Management/
Corporate Finance

Lombard Odier Darier Hentsch Trust (Bermuda) Limited
The Corner House, 20 Parliament Street
PO Box HM 2271
Hamilton, HM JX, Bermuda
Telephone: (441) 292-7817
Fax: (441) 299-8798
Incorporation/Trusts/Management/Tax Planning

St. George's Trust Company Limited
PO Box HM 3051
Hamilton, HM NX, Bermuda
Telephone: (441) 295-1820
Fax: (441) 295-5491
E-mail: stgeorges@lom.bm
Web site: www.stgeorges.com
Trust Services

Cox Hallett Wilkinson
Milner House, 18 Parliament Street
PO Box 1561,
Hamilton, HM FX, Bermuda
Telephone: (441) 295-4630
Fax: (441) 292-7880
E-mail: cw@cw.bm
Web site: www.cw.bm
International Business Transactions

British Virgin Islands

Affiliation: Overseas Territory of the United Kingdom.
Location: A group of islands 60 miles southeast of Puerto Rico in the Caribbean.
Capital and Largest City: Road Town.
Government: Self-governing British Crown Colony.
Legal System: English common law.
Official Language: English.
Stability: Stable.
Currency: U.S. dollar.
International Time: –4 hrs. GMT.
Country Code: 809.
Embassy: British Embassy, 3100 Massachusetts Avenue, NW, Washington, DC 20008. Telephone: (202) 588-7800.
Type of Legal Entities: International Business Company (IBC). Bearer shares are permitted. All types of trusts. Unrestricted and restricted banking licenses.
Unique Characteristics: Trademark registrations. Flag of convenience. Popular for IBCs, banking, mutual funds, and insurance. Great sailing waters!
Taxation: A no-tax haven.
Exchange Controls: None.
Treaties with the United States: No income tax treaty. There is a TIEA and an MLAT.
Useful Web Site: www.loc.gov
Business Contacts:

ILS Fiduciary (BVI) Limited
Mill Mall, Wickhams Cay 1
PO Box 3085
Tortola, B.V.I.
Telephone: (284) 494-2999
Fax: (284) 494-5076
E-mail: ilsbvi@ils-world.com
Web site: www.ils-world.com
Incorporation/Management

Quijano & Associates (BVI) Limited
R. G. Hodge Plaza, 2nd Floor, Wickhams Cay 1
PO Box 313
Road Town, Tortola, B.V.I.
Telephone: (284) 494-3638
Fax: (284) 494-7274
E-mail: quijano@quijano.com

Web site: www.quijano.com
Incorporation/Trusts

AMS Trustees Limited/AMS Fund Management Limited/Arawak Trust Company Limited
Sea Meadow House
PO Box 116
Road Town, Tortola, B.V.I.
Telephone: (284) 494-3399
Fax: (284) 494-3041
E-mail: ams@amsbvi.com
Web site: www.amsbvi.com
Offshore Financial and Trust Services/E-Commerce

Arawak Trust Company Limited
PO Box 173
Road Town, Tortola, B.V.I.
Telephone: (284) 494-3399
Fax: (284) 494-3041
E-mail: arawak@amsbvi.com
Offshore Financial Services/E-Commerce

Barclays Bank PLC (International Banking Center)
PO Box 70
Road Town, Tortola, B.V.I.
Telephone: (284) 494-2171
Fax: (284) 494-7405
E-mail: barcbvi@caribsurf.com
Major Currencies/Credit Cards/Mutual Funds/Int'l. Mortgages

Caribbean Corporate Services Limited
Omar Hodge Building, Wickhams Cay 1
PO Box 362
Road Town, Tortola, B.V.I.
Telephone: (284) 494-5108
Fax: (284) 494-4704
E-mail: Ccsl@surfbvi.com
Incorporation/Management/Trust Services

Deloitte & Touche
Omar Hodge Building, Wickhams Cay 1
PO Box 3083
Road Town, Tortola, B.V.I.
Telephone: (284) 494-2868

Fax: (284) 494-7889
E-mail: deloitte@deloitte.vg
Web site: www.deloitte.vg
Accounting/Taxation

Harney Westwood & Riegels/HWR Services Limited
Craigmuir Chambers
PO Box 71
Road Town, Tortola, B.V.I.
Telephone: (284) 494-2233
Fax: (284) 494-3547
Web site: www.harneys.com
E-mail: mail@harneys.com
Full Service Law Firm/Tax Planning

Jordans (Caribbean) Limited
Geneva Place, Waterfront Drive
PO Box 3469
Road Town, Tortola, B.V.I.
Telephone: (284) 494-6643
Fax: (284) 494-6615
E-mail: jordans@surfbvi.com
Web site: www.jordans-international.com
Incorporation/Management/Advice

Maitland International (Maitland & Co—Fiduciary Division)/
Midocean Management & Trust Services (BVI) Limited
9 Columbus Center, Pelican Drive
PO Box 805
Road Town, Tortola, B.V.I.
Telephone: (284) 494-4567
Fax: (284) 494-4568
E-mail: midocean@bvi.co
Web site: Maitlandgroup.com
International Accounting Firm

Moore Stephens International Services (BVI) Limited
PO Box 3186
Road Town, Tortola, B.V.I.
Telephone: (284) 494-4311
Fax: (284) 494-4312
E-mail: moorestephens@surfbvi.com
Financial Services

Morgan & Morgan Trust Corporation Limited (Belize) Ltd.
PO Box 958
Road Town, Tortola, B.V.I.
Telephone: (284) 494-2011
Fax: (284) 494-2015
E-mail: bvi@morimor.com
Web site: www.morimor.com
Full Service Law Firm

Mossack Fonseca & Co. (BVI) Limited
Akara Building, 24 De Castro Street, Wickhams Cay 1
PO Box 3136
Road Town, Tortola, B.V.I.
Telephone: (284) 494-4840
Fax: (284) 494-4841
E-mail: general@mossfon-bvi.com
Web site: www.mossfon-bvi.com
Incorporation/Management/Legal

Smith-Hughes Raworth & McKensie
PO Box 173
Road Town, Tortola, B.V.I.
Telephone: (284) 494-3384
Fax: (284) 494-2914
E-mail: mail@s-hrm.com
Commercial Law/Incorporation/Trusts/E-Commerce

Brunei Darussalam

Affiliations: Association of Southeast Asian Nations; Commonwealth of Nations; United Nations.
Location: In the South China Sea off the northwest coast of Borneo.
Capital and Largest City: Bandar Seri Begawan.
Government: Independent Constitutional Sultanate.
Legal System: Civil law is based on English common law.
Official Language: Malay. Also speak English and Chinese.
Stability: Stable.
Currency: Brunei dollar.
International Time: +8 hrs. GMT.
Country Code: 673.
Embassy: Embassy of Brunei Darussalem, 3520 International Court, NW, Washington, DC 20008. Telephone: (202) 237-1838.
Type of Legal Entity: International Business Company (IBC) limited by shares.

Unique Characteristics: Tax advantages for banking, insurance, investment funds, and trust management.

Taxation: A no-tax haven.

Exchange Controls: None.

Treaties with the United States: No income tax treaty. No TIEA. No MLAT.

Useful Web Site: www.brunei.gov.bn/index.htm

Business Contacts:

Dr. Colin Ong Legal Services, Advocates & Solicitors
Suites 2.2 to 2.4
Gadong Properties Center
KM 3.5 Jalan Gadong
Bandar Seri Begawan BE4119
Negara Brunei Darussalam
Telephone: (673) 242-0913
Fax: (673) 242-0911
E-mail: onglegal@brunet.bn
Banking/Business/Insurance

PricewaterhouseCoopers
No. 1, 4th Floor, Wisma Setia
PO Box 1628
Bandar Seri Begawan BS 8673
Brunei Darussalam
Telephone: (673) 222-3341
Fax: (673) 224-2402
E-mail: pwc@brunet.bn
Accounting/Tax/Company Services

Campione (Italy)

Affiliations: Italy and Switzerland; NATO; European Union.

Location: "Campione d'Italia" is an Italian enclave surrounded by Switzerland on Lake Lugano in the Swiss canton of Ticino.

Capital and Largest City: Rome, Italy.

Government: Republic (Italy); Campione is self-governing.

Legal System: The Italian judicial system is based on Roman law modified by the Napoleonic Code and subsequent statutes.

Official Language: Italian.

Stability: Stable.

Currency: Swiss franc; Euro (Italy).

International Time: +1 hr. GMT.

Country Code: 41.

Embassy: Embassy of Italy, 3000 Whitehaven Street, NW, Washington, DC 20008. Telephone: (202) 612-4400.

Type of Legal Entity: Incorporated company. Consult with an Italian lawyer. A good alternative to using a Swiss company.

Unique Characteristics: An excellent expatriate haven and good for real estate investment. Refer to Appendix under "Offshore Citizenship and Retirement Opportunities." Campione is the backdoor to Switzerland. Unrestricted access to Switzerland and Liechtenstein. Lake Lugano, Switzerland, has 40 Swiss banks that are conveniently located to Campione. The Italian enclave shares other common features with Switzerland such as license plates, Swiss postal address, telephones, the Swiss country code 41, traffic laws, and more. Italy is a member of the Financial Action Task Force (FATF).

Taxation: A little-known no-tax haven. No income tax or local tax in Campione. Italians have never imposed taxes on Campione and the Swiss have no jurisdiction. Campione raises revenues for the Italian government from its only casino.

Exchange Controls: None.

Treaties with the United States: No income tax treaty. No TIEA. There is an MLAT with Italy.

Useful Web Site: www.loc.gov

Business Contacts:

Dr. Ernst Zimmer
2 Corso Italia
CH-6911 Campione d'Italia, Switzerland
Telephone: 41 (91) 649-3340
Fax: 41 (91) 649-4268
Residency/Real Estate

Audit Consulting
Dott. Luca Bassi
Via Adamo del Pero 38
I-22100 Como, Italy
Fax: 39 (031) 26-26-47
E-mail: auditconsulting@tin.it
Campoine Company Formation Services

Maurizio Codurri, Managing Partner
Frau & Partners
via C. Poerio 15, I-20129 Milan, Italy
Telephone: 39 (02) 7600-3199
Fax: 39 (02) 7600-3311
E-mail: Maurizio-codurri@fraupartners.org
Lawyers/International Tax Planning/Banking

Consulting International
2 Corso Italia
CH-6911 Campione, Switzerland
Telephone: 41 (91) 649-5510
Fax: 41 (91) 649-4268
E-mail: consulting@swissonline.ch.com
Real Estate

Avv. Daniele Funghini
Via Diaz 58
I-22100 Como, Italy
Telephone: 39 (031) 26-74-22
Fax: 39 (031) 26-73-10
E-mail: avvfunghini@email.it
Italian Lawyer Located Near Campione

Immobiliare Wehner
Viale Marco 27
CH-6911 Campione, Italy
Telephone: 41 (0) 91-649-7549
Fax: 41 (0) 91-649-6345
Mobile: 41 (0) 79-620-6080
E-mail: info@immowehner.ch
Web site: www.immowehner.ch
Oldest Real Estate Agency Serving Campione

International Real Estate Services
Telephone Switzerland: 41 (79) 358-2826
Telephone Italy: 39 (348) 292-4588
Telephone Liechtenstein: (423) 370-2777
Fax Switzerland: 41 (1) 274-2515
E-mail: info@lakelugano.com
Web sites: www.lofts-tessin.com; www.italianlakesproperty.com
Lake Lugano and Campione Real Estate

Christian H. Kalin
Henley & Partners AG
Kirchgasse 22
CH-8001 Zurich, Switzerland
Telephone: 41 (44) 266-22-22
Fax: 41 (44) 266-22-23

E-mail: chris.kalin@henleyglobal.com
Web site: www.henleyglobal.com
Swiss Residency/Citizenship

Avv. Andrea Marcinkiewicz
Via Rovelli 36
I-22100 Como, Italy
Telephone: 39 (031) 27-18-55
Fax: 39 (031) 26-28-38
E-mail: assolex@tin.it
Italian Lawyer Located Near Campione

Massimo Cremona, Pirola Pennuto Zei & Associati
Via Vittor Pisani 16
20124 Milan, Italy
Telephone: 39 (02) 6699-5241
Fax: 39 (02) 669-3131
E-mail: Massimo.cremon@studiopirola.com
Web site: www.studiopirola.com
Lawyers/International Tax Planning/Mergers and Acquisitions

Studio Avvocato Giovanni Acampora
Via Pompeo Magno 1
00192 Rome, Italy
Telephone: 39 (06) 321-2506
Fax: 39 (06) 321-1458
E-mail: Giordano@acampora.net
Web site: www.acampora.net
Lawyers/International Tax Planning/Asset Protection/Business trusts

Wetag Consulting
Lugano Riva Caccia 3
Lugano, Switzerland
Telephone: 41 (91) 994-6851
Fax: 41 (91) 994-6852
E-mail: info@wetag.ch
Real Estate

Cayman Islands

Affiliation: Overseas Territory of the United Kingdom.
Location: In the western Caribbean just south of Cuba.
Capital and Largest City: George Town (Grand Cayman Island).

Government: Self-governed.
Legal System: English common law.
Official Language: English.
Stability: Stable.
Currency: Cayman Island dollar.
International Time: –5 hrs. GMT.
Country Code: 809.
Embassy: British Embassy, 3100 Massachusetts Avenue, NW, Washington, DC 20008. Telephone: (202) 588-7800.
Type of Legal Entities: Exempted Company; Ordinary Non-Resident; Ordinary Resident; Limited Duration Company; Limited Liability Company (LLC); Guarantee Company. Bearer shares are permitted in exempt companies only. Many types of companies can be formed for special purposes; a variety of partnerships and trusts. Class A and Class B bank licenses are obtainable.
Unique Characteristics: Popular offshore banking center; flag of convenience; investment funds; securities and insurance companies. Home of the Cayman Island Stock Exchange.
Taxation: A no-tax haven.
Exchange Controls: None.
Treaties with the United States: No income tax treaty. There is a TIEA and an MLAT.
Useful Web Site: www.gov.ky; http://cayman.com.ky
Business Contacts:

AALL Trust & Banking Corporation Limited
PO Box 1166
George Town, Grand Cayman, Cayman Islands
Telephone: (345) 949-5588
Fax: (345) 949-8265
E-mail: aall@candw.ky
Private Banking/Incorporations/Trusts

Ansbacher (Cayman) Limited
PO Box 887
Grand Cayman, Cayman Islands
Telephone: (345) 949-8655
Fax: (345) 949-7946
E-mail: info@ansbacher.com.ky
Trusts/Management/Investments/Banking

Bank of Butterfield International (Cayman) Ltd.
Butterfield House, 68 Fort Street
PO Box 705 GT
Grand Cayman, Cayman Islands

Telephone: (345) 949-7055
Fax: (345) 949-7004
E-mail: info@bankofbutterfield.ky
Web site: bankofbutterfield.ky
Management/Investment Portfolio/Custody

Caledonian Bank & Trust Limited
Caledonian House
PO Box 1043 GT
Grand Cayman, Cayman Islands
Telephone: (345) 949-0050
Fax: (345) 949-8062
E-mail: info@caledonian.com
Web site: www.caledonian.com
Full Financial Services Provider

Cayman National Corporation
PO Box 1097 GT
Grand Cayman, Cayman Islands
Telephone: (345) 949-4655
Fax: (345) 949-0774
E-mail: cnc@caymannational.com
Web site: www.caymannational.com
Banking/Trust/Corporate/Investments/Insurance

Charles Adams, Ritchie & Duckworth
Attorneys-at-Law
PO Box 709 GT
2nd Floor, Zephyr House, Mary Street
Grand Cayman, Cayman Islands
Telephone: (345) 949-4544
Fax: (345) 949-7073
Full Service Legal Firm

Dextra Bank & Trust Co. Ltd.
Global House, North Church Street
PO Box 2004 GT
George Town, Grand Cayman, Cayman islands
Telephone: (345) 949-7844
Fax: (345) 949-2795
E-mail: dextra@candw.ky
Banking/Trusts/Investment Management

Five Continents Financial Limited/Rothschild Trust Cayman Limited
2nd Floor, Anchorage Center
PO Box 30715 SMB
George Town, Grand Cayman, Cayman Islands
Telephone: (345) 949-3022
Fax: (345) 949-3177
International Investment Advisors

Julius Baer Trust Company (Cayman) Limited
Windward III, SafeHaven Corporate Center, West Bay Road
George Town, Grand Cayman, Cayman Islands
Telephone: (345) 949-7212
Fax: (345) 949-0993
Trusts/Management/Mutual Funds

KPMG
Century Yard, Cricket Square
PO Box 493
George Town, Grand Cayman, Cayman Islands
Telephone: (345) 949-4800
Fax: (345) 949-7164
E-mail: KPMG@kpmg.ky
Web site: www.kpmg.ky
Accounting/U.S. Taxation/Management

Lines Overseas Management (Cayman) Ltd.
Buckingham Square, West Bay Road
PO Box 30997 SMB
Grand Cayman, Cayman Islands
Telephone: (345) 949-5808
Fax: (345) 949-1338
E-mail: john.swain@lom.bm
Securities Brokerage/Discretionary Asset Management

Moore Stephens
3rd Floor, West Wind Building
PO Box 1782 G
Grand Cayman, Cayman Islands
Telephone: (345) 945-5889
Fax: (345) 945-5907
E-mail: msci@candw.ky
International Professional Services

Schroder Cayman Bank and Trust Company Ltd.
PO Box 1040 GT, Harbour Center
Grand Cayman, Cayman Islands
Telephone: (345) 949-2849
Fax: (345) 949-5409
E-mail: schroder@candw.ky
Banking/Trust Services/Investment Management

Channel Islands—Guernsey

Affiliation: The Channel Islands are a Crown dependency of the United Kingdom.

Location: A group of islands located 40 miles north of France and 110 miles south of Britain in the English Channel.

Capital and Largest City: St. Peter Port (Guernsey).

Government: Independent jurisdiction with their own constitution. They were once a part of the Dutchy of Normandy.

Legal System: They maintain their own legal system based on Norman law, but local legislation is directly influenced by English common law.

Official Language: English.

Stability: Stable.

Currency: Guernsey pound.

International Time: Ground Zero—GMT.

Country Code: 44 1534.

Embassy: British Embassy, 3100 Massachusetts Avenue, NW, Washington, DC 20008. Telephone: (202) 588-7800.

Type of Legal Entities: Exempt Company; International Business Company (IBC); cell companies. All companies have limited liability. No bearer shares are allowed. Shareholder identities have to be disclosed to the Financial Services Commission. Must apply for IBC status.

Unique Characteristics: Popular for banking, trusts, investment funds, and insurance companies. Home of the Channel Island Stock Exchange.

Taxation: Exempt companies pay a flat nominal annual tax to be exempt from income tax. International Business Companies pay between 0.50 percent and 2 percent tax on international profits; and 30 percent on local-source income.

Exchange Controls: None.

Treaties with the United States: No income tax treaty. There is a TIEA and an MLAT.

Useful Web Sites: www.gov.gg; www.legisgroup.com

Business Contacts:

Michael Doyle
Sark Offshore Consultancy

Castle Company Management LLC LTD
La Connellerie
Isle of Sark, Channel Islands, GY9 OSF
Telephone: 44 (01481) 832119
Fax: 44 (01481) 832738
E-mail: sales@sarkoffshore.demon.co.uk
Company Management/Full Administration Services for Channel Island and Offshore Entities

Ansbacher (Channel Islands) Limited
PO Box 79, La Plaiderie House
St. Peter Port, Guernsey, Channel Islands, GY1 3DQ
Telephone: 44 (01481) 726421
Fax: 44 (01481) 726526
Multicurrency Banking/Investment Management

Bachmann Trust Company Limited
PO Box 175, Frances House, Sir William Place
St. Peter Port, Guernsey, Channel Islands, GY1 3DQ
Telephone: 44 (01481) 723573
Fax: 44 (01481) 711353
E-mail: enquiries@bachmanngroup.com
Web site: www.bachmanngroup.com
Full Range of Offshore Financial Services

Bank of Butterfield International (Guernsey) Limited
PO Box 25
Roseneath, The Grange
St. Peter Port, Guernsey, Channel Islands GY1 3AP
Telephone: 44 (01481) 711521
Fax: 44 (01481) 714533
E-mail: info@butterfield.gg
Banking/Trust and Corporate Services/Investment Management

Baring Asset Management (C.I.) Limited
PO Box 71
Trafalgar Court, Les Banques
St. Peter Port, Guernsey, Channel Islands GY1 3DA
Telephone: 44 (01481) 745010
Fax: 44 (01481) 745064
E-mail: enquiries@bamci.com
Web site: www.baring-asset.com
Investment Management

Barings (Guernsey) Limited
PO Box 71
Trafalgar Court, Les Banques
St. Peter Port, Guernsey, Channel Islands GY1 3DA
Telephone: 44 (01481) 745000
Fax: 44 (01481) 745050
E-mail: enquiries@bamci.com
Web site: www.baring-asset.com
International Banking/Foreign Exchange

Dixcart Trust Corporation Limited
Dixcart House
PO Box 161, Sir William Place
St. Peter Port, Guernsey, Channel Islands GY1 4EZ
Telephone: 44 (01481) 723996
Fax: 44 (01481) 727417
E-mail: advice@dixcart.co.gg
Web site: www.dixcart.com
Formations/Investment Management/Tax Planning/E-Commerce

Generali International
Generali Worldwide
PO Box 613
Les Echelons Court, South Esplanade
St. Peter Port, Guernsey, Channel Islands GY1 4PA
Telephone: 44 (01481) 714108
Fax: 44 (01481) 712424
E-mail: enquiries@generali-guernsey.com
Web site: www.generali-gi.com
Investment Life Products

Investec Bank (Channel Islands) Limited
PO Box 188
La Vieille Cour
St. Peter Port, Guernsey, Channel Islands GY1 3LP
Telephone: 44 (01481) 723506
Fax: 44 (01481) 720844
E-mail: enquiries@investec-ci.com
Web site: www.investec-ci.com
Private Banking for International Investors

KPMG
PO Box 235
2 Grange Place, The Grange
St. Peter Port, Guernsey, Channel Islands GY1 4LD
Telephone: 44 (01481) 721000
Fax: 44 (01481) 722373
International Tax Planning/Accounting

Leopold Joseph & Sons (Guernsey) Limited
PO Box 244
Albert House, South Esplanade
St. Peter Port, Guernsey, Channel Islands GY1 3QB
Telephone: 44 (01481) 712771
Fax: 44 (01481) 727025
E-mail: info@leopoldjoseph.com
Private Global Banking

Old Mutual International (Guernsey) Limited
Fairbairn House
PO Box 121, Rohais
St. Peter Port, Guernsey, Channel Islands GY1 3HE
Telephone: 44 (01481) 726726
Fax: 44 (01481) 728953
Wide Range of Investment Funds

Olsen Ferbrache Morgan
PO Box 212
Hadsley House, Lefebvre Street
St. Peter Port, Guernsey, Channel Islands GY1 4JE
Telephone: 44 (01481) 712277
Fax: 44 (01481) 710900
E-mail: enquiry@ofmlaw.com
Web site: www.ofmlaw.com
Investment Funds/Banking/Trust/Fiduciary/Corporate

Ozannes
PO Box 186
1 Le Marchant Street
St. Peter Port, Guernsey, Channel Islands GY1 4HP
Telephone: 44 (01481) 723466
Fax: 44 (01481) 727935
E-mail: advocates@ozannes.com

Web site: www.ozannes.com
Banking/Finance/E-Commerce/Investment Funds

St. Peters Trust Company Limited
Quay House, South Esplanade
St. Peter Port, Guernsey, Channel Islands GYl 4EJ
Telephone: 44 (01481) 723674
Fax: 44 (01481) 711541
E-mail: quay@quayport.demon.co.uk
Trust and Management Services/Asset Protection Strategies

Channel Islands—Jersey

Affiliation: The Channel Islands are a Crown dependency of the United Kingdom.

Location: A group of islands located 40 miles north of France and 110 miles south of Britain in the English Channel.

Capital and Largest City: St. Helier (Jersey).

Government: Independent jurisdiction with their own constitution. They were once a part of the Dutchy of Normandy.

Legal System: They maintain their own legal system based on Norman law, but local legislation is directly influenced by English common law.

Official Language: English.

Stability: Stable.

Currency: Jersey pound.

International Time: Ground Zero—GMT.

Country Code: 44 1539.

Embassy: British Embassy, 3100 Massachusetts Avenue, NW, Washington, DC 20008. Telephone: (202) 588-7800.

Type of Legal Entities: Exempt Private Company limited by shares. International Business Company (IBC). Private and public companies are recognized.

Unique Characteristics: Popular for fixed interest and discretionary trusts. Not appropriate for clients who require maximum privacy. Not the most cost-effective offshore jurisdiction.

Taxation: Exempt companies pay a flat nominal annual tax to become exempt from income tax. International companies can negotiate an income tax rate between 0 and 30 percent. There is a minimum 2 percent income tax on foreign-source income and 30 percent on local-source income.

Exchange Controls: None.

Treaties with the United States: No income tax treaty. There is a TIEA and an MLAT.

Useful Web Site: www.gov.je

Business Contacts:

Michael Doyle
Sark Offshore Consultancy
Castle Company Management LLC LTD
La Connellerie
Isle of Sark, Channel Islands, GY9 OSF
Telephone: 44 (01481) 832119
Fax: 44 (01481) 832738
E-mail: sales@sarkoffshore.demon.co.uk
Company Management/Full Administration Services for Channel Island and Offshore Entities

Abbey National Offshore
PO Box 545, International House
41 the Parade
St. Helier, Jersey, Channel Islands JE4 8XG
Telephone: 44 (01534) 885100
Fax: 44 (01534) 828884
E-mail: sales@abbeynationaloffshore.com
Web site: www.abbeyinternational.com
Offshore Banking/Multiple Currencies

AIB Bank (CI) Limited
PO Box 468
AIB House, Grenville Street
St. Helier, Jersey, Channel Islands JE4 8WT
Telephone: 44 (01534) 883000
Fax: 44 (01534) 883112
E-mail: one@aiboffshore.com
Web site: www.aiboffshore.com
Offshore Financial Services/Wealth Management

Ashburton (Jersey) Limited
PO Box 239
17 Hilary Street
St. Helier, Jersey, Channel Islands JE4 8SJ
Telephone: 44 (01534) 512000
Fax: 44 (01534) 512022
E-mail: enquiries@ashburton.com
Web site: www.ashburton.com
Discretionary Investment Management

Bank of Scotland International
PO Box 664

Halifax House
31–33 New Street
St. Helier, Jersey, Channel Islands JE4 8YW
Telephone: 44 (01534) 613500
Fax: 44 (01534) 759280
Comprehensive Banking and Investment Products and Services

Basel Trust Corporation (Channel Islands) Limited
PO Box 484
3 Old Street
St. Helier, Jersey, Channel Islands JE4 5SS
Telephone: 44 (01534) 500900
Fax: 44 (01534) 500901
E-mail: info@baseltrustjersey.com
Web site: www.baseltrustjersey.com
Estate Planning Services/Offshore E-Commerce

The Beresford Group
Beresford House, Bellozanne Road
St. Helier, Jersey, Channel Islands JE2 3JW
Telephone: 44 (01534) 879502
Fax: 44 (01534) 733405
E-mail: gary@bergroup.com
Web site: www.bergroup.com
Company/Trust/Tax/Asset Protection/Investments

Citco Jersey Limited
Le Masurier House
La Rue Le Masurier
St. Helier, Jersey, Channel Islands JE4 8RD
Telephone: 44 (01534) 756700
Fax: 44 (01534) 756799
E-mail: jersey-trust@citgo.com
Web site: www.citgo.com
Incorporation/Management/Funds

Deutsche Bank Offshore
PO Box 727
St. Paul's Gate
St. Helier, Jersey, Channel Islands JE4 8ZB
Telephone: 44 (01534) 889900
Fax: 44 (01534) 889911
E-mail: db.offshore@db.com

Web site: www.dboffshore.com/offshore
Discretionary Investment Management/Corporate Services

Ernst & Young LLP
Unity Chambers
28 Halkett Street
St. Helier, Jersey, Channel Islands JE1 1EY
Telephone: 44 (01534) 288600
Fax: 44 (01534) 288688
Web site: www.ey.com/channel_islands
International Tax Planning

Galsworthy & Stones
PO Box 145
Hawksford House
Caledonia Place
St. Helier, Jersey, Channel Islands JE4 8QP
Telephone: 44 (01534) 836800
Fax: 44 (01534) 836999
E-mail: mail@galsworthy.com
Web site: www.galsworthy.com
Banking and Finance/Trusts/Wills/Estates

Gerrard Private Bank (Jersey) Limited
28 New Street
St. Helier, Jersey, Channel Islands JE2 3TE
Telephone: 44 (01534) 887889
Fax: 44 (01534) 509725
E-mail: jer@gerrardpb.com
Web site: www.gerrardpb.com
Private Banking/Discretionary Investment Management

Hill Samuel Jersey Limited
PO Box 63, 7 Bond Street
St. Helier, Jersey, Channel Islands JE4 8PH
Telephone: 44 (01534) 604604
Fax: 44 (01534) 604606
E-mail: hsj@hillsamjsy.co.uk
Web site: www.hillsamjsy.co.uk
Private Banking/Discretionary Investment Management

HSBC Bank International Limited
PO Box 26
28/34 Hill Street

St. Helier, Jersey, Channel Islands JE4 8NR
Telephone: 44 (01534) 606000
Fax: 44 (01534) 606001
Web site: www.offshore.hsbc.com
Personal and Corporate Banking and Investment Services

Insinger de Beaufort (International) Limited
PO Box 177
38–39 Esplanade
St. Helier, Jersey, Channel Islands JE4 8RF
Telephone: 44 (01534) 708090
Fax: 44 (01534) 708050
E-mail: infojrs@int.insinger.com
Asset Management/Securities Dealer

Lloyds TSB Bank
Jersey International
PO Box 788, 25 New Street
St. Helier, Jersey, Channel Islands JE4 82E
Telephone: 44 (0134) 736626
Personal Offshore Banking/Debit Cards

Regent Tax Consultants Limited
PO Box 621, Le Galais Chambers
54 Bath Street
St. Helier, Jersey, Channel Islands JE4 8YD
Telephone: 44 (01534) 501311
Fax: 44 (01534) 501313
E-mail: tax enquiries@rbc.com
Web site: www.rbc.com
Tax Advisors for U.S./U.K. Persons

Standard Bank Offshore
Standard Bank House
PO Box 583
47–49 La Motte Street
St. Helier, Jersey, Channel Islands JE4 8XR
Telephone: 44 (01534) 881188
Fax: 44 (01534) 881133
E-mail: sboff@sboff.com
Web site: www.sboff.com
Offshore Bank Services/Securities/Investment Management
Banking and Investment Services for International Clients

Voisin & Co.
PO Box 31
Templar House, Don Road
St. Helier, Jersey, Channel Islands JE4 8NU
Telephone: 44 (01534) 500300
Fax: 44 (01534) 500350
E-mail: mail@voisinlaw.com
Web site: www.voisinlaw.com
International Commercial Law Firm

Cook Islands

Affiliation: New Zealand.
Location: This group of 15 islands is strung across the South Pacific between Samoa to the west and French Polynesia to the east.
Capital and Largest City: Avarua (Rarotonga).
Government: Self-governing New Zealand territory under their own constitution.
Legal System: English common law.
Official Language: English. Also speak Maori.
Stability: Stable.
Currency: New Zealand dollar.
International Time: –10.5 hrs. GMT.
Country Code: 682.
Embassy: Embassy of New Zealand, 37 Observatory Circle, NW, Washington, DC 20008. Telephone: (202) 328-4800.
Type of Legal Entities: International Business Company (IBC). Optional limited by shares or guarantee and no liability and unlimited liability. Modern and innovative trust legislation. Class A and Class B bank licensing.
Unique Characteristics: Special penal code for bank confidentiality. Excellent jurisdiction for establishing an asset protection trust, like Nevis and Belize. A very favorable tax haven with good legal and financial support.
Taxation: A no-tax haven.
Exchange Controls: None.
Treaties with the United States: No income tax treaty. No TIEA. No MLAT.
Useful Web Sites: www.ck/govt.htm; www.cook-islands.gov.ck
Business Contacts:

ANZ Banking Group Ltd.
PO Box 907
Rarotonga, Cook Islands
Telephone: (682) 21750
Fax: (682) 21760
Bank and Financial Services

Asiaciti Trust Pacific Limited
Level 3, CIDB Building
PO Box 822
Rarotonga, Cook Islands
Telephone: (682) 23387
Fax: (682) 23385
E-mail: altaylor@asiaciti.com
Web site: www.asiaciti.com
Incorporation/Management/Asset Protection Trusts

Clarkes P.C.
PO Box 123
Rarotonga, Cook Islands
Telephone: (682) 24567
Fax: (682) 21567
Solicitors

Cook Islands Savings Bank
PO Box TX
Rarotonga, Cook Islands
Telephone: (682) 29471
Fax: (682) 20471
Bank and Financial Services

Cook Islands Trust & Banking Corporation Ltd.
1st Floor, CIDB Building, Main Road
Rarotonga, Cook Islands
Telephone: (682) 24538
Fax: (682) 24539
E-mail: trustbk@citrust.org.ck
Financial Structures/Asset Protection/Trusts

KPMG Peat Marwick
Parekura Place Tutakimoa Road
PO Box 691
Avarua Rarotonga, Cook Islands
Telephone: (682) 20486
Fax: (682) 21486
E-mail: office@kpmg.co.ck
Accounting/Tax Management

Miller Howard & Lynch
PO Box 39
Panama, Rarotonga, Cook Islands
Telephone: (682) 21043

Fax: (682) 21143
Solicitors

Short, Carolyn & Associates
PO Box 632
Rarotonga, Cook Islands
Telephone: (682) 24530
Fax: (682) 24531
Accountants

Southpac Trust Limited
ANZ House, Main Street
PO Box 11
Avarua, Rarotonga, Cook Islands
Telephone: (682) 20514
Fax: (682) 20667
E-mail: offshore@southpak.co.uk
Banking and Financial Services/Asset Protection Trusts

TrustNet (Cook Islands) Limited
CIDB Building, Avarua
PO Box 208
Rarotonga, Cook Islands
Telephone: (682) 21080
Fax: (682) 21087
E-mail: invest2trustnet.co.uk
Offshore Corporate and Trustee Services

Westpac Banking Corporation
PO Box 42
Rarotonga, Cook Islands
Telephone: (682) 22014
Fax: (682) 20802
Bank and Financial Services

Cyprus

Affiliations: European Union; Commonwealth of Nations; North Atlantic Treaty Organization; United Nations.

Location: In the eastern Mediterranean Sea off the coast of Turkey near the western coast of Syria.

Capital and Largest City: Lefkosia (Nicosia).

Government: Republic.

Legal System: Predominantly based on English common law.

Official Language: Greek, Turkish. Also speak English.

Stability: There is ongoing hostility between the Turkish Cypriots and the Greek Cypriots. The United Nations has established a UN-occupied cease-fire zone while negotiations continue. At stake are recent European Union economic benefits, which are an incentive to both sides, to resolve differences.

Currency: Cyprus pound.

International Time: +2 hrs. GMT.

Country Code: 357.

Embassy: Embassy of the Republic of Cyprus, 2211 R Street, NW, Washington, DC 20008. Telephone: (202) 462-5772.

Type of Legal Entities: Offshore Limited Company. Application must be made to the Central Bank along with references on shareholders.

Unique Characteristics: Flag of convenience. All types of business activities are based in Cyprus.

Taxation: The offshore company pays 10 percent tax on net profits. With proper tax planning and an understanding of the available tax treaties, Cyprus is a favorable low-tax jurisdiction within the European Union (EU).

Exchange Controls: Nonresident-owned companies are exempt from exchange controls.

Treaties with the United States: There is an income tax treaty. No TIEA. No MLAT.

Useful Web Sites: www.cyprus.gov.cy; http://kypros.org/Government

Business Contacts:

Andreas Neocleous & Co
Advocates & Legal Consultants
Neocleous Huose
199, Arch Makarios III Avenue
PO Box 50613
Limassol, Cyprus
Telephone: 357 (25) 362-818
Fax: 357 (25) 359-262
E-mail: david.stokes@neocleous.com
Web site: www.neocleous.com
Incorporation/Management/International Tax Law

Areti Charidemou & Associates
Law Office
21 Vasili Michailidi Street
3026 Limassol, Cyprus
Telephone: 357 (25) 746-103
Fax: 357 (25) 344-019

E-mail: areti@aretilawyers.com
Web site: www.aretilawyers.com
Incorporation/Management/Taxation/Trusts

Bank of Cyprus Ltd.
51 Stassinos Street
Ayia Paraskevi Strovolos
PO Box 21472
1599 Nicosia, Cyprus
Telephone: 357 (22) 237-8000
Fax: 357 (22) 237-8327
Banking and Financial Services

The Bonalbo Group
4th Floor, 5 Costis Palamas Street
PO Box 29000
2084 Nicosia, Cyprus
Telephone: 357 (22) 846-000
Fax: 357 (22) 846-111
E-mail: cyprus@bonalbo.com
Web site: www.bonalbo.com
Incorporation/Management/Trusts/Taxation

Costas P. Erotocritou
C. P. Erotocritou & Co.
Libra Tower, 23 Olympion Str.
PO Box 50437
3605 Limassol, Cyprus
Telephone: 357 (25) 363-665
Fax: 357 (25) 341-500
E-mail: themis@cperotocritou.com
Web site: www.cperotocritou.com
Incorporations/Partnerships/Trusts/Ship Registrations

Ernst & Young
Nicosia Tower Center
36 Byron Avenue
PO Box 1656
Nicosia, Cyprus
Telephone: 357 (22) 467-000
Fax: 357 (22) 365-870
E-mail: lakoufis@logos.cy.net
International Tax Planning

Financial Consultants International (FCI) Ltd.
2 Chr Sozos Street, Eiffel Tower, 3rd Floor
PO Box 21439
1508 Nicosia, Cyprus
Telephone: 357 (22) 673-801
Fax: 357 (22) 665-297
E-mail: horwath@horwathpk.com.cy
Web site: www.horwathpk.com.cy
Incorporation/Management/Accounting/Tax Advice

Horwath P. Kalopetrides & Co.
2 Chr Sozos Street, Eiffel Tower, 3rd & 6th Floors
PO Box 21855
1514 Nicosia, Cyprus
Telephone: 357 (22) 669-017
Fax: 357 (22) 665-297
E-mail: horwath@horwathpk.com.cy
Web site: www.horwathpk.com.cy
Incorporation/Management/Tax Advice

Jordan National Bank PLC (International Banking Unit)
1 Anexartissias Street
Pecora Tower, 2nd Floor
PO Box 53587
3303 Limassol, Cyprus
Telephone: 357 (25) 356-669
Fax: 357 (25) 356-673
E-mail: jnb@cytanet.com.cy
Private and Commercial Banking

Jordans (Cyprus) Limited
Klimentos Tower, No. 13, 41–43, Klimentos Street
PO Box 26692
1646 Nicosia, Cyprus
Telephone: 357 (22) 767-294
Fax: 357 (22) 767-202
E-mail: info@jordans.com.cy
Web site: www.jordans-international.com
Incorporation/Management/Tax Advice

KPMG
Elma House, 10 Mnasiadou Street
PO Box 21121

1502 Nicosia, Cyprus
Telephone: 357 (22) 678-700
Fax: 357 (22) 678-200
E-mail: Nicosia@kpmg.com.cy
Web site: www.kpmg.com.cy
Offshore Tax Specialists

L. Papaphilippou & Co.
1, Costakis Pantelides Avenue
1010 Nicosia, Cyprus
PO Box 22313
1520 Nicosia, Cyprus
Telephone: (357) 226-74141
Fax: (357) 226-73388
E-mail: papaphilippou@lawcy.com
Web site: www.lawcy.com
Law Firm

The National Bank of Greece (Cyprus) Ltd.
15 Arch Makarios Avenue
PO Box 21191
1597 Nicosia, Cyprus
Telephone: 357 (22) 840-000
Fax: 357 (22) 762-080
E-mail: nbgibu@spidernet.com.cy
International Banking/Financial Services

P. G. Economides & Co.
Totalserve House, 17, Gr. Xenopoulou Street
PO Box 53117
3300 Limassol, Cyprus
Telephone: 357 (25) 866-300
Fax: 357 (25) 866-301
E-mail: audit@pgeconomides.com
Offshore Accounting and Taxation

Dubai, United Arab Emirates

Affiliations: Arab League; Organization of Petroleum Exporting Countries; United Nations.

Location: Eastern portion of the Arabian peninsula, strategically located between the Persian Gulf and the Gulf of Oman. Nearby countries are Saudi Arabia, Oman, and Qatar.

Capital and Largest City: Abu Dhabi (Capital); Dubai (largest).

Government: Federation formed by seven emirates known collectively as Trucial States.

Legal System: Federal court system introduced in 1971, except Dubai and Ra's al Khaymah, which are not fully integrated into the federal court system. All emirates have secular courts to adjudicate criminal, civil, and commercial matters.

Official Language: Arabic. Also speak Persian, Hindi, Urdu. Fluent English spoken in Dubai's business world.

Stability: Stable.

Currency: U.A.E. dirham.

International Time: +4 hrs. GMT.

Country Code: 971.

Embassy: Embassy of the United Arab Emirates, 3522 International Court, NW, Washington, DC 20008. Telephone: (202) 243-2400.

Type of Legal Entities: There are seven types of business establishments, including private and public companies, joint venture companies, and various partnerships.

Taxation: No corporate income tax on profits; exempt for 15 years. No withholding taxes.

Exchange Controls: None in Dubai.

Unique Characteristics: Dubai is quickly becoming the "Hong Kong of the Middle East." The Dubai International Financial Center and several other free trade zones are the hub of the offshore trade. Encourages e-commerce through the Dubai Internet City formerly known as Dubai Technology, Electronic Commerce, and Media Free Zone. The ruling family are known worldwide as owners and breeders of fine Thoroughbred racehorses. They actively support the sport with an outstanding program of important international races within their own country.

Treaties with the United States: No MLAT.

Useful Web Site: http://web-vgn.dubai-e.gov.ae:8083

Business Contacts:

Arab Emirates Investment Bank PJSC
Office No. 904, Twin Towers, Baniyas Street
Deira, PO Box 5503
Dubai, United Arab Emirates
Telephone: 971 (4) 2222-191
Fax: 971 (4) 2274-351
E-mail: aeibank@emirates.net.ae
Equity and Bond Market Investments/Portfolio Management

BDO Patel & Al Saleh
Al Futtaim Tower, Suite 304/305, Al Maktoum Street

Deira, PO Box 1961
Dubai, United Arab Emirates
Telephone: 971 (4) 222-2869
Fax: 971 (4) 227-4867
E-mail: bdopatel@emirates.net.ae
Incorporation/Financial Consulting/Tax Planning

Mahendra Asher & Co., Chartered Accountants
Nasa Building, Flat #203, Al Maktoum Street
Deira, PO Box 4421
Dubai, United Arab Emirates
Telephone: 971 (4) 2227-580
Fax: 971 (4) 2233-715
E-mail: masherdb@emirates.net.ae
Web site: mahendraasherco.com
Incorporation/Management/Accounting

Pannell Kerr Foster
301–303 Al Maiden Tower-2, Al Maktoum Street
PO Box 13094
Dubai, United Arab Emirates
Telephone: 971 (4) 223-6508
Fax: 971 (4) 223-4524
E-mail: Dubai@pkfuae.com
Web site: pkfuae.com
International Tax Planning

Sovereign Corporate Services
Suite 201, National Bank of Umm Al Qaiwain Building
Khalid Bin Al Waleed Road
Bur Dubai, PO Box 62201
Dubai, United Arab Emirates
Telephone: 971 (4) 397-6552
Fax: 971 (4) 397-8355
E-mail: Dubai@sovereigngroup.com
Web site: www.sovereigngroup.com
Incorporation/Management/Trustees/Tax Planning/E-Commerce

Gibraltar

Affiliations: Overseas Territory of the United Kingdom; European Union.

Location: At the tip of the Iberian peninsula in the southernmost part of Spain at the Strait of Gibraltar. This is the narrowest point between Europe and Africa at the west end of the Mediterranean Sea.

Capital and Largest City: Gibraltar.

Government: Self-governing under its own constitution. Spain has attempted to gain sovereignty away from Britain for years without success.

Legal System: English common law.

Official Language: English. Also speak French and Spanish.

Stability: Stable.

Currency: Gibraltar pound.

International Time: +1 hr. GMT.

Country Code: 350.

Embassy: British Embassy, 3100 Massachusetts Avenue, NW, Washington, DC 20008. Telephone: (202) 588-7800.

Type of Legal Entities: Exempt company; a nonresident company; a Gibraltar 1992 company; a hybrid company. Partnerships, trusts, and foundations can also be established.

Unique Characteristics: Flag of convenience. Known for banking, insurance companies, fund management, holding companies, and trusts. An exempt company pays no taxes of any kind for 25 years.

Taxation: Qualifying exempt companies pay between 0 and 35 percent annual corporate income tax.

Exchange Controls: None.

Treaties with the United States: No income tax treaty. No TIEA. There is an MLAT.

Useful Web Site: www.gibraltar.gov.gi

Business Contacts:

Argenta & Magnum Management Company Ltd.
206 Neptune House, Marina Bay
PO Box 268
Gibraltar
Telephone: (350) 45460
Fax: (350) 45450
E-mail: argenta@gibnynex.gi
Incorporation/Management/Alternative Citizenships

Attias & Levy
First Floor Suites, 3a Irish Town
Gibraltar
Telephone: (350) 72150
Fax: (350) 74986
E-mail: attlev@gibraltar.gi
Web site: www.attiaslevy.gi
Corporate Services/Trusts/Banking/Ship Registration

Europa Trust Company Limited
Suite 24, Watersgardens 6

PO Box 629
Gibraltar
Telephone: (350) 79013
Fax: (350) 70101
E-mail: info@europa.gi
Web site: www.europa.gi
Incorporations/Trusts/ Yacht Registration

Hodgson Bilton
3rd Floor, Mansion House
143 Main Street
Gibraltar
Telephone: (350) 76498
Fax: (350) 76487
E-mail: jhodgson@sovereigngroup.com
Business Law/Tax/Estate/Trusts

Jordans (Gibraltar) Limited
Suite 3C, Eurolife Building, 1 Corral Road
PO Box 569
Gibraltar
Telephone: (350) 75446
Fax: (350) 79902
E-mail: jordans@gibnet.gi
Web site: www.jordans-international.com
Incorporation/Management/Tax

KPMG Administrative Services Limited
Regal House, Queensway
PO Box 191
Gibraltar
Telephone: (350) 74015
Fax: (350) 74016
E-mail: kpmggib@gibnynex.gi
Offshore Tax Planning

LPS Securities Ltd.
28 Irish Town
Gibraltar
Telephone: (350) 79120
Fax: (350) 78428
E-mail: ipsfutures@gibnynex.gi
Investment Advisors

Marrache & Co.
5 Cannon Lane
PO Box 85
Gibraltar
Telephone: (350) 79918
Fax: (350) 73315
E-mail: Marrache@marrache.com
Web site: www.marrache.com
International Law/Offshore Taxation

The Royal Bank of Scotland (Gibraltar) Limited
1 Corral Road
PO Box 766
Gibraltar
Telephone: (350) 73200
Fax: (350) 70152
Private Banking

Triay & Triay
Attorneys at Law
28 Irish Town
PO Box 15
Gibraltar
Telephone: (350) 72020
Fax: (350) 72270
E-mail: triay@triay.com
Web site: www.triay.com
Law/Financial Services/Investments

Triay Stagnetto Neish
Attorneys at Law
Suites C & D, 2nd Floor, Queensway
PO Box 147
Gibraltar
Telephone: (350) 79423
Fax: (350) 71405
E-mail: tsn@tsnlaw.com
Web site: www.tsnlaw.com
International Tax Planning/Wealth Preservation

Grenada

Affiliations: Commonwealth of Nations; United Nations.
Location: In the Windward Islands of the Caribbean.

Capital and Largest City: St. George's.
Government: Constitutional monarchy with Westminster-style Parliament.
Legal System: English common law.
Official Language: English, Also speak French patois.
Stability: Stable.
Currency: East Caribbean dollar.
International Time: –4 hrs. GMT.
Country Code: 809.
Embassy: Embassy of Grenada, 1701 New Hampshire Avenue, NW, Washington, DC 20009. Telephone: (202) 265-2561.
Type of Legal Entities: International Business Company (IBC). Offshore bank licenses.
Unique Characteristics: A no-tax haven. IBCs are exempt from taxation for 25 years. Dozens of bank licenses have been revoked over the recent years because of illegal activity.
Taxation: No tax on offshore business.
Exchange Controls: None.
Treaties with the United States: No income tax treaty. There is a TIEA and an MLAT.
Useful Web Site: www.geographia.com/grenada
Business Contact:

Sterling International Bank & Trust Corporation
Morne Rouge Road
PO Box 1711
Grand Anse, St. George's, Grenada
Telephone: (473) 444-5900
Fax: (473) 444-5912
Incorporation/Trust/Banking/Credit Cards

Hong Kong, China

Affiliation: Special Administration Region of China.
Location: South of mainland China on the South China Sea.
Capital and Largest City: Victoria.
Government: This western-style financial center operates within the communist state of China under a policy of "one country, two systems" to preserve its economic independence in compliance with its former lease agreement with Britain which expired on July 1, 1997. This status-quo position is to remain effective for 50 years past the expiration of the lease. That remains to be seen; the Chinese have been relatively laissez-faire to date, but that could change.
Legal System: English common law.
Official Language: Chinese and English.

Stability: Stable.

Currency: Hong Kong dollar.

International Time: +8 hrs. GMT.

Country Code: 852.

Embassy: Embassy of the People's Republic of China, 2300 Connecticut Avenue, NW, Washington, DC 20008. Telephone: (202) 328-2500.

Type of Legal Entities: Private Company Limited by Shares; partnerships and trusts.

Unique Characteristics: A T-7 tax haven. Flag of convenience. Popular for holding, insurance, and trading companies and investment funds. Major international banking center and shipping port. Strict bank secrecy laws. Home of the Hong Kong Stock Exchange. Possible expatriate haven under their Business Investment Visa. Member of the Financial Action Task Force (FATF).

Taxation: A low-tax haven. Maximum profit tax rate is 17 percent. Foreign-source profits are not taxed. On local business there are profits, salary, and property taxes. No withholding, capital gains net worth, or value-added tax (VAT).

Exchange Controls: None.

Treaties with the United States: No income tax treaty. No TIEA. There is an MLAT.

Useful Web Site: www.info.gov.hk

Business Contacts:

Barber Financial Advisors
355 Burrard Street, Suite 1000
Vancouver, BC V6C 2G8 Canada
Telephone: (604) 608-6177
Fax: (604) 608-2984
E-mail: Info@BarberFinancialAdvisors.com
Web site: www.BarberFinancialAdvisors.com
Incorporations/Management/Bank Accounts

AMS Trustees (H.K.) Limited
Room 1210, 12/F Wing on Center
111 Connaught Road Central
Hong Kong
Telephone: (852) 2147-2108
Fax: (852) 2147-2119
Offshore Financial Services/Investment Funds/E-Commerce

Asiaciti Trust Hong Kong Limited
Room 610–11 Bank of America Tower
12 Harcourt Road
Hong Kong

Telephone: (852) 2591-9009
Fax: (852) 2891-2436
Incorporation/Management/Tax and Asset Protection Strategies

Baker & McKenzie
14/F Hutchison House
10 Harcourt Road
Hong Kong
Telephone: (852) 2846-1888
Fax: (852) 2845-0476
Banking/Finance/Legal/Tax/Investments

The Bank of East Asia, Limited
Legal Division, Bank of East Asia Building
10 Des Voeux Road, Central
Hong Kong
Telephone: (852) 2842-3238
Fax: (852) 2537-1663
Incorporation/Management/Trust Services

Bryan Cave
Suite 3704, Tower One, Lippo Center
89 Queensway
Hong Kong
Telephone: (852) 2522-2821
Fax: (852) 2522-3830
Large International Commercial Law Firm

CMG First State Investments (Hong Kong) Limited
6/F Three Exchange Square
8 Connaught Place, Central
Hong Kong
Telephone: (852) 2846-7555
Fax: (852) 2868-4742
Investment Management

Ernest Maude Continental Investments Limited
Suite 2201–03, Universal Trade Center
3 Arbuthnot road, Central
Hong Kong
Telephone: (852) 2521-9188
Fax: (852) 2526-2993
Personal Financial and Investment Advisory

Grant Thornton
13th Floor, Gloucester Tower, The Landmark
11 Pedder Street, Central
Hong Kong
Telephone: (852) 2218-3000
Fax: (852) 2218-3500
Accounting and Taxation for Business

Henley & Partners Far East Ltd.
13/F Silver Fortune Plaza
1 Wellington Street
Central Hong Kong
Telephone: (852) 2525-7717
Fax: (852) 2140-6833
E-mail: jflader@zetland.biz
Residency and Business Visa

Insinger de Beaufort Trust (HK) Limited
11/F, Standard Chartered Bank Building
4–4A Des Voeux Road, Central
Hong Kong
Telephone: (852) 2526-3665
Fax: (852) 2530-4898
Incorporation/Management/Trust Services/Private Banking

International Taxation Advisory Services Limited
Suite 4002 A, Central Plaza
18 Harbour Road, Wanchai
Hong Kong
Telephone: (852) 2868-3130
Fax: (852) 2523-8549
Offshore Tax Planning/Asset Protection Strategies

LGT Bank in Liechtenstein AG
29th Floor, Two Exchange Square
8 Connaught Place, Central
Hong Kong
Telephone: (852) 2523-6180
Fax: (852) 2868-0059
Discretionary Portfolio Management/Investment Advisory

Overseas Company Registration Agents Asia Limited (OCRA Hong Kong)
1301 Bank of America Tower

12 Harcourt Road, Central
Hong Kong
Telephone: (852) 2522-0172
Fax: (852) 2521-1190
E-mail: ocra@ocra-asia.com
Web site: www.ocra-worldwide.com
Offshore Corporate, Trust and Taxation Services

Rabobank
2 Exchange Square
Central, Hong Kong
Telephone: (852) 2103-2000
Fax: (852) 2530-1728
Bank and Financial Services

Isle of Man

Affiliations: United Kingdom; Special EU status.
Location: Between Ireland and England in the Irish Sea.
Capital and Largest City: Douglas.
Government: Self-governed British Crown sovereign dependency.
Legal System: English common law.
Official Language: English.
Stability: Stable.
Currency: Isle of Man pound.
International Time: Ground Zero—GMT.
Country Code: 44 1624.
Embassy: British Embassy, 3100 Massachusetts Avenue, NW, Washington, DC 20008. Telephone: (202) 588-7800.
Type of Legal Entities: Limited Liability Company (LLC). Private and public companies are recognized.
Unique Characteristics: Known for their investment funds, offshore banking, Manx trusts, hybrid companies, and insurance companies. E-commerce center. Good jurisdiction for doing business within the European Union. Pressure from the EU and OECD on "harmful tax competition" and information disclosure on company accounts.
Taxation: An international company can be taxed on all or part of its income up to 35 percent. An exempt company is free of taxation on foreign-source income. Nonresidents pay no tax on a nonresident company. No capital gains, wealth, property, death, or capital transfer taxes.
Exchange Controls: None.

Treaties with the United States: There is an income tax treaty, a TIEA, and an MLAT.

Useful Web Site: www.gov.im

Business Contacts:

Charles Cain
Skye Fiduciary Services
Skyefid Limited
2 Water Street
Ramsey, Isle of Man 1M8 1JP
Telephone: 44 (01624) 811611
Fax: 44 (01624) 816645
E-mail: charles.cain@skyefid.com
Web site: www.skyefid.com
Asset Protection and Fiduciary Structures for Americans

David Ashton
Chris Eaton
ILS (Corporate Services) Limited
2nd Floor, Atlantic House
Circular Road
Douglas, Isle of Man IM1 1SQ
Telephone: 44 (01624) 682500
Fax: 44 (01624) 628488
E-mail: ilscorp@ils-world.com
Web site: www.ils-world.com
Incorporation/Management/Multiple Jurisdictions

Isle of Man Assurance Group
IOMA House, Hope Street
Douglas, Isle of Man IM1 1AP
Telephone: 44 (01624) 681200
Fax: 44 (01624) 681397
E-mail: ioma@ioma.co.im
Web site: www.ioma.co.im
Customized Life Products/Company Management

Abbey National Treasury International Ltd.
PO Box 150, Carrick House
Circular Road
Douglas, Isle of Man IM99 1NH
Telephone: 44 (01624) 644800
Fax: 44 (01624) 644691
Personal Banking Products and Services

AIB Bank (Isle of Man) Limited
PO Box 186
Douglas, Isle of Man, IM99 1QE
Telephone: 44 (01624) 639772
Fax: 44 (01624) 639636
E-mail: one@aiboffshore.com
Web site: www.aiboffshore.com
Offshore Banking and Investment Services

AXA Isle of Man Limited
Royalty House
Walpole Avenue
Douglas, Isle of Man IM1 2SL
Telephone: 44 (01624) 643300
Fax: 44 (01624) 643444
E-mail: amtc@amtcltd.com
Single Premium Investments/Life Insurance

Bank of Ireland
PO Box 246
Christian Road
Douglas, Isle of Man IM99 1XF
Telephone: 44 (01624) 644222
Fax: 44 (01624) 644245
E-mail: info@boifsharp.com
Banking and Investments for Expatriats

Canada Life International Limited
St. Mary's, The Parade
Castletown, Isle of Man 1M9 1RJ
Telephone: 44 (01624) 8202000
Fax: 44 (01624) 820201
E-mail: info@canadalifeint.com
Web site: www.canadalifeint.com
Flexible Investment Products

Caymanx Trust Company Limited
34 Athol Street
Douglas, Isle of Man IM1 1RD
Telephone: 44 (01624) 646900
Fax: 44 (01624) 662192
E-mail: mail@cncoim.com
Private Banking and Trust Services/Investment Management

Crossman Trust Company Limited
Portland House, Station Road
Ballasalla, Isle of Man 1M9 2AE
Telephone: 44 (01624) 825805
Fax: 44 (01624) 824570
E-mail: Crossman trust@enterprise.net
Web site: www.crossleys.com
Corporate/Trust/Estate/Asset Protection

Ernst & Young Trust Company Limited
Jubilee Buildings, Victoria Street
Douglas, Isle of Man IM1 1SH
Telephone: 44 (01624) 6990000
Fax: 44 (01624) 699001
Web site: www.ey.com.im
International Tax Planning

Friends Provident International Limited
Royal Court
Castletown, Isle of Man 1M9 1RA
Telephone: 44 (01624) 821212
Fax: 44 (01624) 824405
E-mail: servicedesk@fpiom.com
Single and Regular Premium Investments Products

Horwath Clark Whitehill
7th Floor, Victory House
Prospect Hill
Douglas, Isle of Man IM1 1EQ
Telephone: 44 (01624) 627335
Fax: 44 (01624) 677225
E-mail: mail@horwath.co.im
Web site: www.horwath.com.im
Incorporation/Management/Tax Planning

Irish Permanent, International (IOM) Ltd.
12–14 Ridgeway Street
Douglas, Isle of Man IM1 1EN
Telephone: 44 (01624) 641641
Fax: 44 (01624) 676795
E-mail: hanrahang@ip-intl.com
Web site: www.ip-intl.com
Management/Banking/Trust/Funds

Jordans (Isle of Man) Limited
1st Floor, Atlantic House
4–8 Circular Road
Douglas, Isle of Man IM1 2AG
Telephone: 44 (01624) 693000
Fax: 44 (01624) 693001
E-mail: angela-seabrook@jordans-iom.com
Web site: www.jordans-international.com
Incorporation/Management/Trusts/Accounting/Tax

Lloyds TSB Offshore Limited
Corporate Banking
PO Box 8, Victory House, Prospect Hill
Douglas, Isle of Man IM99 1AH
Telephone: 44 (01539) 448019
Fax: 44 (01624) 626033
Web site: www.lloydstsb-offshore.com
Corporate Offshore Banking/Debit Cards

OCRA (Overseas Company Registration Agents Limited)
Tower Street
Ramsey, Isle of Man 1M8 1JA
Telephone: 44 (01624) 811000
Fax: 44 (01624) 811001
E-mail: ocra@ocra.com
Offshore Corporate Services/Tax Planning

Royal Skandia Life Assurance Limited
Skandia House, Finch Road
Douglas, Isle of Man IM99 1NN
Telephone: 44 (01624) 611611
Fax: 44 (01624) 611715
E-mail: info@royalskandia.com
Web site: www.royalskandia.com
Tax-Efficient Investment Plans

Scottish Provident International Life Assurance Limited
Provident House
Ballacottier Business Park, Cooil Road
Douglas, Isle of Man IM2 2SP
Telephone: 44 (01624) 681681
Fax: 44 (01624) 677336
E-mail: customer_services_iom@spila.com

Web site: www.spila.com
Investment/Life Insurance/Retirement Plans

Simcocks Advocates Limited
Ridgeway house, Ridgeway Street
Douglas, Isle of Man IM99 1PY
Telephone: 44 (01624) 690300
Fax: 44 (01624) 690333
E-mail: mail@simcocks.com
Web site: www.simcocks.com
Law Firm Specializing in Offshore Activities

Standard Bank Stockbrokers (Isle of Man) Limited
Standard Bank House
1 Circular Road
Douglas, Isle of Man IM1 1SB
Telephone: 44 (01624) 643643
Fax: 44 (01624) 643801
Web site: www.sboff.com
Securities Dealers/Portfolio Services

Moore Stephens
PO Box 25
26 Athol Street
Douglas, Isle of Man IM99 1BD
Telephone: 44 (01624) 662020
Fax: 44 (01624) 662430
E-mail: mail@moore-stephens.co.im
Chartered Accounts/Investment Management

Mary Tait, Investment Manager
Lorne House Trust Limited
Lorne House, Castletown, Isle of Man IM9 1AZ
Telephone: 44 (01624) 823579
Fax: 44 (01624) 822952
E-mail: general@lorne-house.com
Web site: www.lorne-house.com
Founded in 1982 by Ronald Buchanan
Investment Management/Trust and Corporate Services

Labuan, Malaysia

Affiliations: Commonwealth of Nations; United Nations; Association of Southeast Asian Nations.

Location: Malaysia.

Capital and Largest City: Kuala Lumpur.
Government: Constitutional monarchy.
Legal System: Based on English common law.
Official Language: Bahasa Melayu. Also speak English, Chinese, and Tamil.
Stability: Stable.
Currency: Malaysian Ringgit (RM).
International Time: +8 hrs. GMT.
Country Code: 60.
Embassy: Embassy of Malaysia, 3516 International court NW, Washington, DC 20008. Telephone: (202) 572-9700.
Type of Legal Entities: Offshore and foreign offshore companies.
Unique Characteristics: No bank secrecy. Confidentiality clauses are incorporated into various Acts. Encourages offshore e-commerce business.
Taxation: No foreign-source income tax on a resident company.
Exchange Controls: No exchange controls for offshore companies and their foreign business.
Treaties with the United States: No income tax treaty. No TIEA. No MLAT.
Business Contacts:

Insinger Brumby Trust (Labuan) Sdn Bhd
Brumby House
1st Floor Jalan Bahasa
PO Box 80148
87011 Labuan F.T., Malaysia
Telephone: 60 (87) 423828
Fax: 60 (87) 417242
E-mail: Raymond.wong@asia.insigner.com
Incorporation/Management/Trustees/Accounting

Maybank International (L) Ltd., Labuan IOFC
Level 16(B), Main Office Tower
Financial Park Labuan, Jalan Merdeka
PO Box 81915
87028 W.P. Labuan, Malaysia
Telephone: 60 (87) 414406
Fax: 60 (87) 414806
E-mail: millmit@tm.net.my
International Banking Services

Portcullis Trust (Labuan) Sdn Bhd & David Chong & Co.
Level 7 (F2) Main Office Tower
Financial Park Labuan, Jalan Merdeka
PO Box 80107
87011 F.T. Labuan, Malaysia

Telephone: 60 (87) 439191
Fax: 60 (87) 439193
E-mail: georgep@pc.jaring.my
Incorporation/Management/Accounting/Tax Planning

Sititrust & Administrator Sdn Bhd
Suite 5(I), 5th Floor Main Office Tower
Financial Park Labuan, Jalan Merdeka
PO Box 81840
87028 F.T. Labuan, Malaysia
Telephone: 60 (87) 421663
Fax: 60 (87) 421662
E-mail: ctrust@tm.net.my
Incorporation/Management/Trusts

ZI Labuan Trust Company Sdn Bhd
Unit Level 13 (E), Main Office Tower
Financial Park Labuan, Jalan Merdeka
87000 F.T. Labuan, Malaysia
Telephone: 60 (87) 451688
Fax: 60 (87) 453688
E-mail: aziaan.com@ziltco.com.my
Incorporation/Management/Trusts/Tax Planning

Liechtenstein

Affiliation: United Nations.

Location: This postage stamp sized enclave is situated in Western Europe and bordered by Switzerland to the west and Austria to the east.

Capital and Largest City: Vaduz.

Government: Hereditary constitutional monarchy.

Legal System: The prince of the state and the legislature pass law. Civil and criminal procedures have an Austrian influence, contract and property law a Swiss orientation, and commercial law a German base.

Official Language: German.

Stability: Stable.

Currency: Swiss Franc.

International Time: +1 hr. GMT.

Country Code: 41 75.

Embassy: No embassy in the United States.

Type of Legal Entities: The Establishment (Anstalt), a novel entity unlike any found in the United States; AG (Aktiengesellscht)—a corporation limited by shares; GmbH (Gesellschaft mit beschrauker Haftung)—a limited liability company; Foundation (Stiftungen)—another unique entity of Liechtenstein. Bearer shares are permitted; holding companies; domiciliary companies; partnerships; trusts; trust enterprises. A more complete description of the Anstalte can be found in Chapter 18.

Unique Characteristics: Strict bank secrecy. A T-7 money haven. Resisting attack from the OECD. A blacklisted country. Known for unique corporate and trust structures, foreign holding companies, banking, and investment funds. Numbered accounts available to high-net worth individuals. Excellent management services available for all types of entity.

Taxation: A low-tax haven. A company of any kind that qualifies as an offshore investor will pay no taxes on income from sources outside Liechtenstein.

Exchange Controls: None.

Treaties with the United States: No income tax treaty. No TIEA. No MLAT.

Business Contacts:

Barber Financial Advisors
355 Burrard Street, Suite 1000
Vancouver, BC V6C 2G8 Canada
Telephone: (604) 608-6177
Fax: (604) 608-2984
E-mail: Info@BarberFinancialAdvisors.com
Web site: www.BarberFinancialAdvisors.com
Personal and Company Bank Accounts

Administrust Services Reg
J. Rheinbergerstrasse 6
PO Box 634
FL 9490 Vaduz, Liechtenstein
Telephone: (423) 232-3021
Fax: (423) 232-5040
Personal Tax and Estate Planning/Portfolio Management/Corporate Services

Audita-Revisions-AG
Bangarten 2 Postfach 119
FL 9490 Vaduz, Liechtenstein
Telephone: (423) 232-5213
Fax: (423) 232-5277
Accounting/Taxation/Management

BBT Banzer & Buchel Treuhand AG
Austrasse 49
FL 9490 Vaduz, Liechtenstein
Telephone: (423) 238-1313

Fax: (423) 238-1300
Corporate Services/Financial Planning/Asset Protection

Credit Suisse Trust Limited
Pradafant 21
FL 9490 Vaduz, Liechtenstein
Telephone: (423) 237-7100
Fax: (423) 237-7111
Incorporation/Management

Roger Frick
Allgemeines Treuunternehmen (ATU)
Aeulestrasse 5
FL 9490 Vaduz, Liechtenstein
Telephone: (423) 237-3434
Fax: (423) 237-3460
Incorporation/Management/Legal and Tax
Advise/Fiduciary/Trusteeships

Jura Trust AG
Mitteldorf 1, PO Box 838
FL 9490 Vaduz, Liechtenstein
Telephone: (423) 237-7575
Fax: (423) 232-1362
Wealth Preservation/Tax Planning/Incorporations/Trusts

LGT Bank Liechtenstein AG
Herrengasse 12
FL 9490 Vaduz, Liechtenstein
Telephone: (423) 235-1122
Fax: (423) 235-1522
Banking/Investment Management

Miselva Etablissement
Josef Rheinberger Strasse 29
FL 9490 Vaduz, Liechtenstein
Telephone: (423) 237-6900
Fax: (423) 237-6910
Incorporation/Management/Legal/Accounting

Praesidial-Anstalt
Aeulestrasse 38, Postfach 583
FL 9490 Vaduz, Liechtenstein

Telephone: (423) 236-5555
Fax: (423) 236-5399
Corporate/Trusts/Asset Protection/Tax Planning

Dr. Norbert Seeger
Advokaturburo
Attorney at Law
Am Schragen Weg 14, PO Box 1618
9490 Vaduz, Liechtenstein
Telephone: (423) 232-0808
Fax: (423) 232-0630
Personal Taxation/Estate Planning/Portfolio Management/Asset Protection

Serica Bank Aktiengesellschaft
Pflugstrasse 16
FL 9490 Vaduz, Liechtenstein
Telephone: (423) 236-5522
Fax: (423) 236-5505
Private Banking

Toendury and Partner AG
Bergstrasse 389, PO Box 777
FL 9497 Triesenberg, Liechtenstein
Telephone: (423) 262-8333
Fax: (423) 262-7989
Accounting/Tax/Legal/Trustees/Investment Management

Luxembourg

Affiliations: North Atlantic Treaty Organization; European Union; United Nations.
Location: Western Europe. Bordered by Belgium, France, and Germany.
Capital and Largest City: Luxembourg.
Government: Constitutional monarchy.
Legal System: Civil law system.
Official Language: Luxembourgish (national). Also speak French, German, and English.
Stability: Stable.
Currency: Euro.
International Time: +1 hr. GMT.
Country Code: 352.

Embassy: Embassy of Grand Dutchy of Luxembourg, 2200 Massachusetts Avenue, NW, Washington, DC 20008. Telephone: (202) 265-4171.

Type of Legal Entities: SA—Societes Anonymes, a corporation; SaRL—Societes a resposabilite limitee, a private limited company; also several types of partnerships. Holding companies include the 1929 holding company; the billionaire holding company; the finance holding company, and the 1990 or SOPARFI holding company.

Unique Characteristics: Excellent banking center. Bank secrecy laws. Numbered accounts. Popular jurisdiction for holding companies and investment companies. A member of the Financial Action Task Force (FATF).

Taxation: Numerous tax incentives. A high-tax jurisdiction. However, there are exceptions, such as on holding companies, that are not subject to corporate income tax. A parent-subsidiary, known as a SOPARFI is exempt under certain circumstances from corporate capital gains and dividends.

Exchange Controls: None.

Treaties with the United States: There is an income tax treaty. No TIEA. There is an MLAT.

Business Contacts:

ABN AMRO Trust Company (Luxembourg) S.A.
46A Avenue J. F. Kennedy
L-1855 Luxembourg, Luxembourg
Telephone: (352) 427-1711
Fax: (352) 421-961
E-mail: aatlux@pt.lu
Web site: www.abnamrotrust.com
Incorporation/Management

AMS Trust (Luxembourg) S.A.
381 Route de Thionville
L-5887 Hesperange, Luxembourg
Telephone: (352) 263-6571
Fax: (352) 263-6572
E-mail: ams@amslux.lu
Web site: www.amsbvi.com
Offshore Financial Services

Bank Sarasin Benelux SA
287–289 Route d' Arlon
L-1105 Luxembourg, Luxembourg
Telephone: (352) 457-8801
Fax: (352) 452-396
E-mail: influx@sarasin.com

Web site: www.sarasin.com
Private Banking/Investment Management

BGL-MeesPierson Trust (Luxembourg) S.A.
12–16 avenue Monterey
L-2136 Luxembourg, Luxembourg
Telephone: (352) 424-22222
Fax: (352) 424-22070
E-mail: info@bglmeespiersontrust.lu
Incorporation/Management/Trust Services

Delma & Cie Sarl
59 rue G.D. Charlotte
9515 WILTZ, Luxembourg
Telephone: (352) 95-05-74
Fax: (352) 95-91-11
E-mail: business@pt.lu
Incorporation/Management/International Tax Advisors

Fingeco Lux S.A.
4A, boulevard G.D. Charlotte
L-1330 Luxembourg, Luxembourg
Telephone: (352) 45-24-22
Fax: (352) 45-35-05
E-mail: bisenius@fingeco.com
Web site: www.fingeco.com
Incorporation/Management/Fiduciary/Accounting/Custodial

Hoogewerf & Cie
19 Rue Aldringen
L-1118 Luxembourg, Luxembourg
Telephone: (352) 46-00-25
Fax: (352) 46-00-27
E-mail: hoogewerf@hermesnet.com
Incorporation/Management/Tax Advise

Maitland Management Services S.A.
Boite Postal 1361
6 rue Adolphe Fischer
L-1520 Luxembourg, Luxembourg
Telephone: (352) 40-25-05-1
Fax: (352) 40-25-05-66
E-mail: service@maitlandtrust.com

Web site: www.maitlandtrust.com
Incorporation/Management/Accounting/Trustee Services

PanEuroLife SA
14 rue Edward Steichen,
B.P. 2408
L-1882 Luxembourg, Luxembourg
Telephone: (352) 45-67-30-1
Fax: (352) 44-67-34
E-mail: info@paneurolife.com
Web site: www.paneurolife.com
Life Assurance Contracts/Capital Redemption Bonds

PFA Pension Luxembourg S.A.
47 Boulevard Prince Henri
L-1724 Luxembourg, Luxembourg
Telephone: (352) 467766
Fax: (352) 467776
Pension Plans for Expatriates

Trust International Luxembourg S.A.
60 Grand'Rue
L-1660 Luxembourg, Luxembourg
Telephone: (352) 22-40-51
Fax: (352) 22-40-55
E-mail: til@pt.lu
Incorporation/Management/International Tax Planning

Madeira

Affiliation: Portugal.
Location: Off the northwest coast of Africa in the Atlantic Ocean, approximately 535 miles southwest of Lisbon, Portugal.
Capital and Largest City: Lisbon.
Government: Parliamentary Democracy.
Legal System: Civil law.
Official Language: Portuguese and Mirandese.
Stability: Stable.
Currency: Euro.
International Time: Ground Zero—GMT.
Country Code: 351 91.

Embassy: Embassy of Portugal, 2125 Kalorama Road, NW, Washington, DC 20008. Telephone: (202) 328-8610.

Type of Legal Entities: Ltd.—Limitada, a limited liability company; SA—Sociedades Anonimas, a stock corporation. Recognizes the common law trust concept.

Unique Characteristics: Flag of convenience.

Taxation: Companies incorporated in 2005–2006 are subject to corporate tax of 2 percent; 2007–2011 are subject to a rate increase to 3 percent on their foreign-source income.

Exchange Controls: None.

Treaties with the United States: No income tax treaty. No TIEA. No MLAT.

Useful Web Site: www.madeira-web.com

Business Contacts:

Banco Comercial Portugues SA/Sucursal Financeira Exterior
Edificio Marina Forum
Av. Arriaga77, 2nd—sala 203
P-9000-060 Funchal, Madeira Islands
Telephone: 351 (291) 20-64-50
Fax: 351 (291) 20-64-69
International Private and Corporate Banking

Banco Espirito Santo E Comercial de Lisboa
Edificio Arriaga
Avenida Arriaga
P-9000-064 Funchal, Madeira Islands
Telephone: 351 (291) 208-990
Fax: 351 (291) 231-227
International Private and Corporate Banking

Madeira Corporate Services
Avenida Arriaga No. 77, 6th Floor
Edificio Marina Forum
P-9004-533 Funchal, Madeira Islands
Telephone: 351 (291) 202-400
Fax: 351 (291) 237-188
Incorporation/Management/Tax Planning

Madeira Fiducia Management LDA
Avenida Arriaga 73, 1st—105
P-9000-533 Funchal, Madeira Islands
Telephone: 351 (291) 200-988
Fax: 351 (291) 200-989

E-mail: m.fiducia@mail.telepac.pt
Incorporation/Management/Trusts/Admiralty

Madeira Management Cia Lda.
PO Box 7
Rua dos Murcas No. 88
P-9000-058 Funchal, Madeira Islands
Telephone: 351 (291) 201-700
Fax: 351 (291) 227-144
E-mail: mmcl@mail.telepac.pt
Web site: www.madeira-management.com
Incorporation/Management/Legal/Accounting

NMIS—New Madeira Investment Servicos S.A.
Rua Dr. Brito Camara, No. 20-1
P-9000-039 Funchal, Madeira Islands
Telephone: 351 (291) 200-988
Fax: 351 (291) 200-989
Incorporation/Management/Accounting/Admiralty

Teiceira de Freitas, Rodriguez e Moura Costa Soc. Advogados
Avenida Arriaga No. 77, 6th Floor, Suite 601
Edificio Marina Forum
P-9004-533 Funchal, Madeira Islands
Telephone: 351 (291) 202-400
Fax: 351 (291) 230-324
Legal

United Management Services Lda
Rua dos Aranhas No. 53, 3rd Floor
P-9000-044 Funchal, Madeira Islands
Telephone: 351 (291) 207-080
Fax: 351 (291) 207-089
E-mail: ums.Madeira@iol.pt
Corporate Services/Tax Planning/Admiralty

Malta

Affiliations: Commonwealth of Nations; European Union; United Nations.
Location: Made up of five Maltese islands in the Mediterranean Sea between Italy to the north and Africa to the south.
Capital and Largest City: Valletta.
Government: Republic.

Legal System: A patchwork overlay of cultures as a result of a multitude of conquests throughout history has shaped the present legal system. However, modern company law and tax laws are based on English models.

Official Language: Maltese and English.

Stability: Stable.

Currency: Maltese lira.

International Time: +1 hr. GMT.

Country Code: 356.

Embassy: Embassy of Malta, 2017 Connecticut Avenue, NW, Washington, DC 20008. Telephone: (202) 462-3611.

Type of Legal Entities: International Holding Company (IHC), a holding company/administration; International Trading Company (ITC), an onshore operating company doing business outside Malta. Bearer shares are permitted.

Unique Characteristics: Flag of convenience. A good expatriate haven. Home of the Malta Stock Exchange. Best place to stay: the Corinthian Palace Hotel across from the Presidential Palace. Historical and unique.

Taxation: Many tax incentives to qualifying companies in areas of activity where business is encouraged. ITC taxed at 4.17 percent; No taxes on an IHC.

Exchange Controls: None.

Treaties with the United States: No income tax treaty. No TIEA. No MLAT.

Useful Web Site: www.investinmalta.com

Business Contacts:

FINAC Limited
Edward J. Zammit, Chief Executive
141, Mriehel Street
Birkirkara, BKR 10, Malta
Telephone: (356) 2149-1127
Fax: (356) 2540-1093
E-mail: ejzammit@onvol.net
Incorporation/Management/Fiduciary/Taxation

Abacus Holdings Limited—PricewaterhouseCoopers
167 Merchants Street
Valletta VLT 03, Malta
Telephone: (356) 2124-7000
Fax: (356) 2124-4768
E-mail: Kevin.valenzia@mt.pwcglobal.com
Incorporation/Management/Trusts/Accounting/Trustees

Azzopardi Investment Management Limited
Il-Piazzeta, 4th Floor, Tower Road
Sliema, Malta, SLM

Telephone: (356) 2131-3100
Fax: (356) 2131-8897
E-mail: pvazzopardi@usa.net
Securities Dealer/Portfolio Management

Cavalier Trust Services Limited
Finance House, First Floor
Princess Elizabeth Street
Ta'Xbiex, MSD 11 Malta
Telephone: (356) 2133-3680
Fax: (356) 2123-2479
E-mail: curmirsm@vol.net.mt
Incorporation/Management/Tax
Planning/Accounting/Legal/Admiralty

Ernst & Young Limited
Valletta Buildings, South Street
Valletta VLT 11, Malta
Telephone: (356) 2124-3258
Fax: (356) 2122-5528
E-mail: cy.malta@mt.eyi.com
Incorporation/Management/Tax Planning/Trusts

Ganado Sammut
35–36 Archbishop Street
Valletta VLT 08, Malta
Telephone: (356) 2124-7109
Fax: (356) 2124-7170
E-mail: gansamm@maltanet.net
Incorporation/Management/Offshore Financial Services

Grant Thorton
Grant Thorton House, Princess Elizabeth Street
Ta'X biex, MSD 11 Malta
Telephone: (356) 2134-4685
Fax: (356) 2133-1161
E-mail: ardemajo@gtmalta.com
Web site: www.gtmalta.com
Incorporation/Management/Support Services

HSBC Bank Malta p.l.c.—International Banking Center
233 Republic Street
Valletta VLT 05, Malta
Telephone: (356) 2124-9801

Fax: (356) 2124-9805
E-mail: hsbc.com.my
Web site: www.hsbc.com.my
Personal and Business Banking/Investment Services/Custody

Medfinco (Nominee) Limited
Rutter Giappone & Associates
166 Old Bakery Street
Valletta VLT 09, Malta
Telephone: (356) 2123-6767
Fax: (356) 2122-5929
E-mail: ruttergiappone@rgalaw.com
Corporate Services/Commercial Law/Trusts/Tax Planning

MSS International Services Ltd.
Regent House, 52 Fifth Floor, Bisazza Street
Sliema SLM 15, Malta
Telephone: (356) 2124-1857
Fax: (356) 2133-6296
E-mail: Info@mss.com.mt
Web site: www.mss.com.mt
Incorporation/Management/Trusts/Taxation

Osiris Corporate Services Limited
Portico Buildings, Marina Street
Pieta' MSD 08, Malta
Telephone: (356) 2123-5888
Fax: (356) 2566-1132
E-mail: osiris@osiris.com.mt
Incorporation/Management/Trusts/Taxation

PKF Fiduciaries International Limited
35 Mannarino Road
B'kara, BKR 08, Malta
Telephone: (356) 2149-3041
Fax: (356) 484-375
E-mail: info@pkfmalta.com
Web site: www.pkfmalta.com
Incorporation/Management/Back Office Operations/Tax Planning

Valletta Offshore Management Nominee Limited International
Corporate Services Limited
The CPS House, The Emporium Building
St. Louis Street

MSIDA MSDO6, Malta
Telephone: (356) 2134-4391
Fax: (356) 2134-4229
E-mail: cps@cps.com.mt
Incorporation/Management/Accounting/Trusts/Tax Planning

Mauritius

Affiliations: Commonwealth of Nations; United Nations.
Location: In the Indian Ocean, an island east of Madagascar.
Capital and Largest City: Port Louis.
Government: Parliamentary Democracy within the British Commonwealth.
Legal System: English common law.
Official Language: English and French. Also speak Creole, Hindi, Urdu, Hakka, Bojpoori.
Stability: Stable.
Currency: Mauritian rupee.
International Time: +4 hrs. GMT.
Country Code: 230.
Embassy: Embassy of the Republic of Mauritius, 4301 Connecticut Avenue, NW, Suite 441, Washington, DC 20008. Telephone: (202) 244-1491.
Type of Legal Entities: There are two types of offshore and international companies: (1) A company with a Category 1 Global Business License, formerly an offshore company, can utilize tax treaties; (2) a company with a Category 2 Global Business License, formerly an international company, is tax-exempt. Bearer shares are permitted.
Unique Characteristic: Flag of convenience.
Taxation: A low-tax haven. GBL1—income tax rate of 15 percent with an 80 percent tax credit on foreign-source income. GBL2—tax-exempt.
Exchange Controls: None.
Treaties with the United States: No income tax treaty. No TIEA. No MLAT.
Useful Web Site: http://ncb.intnet.mu/govt/house.htm
Business Contacts:

A.A.M.I.L. Ltd.
Suite 340–345, Barkly Wharf, Le Caudan Waterfront
PO Box 1070
Port Louis, Mauritius
Telephone: (230) 210-1000
Fax: (230) 210-2000
E-mail: info@aamil.com
Web site: www.aamil.com
Incorporation/Management/Trustee Services/Accounting/Legal

Bank of Baroda—Offshore Banking Unit
4th Floor, Bank of Baroda Building
Sir William Newton Street
Port Louis, Mauritius
Telephone: (230) 212-3900
Fax: (230) 212-5082
E-mail: bobobu@intnet.mu
Offshore Banking

CKLB International Management Ltd.
PO Box 80, Felix House
24 Dr. Joseph Riviere Street
Port Louis, Mauritius
Telephone: (230) 216-8800
Fax: (230) 216-9800
E-mail: cklbmru@cklb.com
Web site: www.cklb.com
Incorporation/Management/Trusts/Trustee Services

Commonwealth Trust Mauritius Limited
314 St. James Court, St. Denis Street
Port Louis, Mauritius
Telephone: (230) 210-8946
Fax: 44 (870) 121-5614
E-mail: services@commonwealthtrust.com
Web site: www.ctl.vg
Incorporation/Management/Trustee Services

Horwath Corporate Finance Limited
3rd Floor, Amod Building, 19 Poudriere Street
Port Louis, Mauritius
Telephone: (230) 211-3350
Fax: (230) 211-1967
E-mail: horwath@intnet.mu
Incorporation/Management/Asset Protection/Accounting

International Management (Mauritius) Ltd.
4th Floor, Les Cascades Building, Edith Cavell Street
Port Louis, Mauritius
Telephone: (230) 212-9800
Fax: (230) 212-9833
E-mail: imm@intnet.mu
Incorporation/Management/Trusts

Jurisconsult Chambers
Cathedral Square
Port Louis, Mauritius
Telephone: (230) 208-5526
Fax: (230) 208-5586
E-mail: jurist@bow.intnet.mu
Incorporation/Legal Advise

Mauritius International Trust Co. Ltd.
4th Floor, Li Wan Po House
Remy Ollier Street
Port Louis, Mauritius
Telephone: (230) 211-3201
Fax: (230) 211-7549
E-mail: mitcomsi@intnet.mu
Incorporation/Management/Tax Planning/Trustee Services

Mutual Trust Management (Mauritius) Limited
608 St. James Court, St. Denis Street
Port Louis, Mauritius
Telephone: (230) 210-9000
Fax: (230) 210-9001
Web site: www.mutrust.com
Incorporation/Management/Trusts/International Taxation

Overseas Company Registration Agents Mauritius Limited
Happy World House, Sir William Newton Street
Port Louis, Mauritius
Telephone: (230) 211-5100
Fax: (230) 211-5400
E-mail: ocra@ocra-mauritius.com
Web site: www.ocra-mauritius.com
Incorporation/Management/Tax Planning/Advice

SBI International (Mauritius) Ltd.
7th Floor, Harbour Front Building
President John Kennedy Street
PO Box 376
Port Louis, Mauritius
Telephone: (230) 212-2054
Fax: (230) 212-2050
E-mail: sbilmaur@intnet.mu
International Banking

Monaco

Affiliation: France.
Location: Western Europe, on the French coast of the Mediterranean Sea next to Italy.
Capital and Largest City: Monte Carlo.
Government: Constitutional monarchy.
Legal System: French civil law system (Napoleonic law).
Official Language: French. Also speak English, Italian, and Monegasque.
Stability: Stable.
Currency: Euro.
International Time: +1 hr. GMT.
Country Code: 33 93.
Embassy: Embassy of France, 4101 Reservoir Road, NW, Washington, DC 20007. Telephone: (202) 944-6000.
Type of Legal Entities: SAM—Societe Anonyme Mongasque, a company limited by shares; also partnerships and trusts.
Unique Characteristics: Foreign companies may be administered from Monaco without registering, providing greater privacy for the owners. A good way to create a solid onshore presence for an offshore corporation. No commercial business permitted within Monaco for such a company, except for management, banking, and financial purposes. Resisting attack from the OECD. A blacklisted country. Although expensive, a good expatriate haven. Many Brits are relocating to this venue. A favorite banking haven of the Italian Mafia.
Taxation: No personal income tax on residents or nonresidents. There are corporate tax breaks and incentives, but the profit tax base is 33⅓ percent.
Treaties with the United States: No income tax treaty. No TIEA. No MLAT.
Useful Web Site: www.monaco.gouv.mc
Business Contacts:

Ansbacher (Monaco) S.A.M.
14 Ave de Grande-Bretagne
MC 98000, Monaco
Telephone: (377) 97-97-21-41
E-mail: ansbacher.mc
Incorporation/Management/Trusts

Berg & Duffy LLP
Gildo Pastor Center
7 rue du Gabian
MC 98000, Monaco
Telephone: (377) 97-97-87-77

Fax: (377) 97-97-87-78
E-mail: jpduffy@bergduffy.com
Web site: www.bergduffy.com
American and International Law Firm

Donald Manasse
4 Boulevard Des Moulins
MC 98000, Monaco
Telephone: (377) 93-50-29-21
Fax: (377) 93-50-82-08
E-mail: dmanasse@monaco.mc
International Law Firm

E.B.C. Trust Corporation
Le Montaigne, 6 Boulevard Des Moulins
MC 98000, Monaco
Telephone: (377) 92-16-59-99
Fax: (377) 93-25-55-60
E-mail: ebctrust@monaco.mc
Incorporation/Management/Asset Protection/Trustees/Fiduciaries

Henley & Partners Inc.
Kirchgasse 22
CH-8001, Zurich, Switzerland
Telephone: 41 (44) 266-22-22
Fax: 41 (44) 266-22-23
Monaco Residency and Citizenship

Moore Stephens Services S.A.M.
L'Estoril, Avenue Princess Grace
MC 98000, Monaco
Telephone: (377) 93-10-41-21
Fax: (377) 93-25-62-70
E-mail: ms@moorestephens-mc.com
Web site: www.moorestephens-mc.com
Incorporation/Management/Trusts/Tax Planning/Accounting

Moores Rowland
2 Avenue de Monte-Carlo, BP 343
MC 98006, Monaco
Telephone: (377) 97-97-00-22
Fax: (377) 93-25-24-12
E-mail: mr@mri.mc
Incorporation/Management/International Tax Planning

Pacor Secoma S.A.
24 Boulevard, Princesse Charlotte
MC 98000, Monaco
Telephone: (377) 97-97-66-77
Fax: (377) 97-97-66-76
E-mail: psg@monaco.mc
Incorporation/Management/Trusts

Palumbo & Palumbo
29 Boulevard Princesse Charlotte
MC 98000 Monaco
Telephone: (377) 92-16-04-97
Fax: (377) 92-16-05-09
Solicitors

The Netherlands

Affiliations: North Atlantic Treaty Organization; European Union; United Nations.

Location: Western Europe, on the coast of the North Sea between Belgium and Germany.

Capital and Largest City: Amsterdam.

Government: Constitutional monarchy.

Legal System: Based on civil and penal law.

Official Language: Dutch and Frisian.

Stability: Stable.

Currency: Euro.

International Time: +1 hr. GMT.

Country Code: 31.

Embassy: Embassy of the Netherlands, 4200 Linnean Avenue, NW, Washington, DC 20008. Telephone: (202) 244-5300.

Type of Legal Entities: NV—Naamloze Vennootschap, a public or private company, bearer or registered shares permitted. BV—Besloten Vennootschap met beperkte Aansprakelijkheid, a private company with only registered shares.

Unique Characteristics: Known for their holding companies. Potential expatriate haven. A member of the Financial Action Task Force (FATF).

Taxation: Complex tax system. Generally high taxes. Many tax ramifications and exemptions.

Exchange Controls: None.

Treaties with the United States: There is an income tax treaty. No TIEA. There is an MLAT. Numerous tax treaties with other countries.

Useful Web Site: www.government.nl

Business Contacts:

ABN AMRO Trust Company (Nederland) BV
"Atrium" Strawinskylaan 3105, 7th Floor
1077 ZX, PO Box 1469
Amsterdam, The Netherlands
Telephone: 31 (20) 406-4444
Fax: 31 (20) 406-4555
E-mail: abnamro.trust.nl@nl.abnamro.com
Web site: www.abnamrotrust.com
Incorporation/Management/Foundations

AMS Trust (Netherlands) BV
Badhuisweg 84
2587 CL's—Gravenhage, The Netherlands
Telephone: 31 (70) 352-2876
Fax: 31 (70) 358-4110
E-mail: amsneth@amslux.lu
Web site: www.amsbvi.com
Offshore Financial Services

Greyfriars Management Services
Tesselschadestraat 4–12
PO Box 58057
Amsterdam 1040 HB, The Netherlands
Telephone: 31 (20) 685-3085
Fax: 31 (20) 683-2733
E-mail: neher@grahamsmith.com
Corporate Services/Financial and Tax Services

Insinger de Beaufort Trust/Equity Trust Co. NV
Officia 1, De Boelelaan7
Amsterdam 1083 HJ, The Netherlands
Telephone: 31 (20) 301-0101
Fax: 31 (20) 642-7675
E-mail: infonltrust@insinger.com
Web site: www.insinger.com
Corporate Services/Accounting/Royalty Licensing/Legal

Mazars Paardekooper & Hoffman
Amsteldijk 194
Amsterdam 1079 LK, The Netherlands
Telephone: 31 (20) 301-0500
Fax: 31 (20) 644-2836
E-mail: Harry.Bosman@mazars.nl

Web site: www.mazars.nl
International Tax Planning

MeesPierson Intertrust BV
Herengracht 548
1017 CG Amsterdam, The Netherlands
Telephone: 31 (20) 527-1678
Fax: 31 (20) 622-7184
Incorporation/Management/Trust Services

MTM/Horwath Tax Holland/Mutual Trust Management Netherlands BV
Westelijke Randweg 37
1118 CR Schiphol
Amsterdam Airport, The Netherlands
Telephone: 31 (20) 653-2336
Fax: 31 (20) 653-0725
E-mail: netherlandsbv@mutrust.nl
Incorporation/Management/Tax Planning

NCS Benelux
Olympic Plaza Building
Frederik Toeskestraat 123
1076 EE, The Netherlands
Telephone: 31 (20) 673-6484
Fax: 31 (20) 675-8869
E-mail: hq@ncs-bv.nl
Incorporation/Management

PricewaterhouseCoopers
Prins Bernhardplein 200
1097 JB Amsterdam, The Netherlands
Telephone: 31 (20) 568-5603
Fax: 31 (20) 568-6888
E-mail: gert.van.veen@nl.pwcglobal.com
International Tax Planning

RijnHove Groep BV, ISO 9001
Baronielaan 139
NL-4818 PD Breda, The Netherlands
Telephone: 31 (76) 522-0252
Fax: 31 (76) 522-0352
E-mail: info@rijnhove.nl
Web site: www.rijnhove.nl
International Tax Planning/Trust/Accounting

Sovereign Trust (Netherlands) BV
Keizersgracht 241
1016 EA Amsterdam, The Netherlands
Telephone: 31 (20) 428-1630
Fax: 31 (20) 620-8046
E-mail: nl@sovereigngroup.com
Web site: www.sovereigngroup.com
Incorporation/Management/Tax Planning/Credit Cards

The Netherlands Antilles

Affiliation: The Netherlands.

Location: The Antilles comprise two groups in the Caribbean near Venezuela. The Leeward Islands of Curaçao and Bonaire, and the Windward Islands of St. Maarten, St. Eustatius, and Saba.

Capital and Largest City: Williamstad (Curaçao).

Government: Autonomous domain of the Kingdom of the Netherlands, a constitutional and parliamentary government.

Legal System: Civil law system paralleling the Netherlands.

Official Language: Dutch. Also speak Papiamento.

Stability: Stable.

Currency: Netherlands Antilles guilder.

International Time: –4 hrs. GMT.

Country Code: 599.

Embassy: Embassy of the Netherlands, 4200 Linnean Avenue, NW, Washington, DC 20008. Telephone: (202) 244-5300.

Type of Legal Entities: NV—Naamloze Vennootschap is the preferred offshore vehicle, a public or private company with bearer shares or registered shares.

Unique Characteristics: Popular for holding companies, investment companies, finance companies, mutual funds, and trading companies. Offshore bank licenses, and captive and reinsurance licensing offered.

Taxation: Holding companies pay a low 2.4 to 3 percent tax on income. Companies receiving royalties, dividends, and capital gains pay no tax on their incomes and profits.

Exchange Controls: None.

Treaties with the United States: There is an income tax treaty. No TIEA. There is MLAT.

Useful Web Site: www.gov.an

Business Contacts:

ABN AMRO Bank NV
Kaya Flamboyan1

Curaçao, Netherlands Antilles
Telephone: 599 (9) 763-8342
Fax: 599 (9) 736-7268
Incorporation/Management/Banking

ABN AMRO Trust Company (Curaçao) N.V.
Pietermaai 15
PO Box 4905
Willemstad, Curaçao, Netherlands Antilles
Telephone: 599 (9) 433-5000
Fax: 599 (9) 461-3395
E-mail: aatrust@cura.net
Web site: www.abnamrotrust.com
Incorporation/Management/Legal

AMACO (Curaçao) NV
Kaya W/F.G. (Jombi) Mensing 36
PO Box 3141
Willemstad, Curaçao, Netherlands Antilles
Telephone: 599 (9) 461-1299
Fax: 599 (9) 461-5392
E-mail: info@amaco.group.com
Incorporation/Management/Legal/Banking

CAK Trustkantoor NV
Scharlooweg #61
Willemstad, Curaçao, Netherlands Antilles
Telephone: 599 (9) 736-7181
Fax: 599 (9) 736-7161
E-mail: cakgroup@attglobal.net
Asset Management/International Cash Flow

Citgo Curaçao, Corporate and Trust Services
De Ruyterkade 62
International Fund Services, Kaya Flamboyan 9
PO Box 812
Curaçao, Netherlands Antilles
Telephone: 599 (9) 732-2555
Fax: 599 (9) 732-2500
E-mail: hvanneutegem@citgo.com
Web site: www.citgo.com
Incorporation/Management/Fiduciary/Accounting

Intertrust (Antilles) NV
Landhuis Joonchi, Kaya Richard J. Beaujon z/n
PO Box 837
Curaçao, Netherlands Antilles
Telephone: 599 (9) 736-6277
Fax: 599 (9) 736-6161
E-mail: intertrust-curacao@compuserve.com
Incorporation/Management/International Legal and Taxation

MeesPierson Intertrust (Curaçao) NV
Berg Arrarat 1
PO Box 3889
Willemstad, Curaçao, Netherlands Antilles
Telephone: 599 (9) 463-9300
Fax: 599 (9) 463-4129
Private Banking and Trust Services

PricewaterhouseCoopers
Julianaplein 38
PO Box 360
Curaçao, Netherlands Antilles
Telephone: 599 (9) 430-000
Fax: 599 (9) 461-1118
E-mail: hans.j.olattel@an.pwcglobal.com
Business, Tax and Assurance Advise

RBTT Bank Antilles NV
Kaya Flamboyan1
Curaçao, Netherlands Antilles
Telephone: 599 (9) 763-8000
Fax: 599 (9) 737-1089
Offshore Banking Services

Van Der Plank, Civil-Law Notary Office
Schottegatweg Oost 191
Curaçao, Netherlands Antilles
Telephone: 599 (9) 461-6833
Fax: 599 (9) 461-5939
E-mail: notaris@cura.net
Incorporation/Legal Advice

Panama

Affiliation: United Nations.

Location: Central America; Costa Rica to the north, Colombia to the south, between the North Pacific Ocean and the Caribbean Sea.

Capital and Largest City: Panama City.

Government: Constitutional Democracy.

Legal System: Civil law system.

Official Language: Spanish. English is also common, especially in business.

Stability: Stable.

Currency: Balboa and U.S. dollar.

International Time: –5 hrs. GMT.

Country Code: 507.

Embassy: Embassy of the Republic of Panama, 2862 McGill Terrace, NW, Washington, DC 20008. Telephone: (202) 483-1407.

Type of Legal Entities: SA—Societe Anonyms with limited liability, a corporation; Private Foundation; civil law trusts. Bearer shares are permitted. Excellent flag of convenience.

Unique Characteristics: The "Hong Kong of Latin America." A T-7 tax haven.

Taxation: No tax on foreign-source income.

Exchange Controls: None.

Treaties with the United States: No income tax treaty. No TIEA. There is an MLAT.

Useful Web Site: www.presidencia.gob.pa

Business Contacts:

Barber Financial Advisors
355 Burrard Street, Suite 1000
Vancouver, BC V6C 2G8 Canada
Telephone: (604) 608-6177
Fax: (604) 608-2984
E-mail: Info@BarberFinancialAdvisors.com
Web site: www.BarberFinancialAdvisors.com
Incorporations/Management/Private Foundations/Personal and Corporate Bank Accounts/Offshore E-Commerce/Ready-Made Companies

American Finance & Development Group S.A.
Calle 61, #23A
PO Box 871047
Panama 7, Republic of Panama
Telephone: (507) 223-3172
Fax: (507) 223-3899
Incorporation/Management/Trusts/Immigration/Fiduciary

Arias & Arias Consultores
Via Cincuentenario, Edificio Coco Bay, Suite 13
PO Box 55-0835
Panama 7, Republic of Panama
Telephone: (507) 226-5833
Fax: (507) 226-8788
Incorporation/Trusts/Foundations/Tax Planning

Benedetti & Benedetti
Comosa Building, 21st Floor
Samuel Lewis and Manuel M. Ycaza Avenue
PO Box 850120
Panama 5, Republic of Panama
Telephone: (507) 263-4444
Fax: (507) 264-5962
Incorporation/Management/Ship Registration/Trusts

Fabrega, Varsallo, Molino & Molino
Omega Building
Samuel Lewis Avenue and 53rd Street
PO Box 4493
Panama 5, Republic of Panama
Telephone: (507) 263-5333
Fax: (507) 263-6983
Incorporation/Management/Trusts/Foundation/Tax and Estate Planning

Henley & Partners
Galindo, Arias and Lopez
Scotia Plaza, 18 Avenue Federico Boyd and 51st Street
Suite 9, 10, 11
PO Box 8629
Panama 5, Republic of Panama
Telephone: (507) 263-5633
Fax: (507) 263-5335
E-mail: gala@gala.com.pa
Web site: www.henleyglobal.com/panama
Immigration/Residency Specialists/Multi-jurisdictions

International Management and Trust Corporation (Intertrust)
10 Elvira Mendez Street, Penthouse
PO Box 0816-03012
Panama 1, Republic of Panama

Telephone: (507) 263-6300
Fax: (507) 263-6392
Incorporation/Management/Foundations/Ship Registrations

Morgan & Morgan
Swiss Tower, 16th Floor, 53E Street, Urb. Marbella
PO Box 0832-00232, World Trade Center
Panama, Republic of Panama
Telephone: (507) 265-7777
Fax: (507) 265-7700
Full Service Law Firm

Pardini & Associates
Plaza 2000 Tower, 10th Floor
50th Street
PO Box 9654
Panama 5, Republic of Panama
Telephone: (507) 223-7222
Fax: (507) 264-4730
Offshore Incorporations/Investment Immigration

Quijano & Associates, Attorneys-at-Law
Salduba Building, 3rd Floor
PO Box 0816-02884
Panama, Republic of Panama
Telephone: (507) 269-2641 or (507) 269-2743
Fax: (507) 269-2591 or (507) 263-8079
E-mail: quijano@quijano.com
Web site: www.quijano.com
Full Service Law Firm/Immigration/Residency

Rainelda Mata-Kelly, Attorney at Law
PO Box 9012
No. 414, 4th Floor, Balboa Plaza, Balboa Avenue
Panama 6, Republic of Panama
Telephone: (507) 263-4305
Fax: (507) 264-2868
E-mail: rmk@mata-kelly.com
Web site: www.mata-kelly.com
Immigration/Residency

Derek Sambrook
Trust Services Ltd.

Balboa Plaza, Suite 522
Avenida Balboa, Panama, Republic of Panama
Mailing address: Apartado 0832-1630, World Trade Center
Panama, Republic of Panama
Telephone: (507) 269-2438
Fax: (507) 269-4922
E-mail: Sambrook@trustserv.com
Web site: www.trustserv.com
Offshore Immigration Trusts/Trust and Estate Planning

Stern & Co. SA
PO Box 871075
Panama 7, Republic of Panama
Telephone: (507) 223-3134
Fax: (507) 223-3899
Comprehensive Business Law Firm

Saint Kitts and Nevis

Affiliations: Commonwealth of Nations; United Nations.
Location: West of Antigua in the Lesser Antilles of the Caribbean Sea.
Capital and Largest City: Basseterre (Capital—Saint Kitts); Charlestown (Largest—Nevis).
Government: Constitutional monarchy.
Legal System: English common law.
Official Language: English.
Stability: Stable.
Currency: East Caribbean dollar.
International Time: –4 hrs. GMT.
Country Code: 809.
Embassy: Embassy of Saint Kitts and Nevis, 3216 New Mexico Avenue, NW, Washington, DC 20016. Telephone: (202) 686-2636.
Type of Legal Entities: International Business Company (IBC). Bearer shares are permitted. Total anonymity. No minimum capitalization required.
Unique Characteristics: A T-7 tax haven. Excellent for offshore and e-commerce business. Strict bank secrecy. Excellent asset protection trusts like Belize and the Cook Islands. One of the two best Economic Citizenship Programs available. Dominica has the other program.
Taxation: A no-tax haven.
Treaties with the United States: No income tax treaty. No TIEA. There is an MLAT.
Useful Web Site: www.embassy.gov.kn

Business Contact:

Barber Financial Advisors
355 Burrard Street, Suite 1000
Vancouver, BC V6C 2G8 Canada
Telephone: (604) 608-6177
Fax: (604) 608-2984
E-mail: Info@BarberFinancialAdvisors.com
Web site: www.BarberFinancialAdvisors.com
Incorporation/Management/Personal and Corporate Bank Accounts/Credit & Debit Cards/Asset Protection Trusts/Offshore E-Commerce/Ready-Made Companies

Saint Vincent and the Grenadines

Affiliations: Commonwealth of Nations; United Nations.
Location: Lies 100 miles west of Barbados in the Caribbean.
Capital and Largest City: Kingstown.
Government: Parliamentary Democracy.
Legal System: English common law.
Official Language: English, French patois.
Stability: Stable.
Currency: East Caribbean dollar.
International Time: –4 hrs. GMT.
Country Code: 809.
Embassy: Embassy of Saint Vincent and the Grenadines, 3216 New Mexico Avenue, NW, Washington, DC, 20016. Telephone: (202) 364-6730.
Type of Legal Entities: International Business Company (IBC); Limited Duration Company (LDC); foreign company; International Insurance Company.
Unique Characteristics: Bank secrecy and confidentiality are protected by stiff civil and/or criminal penalties under the Confidentiality Relationship Preservation (International Finance) Act of 1996.
Taxation: A no-tax haven.
Exchange Controls: None.
Treaties in the United States: No income tax treaty. No TIEA. There is an MLAT.
Useful Web Site: www.svtourism.com
Business Contacts:

Argon Limited
97 Granby Street, 1st Floor
PO Box 1817
Kingstown, St. Vincent and the Grenadines

Telephone: (784) 485-6585
Fax: (784) 485-6586
E-mail: argon@caribsurf.com
Incorporation/Management/Trust Services

Caribbean Financial and Accounting Services Limited
18 Long Lane Upper, Middle Street
PO Box 561
Kingstown, St. Vincent and the Grenadines
Telephone: (784) 456-2669
Fax: (784) 456-1576
E-mail: kpmgsvg@caribsurf.com
Offshore and Accounting Services

Corporate Agents (SVG) Limited
Medical Arts Building, Paul's Avenue
PO Box 1818
Kingstown, St. Vincent and the Grenadines
Telephone: (784) 457-1902
Fax: (784) 457-1906
E-mail: corpagnt@caribsurf.com
Incorporation/Management

Cosmos Trust Limited
78 Halifax Street, PO Box 726
Kingstown, St. Vincent and the Grenadines
Telephone: (784) 457-1258
Fax: (784) 457-2653
E-mail: akin@caribsurf.com
Trust Services

Fidelity International Consultants Ltd.
Stewart Building, Long Wall
PO Box 1758
Kingstown, St. Vincent and the Grenadines
Telephone: (784) 456-1912
Fax: (784) 457-2469
E-mail: gmstewart@caribsurf.com
Incorporation/Management/Trusts/Fiduciary

The Grenadines Trust and Management Co. Ltd.
Murray's Road
PO Box 1693
Kingstown, St. Vincent and the Grenadines
Telephone: (784) 456-2615

Fax: (784) 457-2867
E-mail: gtmc@caribsurf.com
Incorporation/Management/Trust Services

Ramerson Trust Corporation
Granby Street, the Methodist Building
PO Box 597
Kingstown, St. Vincent and the Grenadines
Telephone: (784) 457-2372
Fax: (784) 457-2307
Trust Services

St. Vincent Trust Service Ltd., Caribbean Office
Trust House, 112 Bonadie Street
PO Box 613
Kingstown, St. Vincent and the Grenadines
Telephone: (784) 457-1145
Fax: (784) 457-1961
E-mail: trust house@saint-vencent-trust.com
Incorporation/Management/Trusts/Tax Planning

Sovereign Bank Corporation Ltd.
The Financial Services Center
PO Box 1824
Kingstown, St. Vincent and the Grenadines
Telephone: (784) 456-2458
Fax: (784) 456-1605
E-mail: sovereignfund@caribsurf.com
Offshore Banking Services/Offshore Funds

TBS Management & Trust Co. Ltd.
Cnr. Granby & Sharpe Streets, Suite K643
Kingstown, St. Vincent and the Grenadines
Telephone: (784) 456-2119
Fax: (784) 457-2346
E-mail: tbs@caribsurf.com
Incorporation/Management/Trust Services

Universal Trust Co. (U.T.C.)
White Chapel, PO Box 1281
Kingstown, St. Vincent and the Grenadines
Telephone: (784) 457-1828
Fax: (784) 456-2485
E-mail: kayrab@caribsurf.com
Trust Services

Seychelles

Affiliations: Commonwealth of Nations; United Nations.
Location: Indian Ocean northwest of Madagascar.
Capital and Largest City: Victori.
Government: Socialist Multiparty Republic; Self-governing and independent.
Legal System: Civil law system and common law.
Official Language: Seselwa, Creole, English, and French.
Stability: Stable.
Currency: Seychelles rupee.
International Time: +4 hrs. GMT.
Country Code: 248.
Embassy: Permanent Mission of Seychelles to the United Nations, 800 Second Avenue, Suite 400C, New York, NY 10017. Telephone: (212) 972-1785.
Type of Legal Entities: International Business Companies (IBC); common law trusts; insurance companies; and mutual funds.
Unique Characteristic: Beautiful beaches!
Taxation: IBCs are not subject to taxes.
Exchange Controls: None.
Treaties in the United States: No income tax treaty. No TIEA. No MLAT.
Useful Web Site: www.state.gov/r/pa/ei/bgn/6268.htm
Business Contacts:

A.C.T. Offshore (Pty) Ltd.
The Company Shop
1st Floor, Oliaji Trade Center
PO Box 1377
Victoria, Seychelles
Telephone: (248) 224-899
Fax: (248) 324-777
E-mail: acts@seychelles.net
Web site: www.offshorecompanies.net
Incorporation/Accounting/Legal

FIFCO (Offshore) Services Ltd.
Suite 103, Premier Building
PO Box 308
Victoria, Mahe, Seychelles
Telephone: (248) 323-332
Fax: (248) 324-009
E-mail: fifco@seychelles.net
Incorporation/Management

International Business Registration Agents (Pty) Ltd.
Revolution Avenue
PO Box 18
Victoria, Mahe, Seychelles
Telephone: (248) 612-612
Fax: (248) 612-300
E-mail: ajshah@seychelles.net
Offshore Financial Services

International Corporate Agents Limited
102, AartiChambers, Mont Fleuri
PO Box 870
Victoria, Mahe, Seychelles
Telephone: (248) 225-755
Fax: (248) 225-991
Incorporation/Management/Trustees

Intershore Consult
306 Victoria House
PO Box 673
Victoria, Mahe, Seychelles
Telephone: (248) 225-562
Fax: (248) 225-626
E-mail: interlaw@seychelles.net
Incorporation/Management/Investment Consultants

Switzerland

Affiliation: United Nations.
Location: Western Europe. Bordered by France, Germany, Austria, Liechtenstein and Italy.
Capital and Largest City: Zurich.
Government: Federal Republic.
Legal System: Civil law system.
Official Language: German, French, Italian, Romansch, and English.
Stability: Stable.
Currency: Swiss franc.
International Time: +1 hr. GMT.
Country Code: 41.
Embassy: Embassy of Switzerland, 2900 Cathedral Avenue, NW, Washington, DC 20008. Telephone: (202) 745-7900.

Type of Legal Entities: AG; SA; GmbH; SARL. The AG or Aktiegesellschaft is the most common entity organized under the Laws of Obligation. It is a stock corporation that can issue either bearer or registered shares.

Unique Characteristics: A T-7 country. Famous for banking and bank secrecy. Specialists in portfolio management. Known for investment funds and insurance products. Potential expatriate haven. Refer to Campione, backdoor to Switzerland as a viable alternative to incorporating or living in Switzerland. Home to several securities and commodities exchanges. Member of the Financial Action Task Force (FATF). Getting outside pressures from the EU and OECD. Note: Liechtenstein is a good alternative to Switzerland as a banking center and asset haven.

Taxation: A low-tax haven with a complicated tax structure. Expect to pay around 10 percent on after-tax profit in federal taxes along with cantonal taxes between 15 and 32 percent. An auxiliary or domiciliary company may pay no tax or receive a much lower rate than usual.

Exchange Controls: None.

Treaties with the United States: There is an income tax treaty. No TIEA. No MLAT.

Useful Web Site: www.gov.ch

Business Contacts:

Barber Financial Advisors
355 Burrard Street, Suite 1000
Vancouver, BC V6C 2G8 Canada
Telephone: (604) 608-6177
Fax: (604) 608-2984
E-mail: Info@BarberFinancialAdvisors.com
Web site: www.BarberFinancialAdvisors.com
Personal and Corporate Swiss Bank Accounts/Debit and Credit Cards

ABN AMRO Trust Company (Suisse) S.A.
Rue du Rhone 80
PO Box 3768
CH-1204 Geneva, Switzerland
Telephone: 41 (22) 817-1950
Fax: 41 (22) 817-1955
Incorporation/Management/Swiss, Liechtenstein, and Offshore

Bank Julius Baer
Bahnhofstrasse 36
CH-8010 Zurich, Switzerland
Telephone: 41 (1) 228-5111
Fax: 41 (1) 211-2560
Web site: www.juliusbaer.com
Private Banking/Portfolio Management

Bank Sarasin & Co.
Elisabethenstrasse 62
CH-4002 Basel, Switzerland
Telephone: 41 (61) 277-7777
Fax: 41 (61) 277-7730
Asset Management/Securities Brokerage/Commercial Banking

CAI Conseil (Suisse) SA
19 Rue du Rhone
PO Box 3624
CH-1204 Geneva 11, Switzerland
Telephone: 41 (22) 700-2925
Fax: 41 (22) 700-2933
International Financial Planning

Coutts & Co (Trustees) S.A.
13 Quai de L'ille
PO Box 5511
CH-1211 Geneva 11, Switzerland
Telephone: 41 (22) 319-0101
Fax: 41 (22) 319-0102
Private Banking/Incorporation/Management

EFG Private Bank SA
Bahnhofstrasse 16
PO Box 2255
CH-8022 Zurich, Switzerland
Telephone: 41 (1) 226-1717
Fax: 41 (1) 226-1727
Private Banking

EPS Value Plus AG
Bodmeistr. 9
PO Box 2255
CH-8027 Zurich, Switzerland
Telephone: 41 (43) 344-3800
Fax: 41 (43) 344-3801
Offshore Investments/Life Insurance/Trust Services

JML Portfolio Management Ltd.
Germaniastrasse 55

CH-006 Zurich, Switzerland
Telephone: 41 (58) 800-5440
Fax: 41 (58) 800-5441
Web site: www.jml.com
Swiss Investments and Asset Protection Vehicles for Americans and Others

Marc-Andre Sola
Managing Partner
NMG International Ltd.
Zurich, Switzerland
Telephone: 41 (1) 266-2141
Fax: 41 (1) 266-2149
E-mail: marcsola@nmg-ifs.com
Web site: www.nmg-ifs.com
Swiss Banking and Insurance Specialist

Meespierson Intertrust (Schweiz) AG
Alpenstrasse 15
PO Box 4620
CH-6304 Zug, Switzerland
Telephone: (41) 726-8200
Fax: (41) 726-8250
Company Management/Trust Services/Swiss and Liechtenstein

Rathbone Trust Company SA
1 Place de Saint-Gervais
PO Box 2049
CH-1211 Geneva 1, Switzerland
Telephone: 41 (22) 909-8900
Fax: 41 (22) 909-8939
Offshore Incorporations/Anglo-Saxon Trusts and Foundations

Rickenbach & Partner, Attorneys at Law
Schlossbergstrasse 22
CH-8702 Zollikon-Zurich, Switzerland
Telephone: 41 (1) 391-4477
Fax: 41 (1) 391-7735
Swiss and Liechtenstein Business and Commercial Law

Shahab Malek-Abhari
Wealth Manager
Anker Bank Lausanne
Private Banking

Avenue de la Gare, 50
CH-1001 Lausanne, Switzerland
Telephone: 41 (0) 21-321-07-07
Fax: 41 (0) 21-321-07-98
Direct: 41 (0) 21-321-07-33
E-mail: shahabeddin.malek-abhari@ankerbank.ch
Investment Management. Minimum to establish a portfolio is U.S. $200,000. A personal visit is required.

Dr. Erich Stoeger
Chairman
EurAxxess
Switzerland
Toll-free: (800) 331-0996
E-mail: infor@euraxxess.com
Web site: www.euraxxess.com
A Global Financial Services Company

Von Sury Trust Limited
Spalentorweg 20
PO Box 109
CH-4009 Basle, Switzerland
Telephone: 41 (61) 269-2020
Fax: 41 (61) 269-2000
Swiss and Offshore Incorporations/Management/Asset Management

Turks and Caicos

Affiliation: Overseas Territory of the United Kingdom.
Location: In the Caribbean, south of the Bahamas.
Capital and Largest City: Cockburn Town.
Government: Self-governing British Crown Colony.
Legal System: English common law.
Official Language: English.
Stability: Stable.
Currency: U.S. dollar.
International Time: –5 hrs. GMT.
Country Code: 809.
Embassy: British Embassy, 3100 Massachusetts Avenue, NW, Washington, DC 20008. Telephone: (202) 588-7800.
Type of Legal Entities: Exempt Company. Bearer shares are permitted. Limited partnerships; offshore bank licensing; mutual funds; insurance

company licensing. Attractive trust laws, including asset protection trusts (APTs).

Unique Characteristics: Possible expatriate haven under their Permanent Residency Program or Business Residency.

Taxation: A no-tax haven. The government will guarantee not to impose taxes for 20 years.

Exchange Controls: None.

Treaties with the United States: No income tax treaty. No TIEA. There is an MLAT.

Useful Web Site: www.turksandcaicos.tc/government

Business Contacts:

Barclays Bank PLC (International Banking Center)
PO Box 236, Butterfield Square
Providenciales, Turks & Caicos Islands, West Indies
Telephone: (649) 941-3606
Fax: (649) 941-3430
E-mail: Barclays@tciway.tc
International Banking

The Chartered Trust Company
PO Box 125, Town Center Building
Providenciales, Turks & Caicos Islands, West Indies
Telephone: (649) 946-4881
Fax: (649) 946-4041
Web site: www.chartered-tci.com@tciway.tc
Incorporation/Management/Immigration

Claymore Corporate Services Ltd.
PO Box 564, Market Place
Providenciales, Turks & Caicos Islands, West Indies
Telephone: (649) 941-3216
Fax: (649) 946-4939
Incorporation/Management/Real Estate/Intellectual Property

The Claymore Group
PO Box 64, Building C, Market Place
Providenciales, Turks & Caicos Islands, West Indies
Telephone: (649) 946-4109
Fax: (649) 946-4939
Web site: www.claymore.tc
Incorporation/Asset and Investment Management

Coriats (Caribbean) Limited
PO Box 171, Bristol House, The Center

Providenciales, Turks & Caicos Islands, West Indies
Telephone: (649) 946-4800
Fax: (649) 946-4850
E-mail: trust@coriats.com
Web site: www.coriats.com
Offshore Financial Services/Trust Services

International Company Services (TCI) Limited
PO Box 107 Oceanic House, Duke Street
Providenciales, Turks & Caicos Islands, West Indies
Telephone: (649) 946-2828
Fax: (649) 946-2825
E-mail: icsltci@hotmail.com
Incorporation/Management/Trusts

Kermount Corporate Services Limited
PO Box 191, 1 Runica House, Leeward Highway
Providenciales, Turks & Caicos Islands, West Indies
Telephone: (649) 946-4181
Fax: (649) 946-4040
E-mail: kermount@tciway.tc
Incorporation/Management

Logberg Corporate Services Limited/Twa, Cochrane, Skatfeld
PO Box 209, Chancery Court
Providenciales, Turks & Caicos Islands, West Indies
Telephone: (649) 946-4261
Fax: (649) 946-4410
E-mail: twa@tciway.tc
Incorporation/Management/Trusts

Sovereign Trust (TCI) Limited
PO Box 170, Churchill Building, Front Street
Providenciales, Turks & Caicos Islands, West Indies
Telephone: (649) 946-2050
Fax: (649) 946-1593
E-mail: tci@sovereigngroup.com
Incorporate/Management/Estate/Tax Planning/Taxation

Vanuatu

Affiliations: Commonwealth of Nations; United Nations.
Location: This archipelago of 83 islands stretches 1,400 miles northeast of Australia.

Capital and Largest City: Port Vila.
Government: Independent Republic.
Legal System: English common law.
Official Language: Bislama. Also speak English and French.
Stability: Stable.
Currency: Vatu.
International Time: +11 hrs. GMT.
Country Code: 678.
Embassy: No embassy in the United States.
Type of Legal Entities: International Company, an exempt company; exempt insurance companies; and exempt offshore international bank licensing.
Unique Characteristics: The Government Act protects secrecy. No extradition treaties or diplomatic relations with the United States. Once blacklisted but not any longer. A popular tax haven with Aussies.
Taxation: A no-tax haven.
Exchange Controls: None.
Treaties with the United States: No income tax treaty. No TIEA. No MLAT.
Useful Web Site: www.vanuatugovernment.gov.vu
Business Contacts:

Barber Financial Advisors
355 Burrard Street, Suite 1000
Vancouver, BC V6C 2G8, Canada
Telephone: (604) 608-6177
Fax: (604) 608-2984
E-mail: info@BarberFinancialAdvisors.com;
BarberFinancial@hotmail.com
Web site: www.BarberFinancialAdvisors.com
Private Bank Accounts

ANZ Bank (Vanuatu) Limited
Lini Highway, PMB 003
Port Vila, Vanuatu
Telephone: (678) 22536
Fax: (678) 22814
E-mail: tilbroom2@anz.com
Web site: www.anz.com/vanuatu
International Banking/Internet Banking

European Trust Company Limited—Shareinvest
International Building, PO Box 257
Port Vila, Vanuatu
Telephone: (678) 23410
Fax: (678) 23405

E-mail: security@vanuatu.com.vu
International Securities Dealer

Fidelty Pacific Life Insurance Company Limited
International Building, PO Box 301
Port Vila, Vanuatu
Telephone: (678) 24170
Fax: (678) 25520
E-mail: fidelity@vila.net
Single Premium Life Insurance

Geoffrey Geev & Partners, Barristers & Solicitors
2nd floor, Raffea House, Kumul Highway
PO Box 782
Port Vila, Vanuatu
Telephone: (678) 22067
Fax: (678) 23710
E-mail: geoffgee@vanuatu.com.vu
Offshore Business and Financial Law Firm

George Vasaris & Co.
2nd Floor, Law House, Kumul Highway
PO Box 166
Port Vila, Vanuatu
Telephone: (678) 22457
Fax: (678) 22973
E-mail: lawhouse@vanuatu.com.vu
Offshore Financial and Legal Services

Global Management Services
Moore Stephens House, Lini Highway
PO Box 211
Port Vila, Vanuatu
Telephone: (678) 22159
Fax: (678) 22276
Offshore Financial Services

Guardian Trustees Limited
Windsor House, Kumul Highway
PO Box 1100
Port Vila, Vanuatu
Telephone: (678) 22366
Fax: (678) 23836

E-mail: guardian@guardiantrustees.com
Web site: www.guardiantrustees.com
Incorporation/Management/Trusts/Asset Protection

Hudson & Sugden
1st Floor, Lo Lam House, Lini Highway
PO Box 7
Port Vila, Vanuatu
Telephone: (678) 22166
Fax: (678) 24260
E-mail: hudco@vanuatu.com.vu
Web site: www.hudson.ecn.net.au
Incorporation/Management/Trusts/Legal

Moore Stephens
1st Floor, Moore Stephens House, Kumul Highway
PO Box 95
Port Vila, Vanuatu
Telephone: (678) 22159
Fax: (678) 22276
E-mail: msvila@vanuatu.com.vu
Web site: www.msvanuatu.com.vu
International Tax Planning/Business Services

National Bank of Vanuatu
PO Box 249
Port Vila, Vanuatu
Telephone: (678) 22201
Fax: (678) 22761
Commercial Bank
Pacific International Trust Company Limited
International Building, PO Box 45
Port Vila, Vanuatu
Telephone: (678) 23410
Fax: (678) 23405
E-mail: security@vila.net
Incorporation/Management/Trust Services/Tax Advice

Vanuatu International Trust Company Limited (VITCO)
BDO House, PO Box 240
Kumul Highway
Port Vila, Vanuatu
Telephone: (678) 22280
Fax: (678) 22317

E-mail: bdo@vanuatu.com.vu
Web site: www.bdo.com.vu
Incorporation/Trustee Services/Tax Planning/Investment Advise

Western Samoa

Affiliation: United Nations.
Location: A group of Polynesian islands in the South Pacific northeast of Australia.
Capital and Largest City: Apia.
Government: Parliamentary Government.
Legal System: Based on English common law and local customs.
Official Language: Samoan. A fair amount of English is also spoken.
Stability: Stable.
Currency: Tala.
International Time: –11 hrs. GMT.
Country Code: 685.
Type of Legal Entities: International Companies; offshore bank licensing; insurance companies; and international trusts.
Unique Characteristics: Strict bank secrecy guaranteed by law and confidentiality of company information.
Taxation: No taxes imposed on the legal entities listed.
Exchange Controls: None.
Treaties with the United States: No income tax treaty. No TIEA. No MLAT.
Useful Web Site: www.interwebinc.com/samoa
Business Contacts:

Asiaciti Trust Samoa Limited
Level 2, Lotemau Center
Vaea Street
Apia, Western Samoa
Telephone: (685) 24550
Fax: (685) 21837
E-mail: asiaciti@samoa.ws
Incorporation/Management/Trusts

Intetrust Limited
Level 1, Central Bank of Samoa Building
Beach Road, PO Box 2033
Apia, Western Samoa
Telephone: (685) 20776
Fax: (685) 20777
Incorporation/Management/Trustee Services

PART FOUR

Resources—The Big Picture

Our country is wherever we are well off.

—*John Milton, 1666*

WHAT NEXT?

Armed with the knowledge you have gained, by now you are likely formulating a concrete plan or at least have an idea or two of some potential plans for going offshore. But, what about that *further* step? If you are even toying with the idea of an alternative place to live, whether part-time, temporarily, or permanently, you will enjoy this section. You can find detailed information on 95 country options for a new, a second, or a retirement home.

Some of these countries are better suited than others for expatriating, but a quick review of them will give you a snapshot of whether they might be a match for you. A web site address has been included on each country if you want to explore the possibilities.

Following the 95 country profiles, you will find an invaluable resource guide to assist you in all things offshore. This section contains outstanding hands-on sources for solid information; reliable services; and select financial, investment, and legal contacts. These sources are vital for considering any offshore plans, whether you wish to bank, invest, or do business offshore, travel abroad, or consider expatriating.

I have included some excellent reading references, web sites, and organizations that will offer further insight and enjoyment on topics such as liberty, freedom, your rights and privacy, current events, modern times, our political and cultural climate, and the powers that be.

I wish you every success in your quest!

OFFSHORE CITIZENSHIP AND RETIREMENT OPPORTUNITIES

Presently, there are two Economic Citizenship Programs worth discussing. Both programs are excellent, providing much needed revenue for these countries, and in turn, much desired alternative citizenship opportunities for expatriates who have the money to spend. This is the quickest way to secure foreign citizenship without the usual lengthy residency periods required before being able to apply for citizenship in a foreign country. Here is a closer view of these two Caribbean island nations.

Dominica

This lush tropical paradise is located between two French islands, Guadeloupe and Martinique, in the Leeward Islands of the Eastern Caribbean, and has been an independent nation since 1978. English is the official language as it was formerly a part of the British empire. It is a parliamentary democracy and was explored by Christopher Columbus. The population is approximately 70,000 people, a mix of Black, mixed Black and European, European, Syrian, and Carib Amerindian. They have a high literacy rate of 94 percent and very little crime. The Eastern Caribbean dollar is circulated and is a strong currency used by many Caribbean countries.

Dominica offers full citizenship for life, complete with their national passport, which provides for visa-free travel to 90 countries, without requiring the applicant to make a government-approved investment. The nonrefundable cash contribution to the government is the motivation to grant citizenship.

There are two possibilities for obtaining citizenship: the Family Option and the Single Option. The first plan allows you and your family to apply together for the single payment of U.S. $100,000. This includes your children under 18 years of age. Children over this age, but under 25 years would require an additional U.S. $25,000 each. A single applicant would pay U.S. $75,000. In addition to these required fees, there are professional fees and nonrefundable due diligence fees for each applicant. The processing time is short, only two to three weeks.

Applicants will be required to visit Dominica to take the Oath of Citizenship and to attend a personal interview. This is a good jurisdiction for securing foreign citizenship before relinquishing your current citizenship, as dual citizenship is permitted and will not be reported to your government. This is of particular importance for U.S. citizens, and allows you the window of time you may need to finalize any unfinished business before renouncing your present citizenship and deciding the right moment to act.

Reputable local lawyers are officially appointed by the government to handle applicants for the Economic Citizenship Program. The process is administered professionally and smoothly, and although the government has the final word on accepting you as a new citizen, your chances are excellent for approval.

As a new citizen, you will also benefit from a tax-free status, including no foreign income tax and no capital gains tax or inheritance tax. Dominica is also a tax haven.

Applicant document requirements, typical of these programs, include completion of an application, provision of personal and bank references, evidence of educational background, a copy of current travel documents, passport photos, a medical certificate of good health (including HIV negative), a police certificate showing a clean record, your birth certificate, and, if applicable, marriage certificate and/or divorce decree.

Saint Kitts and Nevis

"The Sisters of the Caribbean" are peaceful, tranquil islands, each adorned with a dormant but scenic volcano and surrounded by sprawling green sugar cane and banana plantations that meet the azure sea. Nevis is famous for its natural spas and the "rich and famous" are known to come here for relaxation and the potential healing properties of these springs. The islands are notably light on the typical tourist facilities although they have been "discovered" in the past decade, and emphasis is on the natural quality of the islands.

Saint Kitts and Nevis are located in the Leeward Islands south of Anguilla, northwest of Montserrat, and southwest of Antigua and Barbuda. This constitutional monarchy was explored by Christopher Columbus and was formerly a part of the United Kingdom, having gained their independence in 1983. They have a literacy rate of 97 percent and little crime. The 40,000 islanders are predominately black, with some British, Portuguese, and Lebanese. The official language is English and the Eastern Caribbean dollar is their currency.

The application for citizenship here covers one family, or a husband, wife, and two unmarried dependent children. The fee is U.S. $35,000 for the applicant and an additional U.S. $15,000 per family member. Additional due diligence and application fees are required, and the cost varies based on the number of persons who are party to the application.

Unlike in Dominica, Economic Citizenship Programs in Saint Kitts and Nevis frequently require a government-approved investment in the country. In the case of Saint Kitts and Nevis, you will need to invest a minimum of U.S. $250,000 in real estate; some outstanding developments are preapproved. This property can be your new home, if and when you choose to move to the country, or it can be managed as vacation rental property that will provide you with income.

The application process is similar to Dominica's, including the required documentation; a local law firm will handle the procedures. The time frame is approximately 6 to 12 weeks to complete and be accepted for citizenship. No personal interview is required so an advance visit to the country is not required. You will likely want to select the property yourself, but this can be handled by a local professional or someone you know acting on your behalf. And, as in Dominica, you can hold dual citizenship and the Saint Kitts-Nevis government will not inform your country where you are presently a citizen.

For either of these Economic Citizenship Programs, I recommend Henley & Partners Inc., with offices in both countries. Refer to "Immigration Services" in the back of this section.

PROFILES OF RETIREMENT HAVENS AND FOREIGN RESIDENCY

Remember that Part Four and the Appendix of this book list resources and information for offshore investors and expatriate services; the Profiles at the end of Part Three describe tax haven countries. The wealth of information provided here will complement your search for a retirement haven or location for temporary or permanent residency. Also, many of these countries permit a foreigner to own real estate.

The following tourist stay information pertains to U.S. citizens, together with the maximum length of stay with proper travel documents acceptable to the visiting country. For travel documents and information about other requirements including longer stays, call or visit the country's U.S. Embassy for more information.

A typical approach to securing permanent residency is to enter a country on a travel visa, then apply for residency while in the country, renewing your tourist visa in advance of each time it is about to expire, until you have satisfied the residency time requirement necessary to apply for permanent residency.

When seeking permanent residency or citizenship in any foreign country, it is best and most efficient to engage the services of a local lawyer with expertise in the area of immigration. In some countries, especially in places like Latin America, connections can make things go much smoother and faster.

Always keep in mind the tax consequences of your choices of countries for living or retiring, just as you would for doing business, including possible tax treaties that might provide tax relief. You can obtain IRS Publication 901 U.S. Tax Treaties, which tells whether a tax treaty exists between the United States and another country offering a reduced tax rate, or the possibility of a complete exemption from U.S. taxes for residents of a particular country who are earning income there. IRS Publication 54, Tax Guide for U.S. Citizens and Resident Aliens Abroad, tells of tax treaties available to U.S. citizens and resident aliens with foreign income. You can download the appropriate publications at www.irs.gov. Other important tax publications and forms can be found at this web site. A local professional or a U.S. international tax planner can give you further advice in these areas.

Andorra

Tourist Stay: No limit. Can rent or purchase real estate and stay indefinitely. An ideal expat haven.

Passport/Residency: The first step to immigrating is to secure a "passive" residence permit good for four years, which grants certain protections under the law. It takes 25 years before you can get citizenship.

Taxes: No income tax. A tax haven country. Strict bank secrecy.

Embassy: New York, NY. Telephone: (212) 750-8064.

Web Site: www.andorra.ad

Office of immigration: Andorra la Vella. Telephone: 376-826222.

Argentina

Tourist Stay: Visa is not required for business; pleasure up to 60 days.

Passport/Residency: After two years of being accepted as an immigrant, you will qualify for naturalization, and the entire time need not be spent in the country. Dual citizenship is acceptable. Excellent passport with visa-free travel to more than 100 countries including the United States, a good part of Europe, and most Latin American countries.

Taxes: No income tax on foreign source income. Special exemptions on income tax for authors and publishers.

Embassy: Washington, DC. Telephone: (202) 238-6460.

Web Site: www.embassyofargentina-usa.org

Austria

Tourist Stay: Visa is not required for tourist stay up to 90 days.

Passport/Residency: Citizenship can be obtained, but on a limited basis, and requires a large government-approved investment of U.S. two million dollars minimum. However, permanent residency can be secured if you have a residence in the country and a minimum annual income of U.S. $25,000. After five years of residency, you can make application for naturalization. Excellent expat haven.

Taxes: As a permanent resident, you avoid the high taxes that citizens typically pay. Strict bank secrecy. A T-7 country.

Embassy: Washington, DC. Telephone: (202) 895-6711.

Web Site: www.austria.org

The Bahamas

Tourist Stay: Up to eight months with proof of U.S. citizenship.

Passport/Residency: Instant permanent residency is touted under "The Bahamas Investment Promotion Program" for three categories of investors: (1) Individual Investors, (2) Group Investors, (3) Entrepreneurs. Many of the "rich and famous" today have chosen the Bahamas as their main or second residence. The minimum investment category starts at U.S. $150,000 in a government-approved project. A Bahamas resident alien passport is obtainable for travel.

Taxes: No income taxes. Formerly an excellent tax haven, but presently best avoided by U.S. citizens for that purpose.

Embassy: Washington, DC. Telephone: (202) 319-2660.

Web Site: www.bahamas.gov.bs

Belize

Tourist Stay: Visa is not required for stay up to 30 days.

Passport/Residency: After living in Belize for one year, you can secure permanent residency after depositing U.S. $700 with a Belize bank. If you are over 45 years of age, and have an minimum annual income of U.S.

$24,000, you can qualify for the Qualified Retired Persons Program (QRP) and receive permanent residency and special tax status.

Taxes: No income tax on foreign source income. Strict bank secrecy. A T-7 tax haven.

Embassy: Washington, DC. Telephone: (202) 332-9636.

Web Site: www.embassyofbelize.org

Bolivia

Tourist Stay: Visa is not required for stay up to 30 days.

Passport/Residency: It is possible to acquire citizenship for a donation with a government-recognized "benefactor to Bolivia" of U.S. $25,000, maybe less, without a personal visit. The casualness of the program has drawn concern. The donor receives an identity card, driver's license, and certificate of citizenship, and is entitled to a five-year passport good for visa-free travel to most of Europe. Another approach is to make an investment or buy real estate, which will qualify you for permanent residency leading to naturalization after five years.

Taxes: No special concessions here, but there are tax-free zones exempting investors from most Bolivian taxes. Not the best expat haven due to taxes, especially as a new citizen, but citizenship may be useful to some people anyway, such as those in need of an alternative country or stepping-stone.

Embassy: Washington, DC. Telephone: (202) 232-4827/28.

Web Site: www.bolivia-usa.org

Brazil

Tourist Stay: Visa is required for stays up to 90 days.

Passport/Residency: You can obtain permanent residency within 60 to 90 days without visiting the country. This gives you the right to enter the country and receive a national ID card and national banking number, entitling the holder to stay as long as desired, get a job, or make investments, the same as citizens. After four years, you will be eligible for naturalization and the Brazilian passport, with visa-free travel to 130 countries and most of Europe. Dual citizenship is recognized. Expect to spend approximately U.S. $35,000 in administrative fees. Another option is to invest a minimum of U.S. $200,000 in the official Economic Investment Permanent Residence Program. If you marry a Brazilian citizen, or have a child by one, you are entitled to citizenship in one year. Brazil is also a backdoor immigration opportunity to Portugal and the European Union, cutting the time in half to three years.

Taxes: Potential expat country. Taxes are on the high side, but lower than most developed countries.
Embassy: Washington, DC. Telephone: (202) 238-2828.
Web Site: www.brasilemb.org

Campione (Italy)

Tourist Stay: Visa is not required for tourist or business stay up to 90 days.
Passport/Residency: Located on Lake Lugano in the Swiss canton of Ticino, Campione is an Italian enclave and is known as the "backdoor to Switzerland" as it is surrounded by Switzerland and its residents have certain Swiss entitlements such as Swiss license plates, post office, Swiss traffic laws, telephone service, and so on. Residents have complete unrestricted access to Switzerland and Liechtenstein as there are no border controls, making Campione a very attractive expat and business haven with easy access to the world's best banking services. Residency rights in Campione are attainable by renting or buying a house or apartment. Real estate is limited and therefore expensive, but in demand, and is a solid investment.
Taxes: No income taxes and no local taxes. A unique little-known no-tax haven. Residents are not subject to Swiss double-taxation agreements. Campione is an attractive tax haven where foreigners can incorporate a Campione company, use a Swiss address, and avoid high Swiss income and withholding taxes. This is a good alternative to using a Swiss company.
Embassy: Washington, DC. Telephone: (202) 328-5500.

Canada

Tourist Stay: Visa is not required. Stay of over 180 days will require a visitor's record issued at the port of entry.
Passport/Residency: Canada provides a unique opportunity for Americans and others to expatriate, and offers several methods for gaining citizenship. For U.S. citizens, it is the least "foreign" country to our own culture, making it an easy place to visit or live. Canadians are generally liked and accepted worldwide unlike their U.S. counterparts, and a Canadian passport provides the holder with a superior travel document.
Taxes: Canada is one of the best places to live in the world, and even with high taxes, certain tax benefits attract Americans and others, which is why it has the highest immigration rate in the world. Expect personal income taxes between federal and provincial to be around 50 percent. Hold on, as a qualified immigrant you become eligible for a complete

moratorium on personal income tax for the first five years that you reside in Canada. And, even better, no taxes at all if your income is derived from an offshore source, non-Canadian trust, or foreign corporation. This is how to avoid U.S. and Canadian income and capital gains taxes altogether. This strategy frequently utilizes the "Five-Year Offshore Immigration Trust." While living in Canada for the required three-year minimum as an expatriate before becoming a Canadian citizen, you can exercise the $80,000 loophole. If you cannot wait that period, you could acquire citizenship quickly through Dominica or St. Kitts-Nevis, so you can renounce your U.S. citizenship before applying to Canada to become a qualified immigrant, thereby effectively eliminating the U.S. tax liability completely while waiting to become a Canadian citizen. Furthermore, as a Canadian citizen, there are no federal estate taxes, making Canada a strategy for wealthy U.S. citizens to avoid giving away more than half their estate to the IRS and, instead, giving it to their rightful heirs. There are also no taxes on worldwide income unlike what U.S. citizens experience. There is another strategy to extend your benefits. Before the full five years of the immigration trust are completed, you can become a lawful resident of another country (such as the ones described in this book), for the tie-breaking sixtieth month, and still be able to visit Canada and the United States for up to six months. As a resident of a foreign country instead of Canada or the United States, you are then free of taxes in both countries. If you maintain this new, but temporary status for 18 months, then repeat the process by returning to Canada to establish residence, you can begin all over again, creating a new immigration trust and the start of another five-year period of tax-free income. Canadian immigration should be explored with a legal professional well versed in the strategy outlined here, but it will be worth the time and expense.

Embassy: Washington, DC. Telephone: (202) 682-1740.
Web Site: www.canadianembassy.org

Chile

Tourist Stay: Visa is not required for stays up to 90 days.
Passport/Residency: With a minimum U.S. $30,000 investment, citizenship can be obtained after five years of residence.
Taxes: A promising future and strong free market economy make Chile attractive for investors in commercial enterprises in remote areas, who receive exemptions from income taxes and other taxes.
Embassy: Washington, DC. (202) 530-4106.
Web Site: www.chile-usa.org

Costa Rica

Tourist Stay: Visa is required for stays up to 90 days.

Passport/Residency: There are two types of residency programs: retired persons who bring in over U.S. $600 a month from an established retirement plan for at least five years; or, a person with a guaranteed passive income from a recognized source of at least U.S. $1,000 a month for the same period. Dual citizenship is acceptable. The new resident is only required to spend four months of the year in the country.

Taxes: No tax on foreign source income. Local income taxes are lower than most developed countries. A tax haven country.

Embassy: Washington, DC. Telephone: (202) 328-6628.

Web Site: www.costarica-embassy.org

Czech Republic

Tourist Stay: Visa is not required for business and tourist stays up to 90 days. Visa is required for longer stays or if planning to conduct business and obtain permanent residency.

Passport/Residency: Not the most attractive expatriate haven, but risk-taking entrepreneurs might like the prospects of starting a business or being self-employed to exploit new opportunities in this country that struggles to become progressive. As incentives, they offer foreigners permanent residency with the right to purchase real estate and a Czech five-year passport with visa-free travel to most of Europe, but not the United States. After five years, residents can apply for naturalization. That will get you visa-free to your bank in Switzerland.

Embassy: Washington, DC. Telephone: (202) 274-9123.

Web Site: www.mzv.cz/washington

Dominica

Tourist Stay: Need proof of citizenship. No visa is required.

Passport/Residency: They have an excellent citizenship program. See the earlier discussion of Economic Citizenship Programs in this section.

Taxes: A tax haven country, but better for alternative citizenship purposes. Investment incentives may include a business tax holiday of up to 15 years and unrestricted repatriation of profits.

Embassy: Washington, DC. Telephone: (202) 364-6781.

Web Site: http://bridgetown.usembassy.gov

Dominican Republic

Tourist Stay: Need proof of citizenship.

Passport/Residency: If residency is desired, a resident visa must be applied for through your nearest Dominican Republic Consulate, and once granted, you have 60 days to arrive in the Dominican Republic (D.R.), at which time you must apply for a provisional residency card with the Immigration Department. The residency card is for one year and renewable each year. Permanent residency can lead to naturalization in six months along with a minimum U.S. $50,000 investment in either real estate or business. Their passport is not the best for travel as a visa is required to most countries. But, it is a beautiful country.

Taxes: Residents are taxed on their worldwide income at the rate of 25 percent for income exceeding U.S. $12,000 a year. Although not a tax haven, D.R. does have special free zones where an offshore company can operate free of the local 30 percent corporate income tax for up to 20 years. There is also no foreign source tax under this scenario. A privately owned offshore banking center is planned, a U.S. $850 million complex, to serve the capital markets for the Caribbean and the Americas, including an electronic exchange, the Latin American International Financial Exchange (LAIFEX). The exchange would like to be the clearinghouse for settlement of the $3 trillion of Caribbean and Latin American debt that is traded annually around the world. D.R. could become an attractive financial hub for the region.

Embassy: Washington, DC. Telephone: (202) 332-6280.

Web Site: www.domrep.org

Ecuador

Tourist Stay: U.S. citizens do not need a visa for the first 90 days. No limit on visa stay if you have a minimum monthly income of U.S. $1,000 or can make a one-time investment of U.S. $15,000. Welcoming to foreign visitors. Good retirement haven.

Passport/Residency: Permanent residency can be acquired with a government-approved investment of at least U.S. $25,000 for one applicant. Each dependent requires investing an additional U.S. $5,000. Citizenship and passport can be obtained after five years of residency. Dual citizenship is recognized.

Taxes: No income tax on foreign-source income. No provincial, county, or municipal taxes. No inheritance or gift tax on assets outside Ecuador. Local income tax is progressive up to 25 percent. No restrictions on real estate ownership by foreigners.

Embassy: Washington, DC. Telephone: (202) 234-7200.
Web Site: www.ecuador.org

Guatemala

Tourist Stay: Passport is required for stays up to 90 days.

Passport/Residency: A short two-year residency qualifies you to obtain naturalization. Two local and reputable sponsors are required to attest to your good character and standing, so a personal visit is likely in order. A good lawyer with connections can probably assist, and even speed up the residency time. Dual citizenship is recognized. At the time of naturalization, you can even change your name. In most cases, their five-year passport is readily accepted throughout Europe without a visa. As a Guatemalan citizen and two years of residency in Spain, you could become naturalized there as well and have dual citizenship even after renouncing your present citizenship.

Taxes: No foreign-source income tax.

Embassy: Washington, DC. Telephone: (202) 745-4952.

Web Site: http://guatemala.usembassy.gov

Hong Kong

Tourist Stay: Visa is not required for stays up to 90 days.

Passport/Residency: There is an opportunity to receive a Business Investment Visa to qualified applicants who intend to start a company that will create local employment. The BIV is easily obtainable for an international businessperson or investor who wants to benefit from doing business in and from Hong Kong.

Taxes: Residents are not taxed on income and profits created from doing business outside Hong Kong. A T-7 tax haven.

Embassy: Washington, DC. Telephone: (202) 328-2500.

Web Site: www.china-embassy.org

Ireland

Tourist Stay: Visa is not required for stays up to 90 days.

Passport/Residency: There are no investment-for-citizenship opportunities in Ireland. Citizenship by ancestry is possible. A permanent resident can become a naturalized citizen after five years. And, a foreign national can marry a person of Irish birth, and qualify for citizenship after three years. Creative types such as writers, artists, and actors also receive favorable treatment.

Taxes: American retirees are obligated to pay Irish taxes at the rate of 26 to 48 percent, but fortunately, you would benefit from the double taxation agreement with the United States. There are other taxes as well. Ireland has had some tax incentives, but these will become nonexistent or passé by 2010 as a result of European Union (EU) pressure. Once upon a time, Ireland was a tax haven, but has chosen to divest itself of this status. A retiree could benefit by incorporating an Irish company to take advantage of various significant tax advantages and engage professional management services to run the operation while retiring and living the life of landed gentry. For more tax information with regard to Americans living in Ireland, contact the Irish Revenue Commissioners, Dublin Castle, Dame Street, Dublin 2. Telephone: 353 (1) 679-2777.

Embassy: Washington, DC. Telephone: (202) 462-3939.

Web Site: www.irelandemb.org

Italy

Tourist Stay: Visa is not required for tourist or business stay up to 90 days.

Passport/Residency: Descendants of Italian nationals are recognized as citizens regardless of birthplace, and other ethnic Italians can gain citizenship through lenient procedures. If you are a foreign citizen and not of Italian origin, a 10-year residency period is required before naturalization. Dual citizenship is recognized. Tourist visas are easily renewable indefinitely if you can show proof of financial means. A good location for offshore investors and financial expats is tax-free Campione, on Lake Lugano, surrounded by Switzerland. Refer to earlier description.

Taxes: Italy is notorious for its taxes and tax dodgers. Resident foreign nationals are not taxed on foreign-source income.

Embassy: Washington, DC. Telephone: (202) 328-5500.

Web Site: www.italyemb.org

Malta

Tourist Stay: Visa is not required for stays up to 90 days.

Passport/Residency: Malta is a favorable expatriate haven and a tax haven. Permanent residency is granted to foreign nationals who are allowed to stay or leave at any time, and who bring in the minimum annual income of U.S. $14,400. Each dependent increases the minimum requirement by U.S. $2,400. The applicant must also have minimum assets of U.S. $360,000 outside Malta. As Malta is an EU country, and party to the

Schengen Area agreement, permanent residents are entitled to travel freely throughout those countries. This lovely, sunny Mediterranean mecca has seen thousands of years of human history and the Maltese typically speak fluent English.

Taxes: Permanent residents pay a flat 15 percent income tax on foreign-source income brought into Malta. There are numerous double taxation agreements that may be beneficial.

Embassy: Washington, DC. Telephone: (202) 462-3611/2.

Web Site: www.investinmalta.com

Monaco

Tourist Stay: No visa is required for stays up to 90 days.

Passport/Residency: Money talks in Monte Carlo. Real estate prices make Monaco an expensive haven, but expats are always welcome. Permanent residency can be secured if you have a minimum net worth of a half million greenbacks; with your good name and professional references in hand, your Monaco lawyer should have you swinging on the Riviera in no time. Besides the rich and famous, creative types are also drawn to Monte Carlo. The pivotal point here is the Principality's relationship with France. Like Liechtenstein, Monaco has come under attack from the Organisation for Economic Co-operation and Development (OECD) with accusations of money laundering. Both countries have refused thus far to concede to outside pressures.

Taxes: No personal income taxes. A tax haven country.

Embassy: New York, NY. Telephone: (212) 759-5227.

Web Site: www.monaco-consulate.com

The Netherlands

Tourist Stay: Visa is not required for tourist or business stay up to 90 days.

Passport/Residency: Foreign nationals must reside for five years in the country for naturalization, whether as a legal resident or not, or three years if married to a Dutch national.

Taxes: No taxes on foreign-source income.

Embassy: Washington, DC. Telephone: (202) 244-5300.

Web Site: www.netherlands-embassy.org

Panama

Tourist Stay: Visa and tourist card valid for 30 days. Stay can be extended up to 90 days.

Passport/Residency: An attractive expat or retirement haven. Permanent residency can be obtained for those with a minimum U.S. $1,000 a month income from a foreign source, or as an executive with an international company, and after five years it can lead to naturalization. Good visa-free passport travel to Latin American, North American, and European countries.

Taxes: Special retirement visas are easy to obtain. No income tax on foreign source income. Substantial tax incentives for any business in the tourism trade. A T-7 tax haven country. Staunch refusal to cooperate with the OECD. Strict bank secrecy. No double taxation agreements or Tax Information Exchange Agreement (TIEA).

Embassy: Washington, DC. Telephone: (202) 483-1407.

Web Site: http://panama.usembassy.gov/panama-esp

Portugal

Tourist Stay: Visa is not required up to 90 days.

Passport/Residency: A residence permit is a slow process, and may take 12 to 18 months. If you keep a low profile, you're not likely to be bothered by officials. Six years' residency is required, sufficient income to live, and a government-approved investment of U.S. $100,000 for naturalization eligibility.

Taxes: The Portuguese, like the United States government, tax worldwide income, and this applies to residents and aliens alike. There is a double-taxation agreement between the two countries, so you won't be paying taxes twice.

Embassy: Washington, DC. Telephone: (202) 332-3007.

Web Site: www.portugalemb.org

Saint Kitts and Nevis

Tourist Stay: Proof of citizenship. Visa is not required for stays up to three months.

Passport/Residency: They have an excellent citizenship program as described earlier in this section.

Taxes: A T-7 tax haven. No taxes. Strict bank secrecy.

Embassy: Washington DC. Telephone: (202) 686-2636.

Switzerland

Tourist Stay: Visa not required for tourism/study stay of less than 90 days.

Passport/Residency: Residency is not easy to obtain unless you start a company that will create local employment. Twelve years of residency can lead to naturalization. It worked for international financier Marc Rich, who had a billion reasons to move, and under the right circumstances, it could be good for you. In his case, he established a legal presence and office in Zug, which is the most favorable canton for business, and moved important business records and operations out of the U.S. government's reach before they aggressively began pursing him. Later, thanks to President Clinton, he was exonerated of all charges against him. An easier resident approach would be to reside in Italy's enclave Campione on Lake Lugano, described earlier. For those who still wish to pursue Swiss residency, consult a Swiss lawyer.

Taxes: Switzerland is not a tax-free haven, but foreign nationals can avoid local taxes on certain investments. There are many tax treaties in place with other nations. Companies and banks are legally obliged to withhold 35 percent tax on interest and dividends earned, which can be offset by a double-taxation agreement, such as the one with the United States. It is an excellent money and asset haven with the world's best banking facilities, and therefore one of my T-7 tax havens.

Embassy: Washington, DC. Telephone: (202) 745-7900.

Web Site: www.swissemb.org

Turks and Caicos

Tourist Stay: Tourists can stay up to three months with a passport.

Passport/Residency: A Permanent Residency Program, established in 1996, offers several ways for expatriates who can invest U.S. $250,000 in a government-approved investment to be entitled to full-time residence. The costs vary: self-employed pay around U.S. $50,000, skilled workers U.S. $30,000, retired persons U.S. $15,000, unskilled workers U.S. $8,000. There is also Business Residency.

Taxes: No taxes. A tax haven country.

Embassy: Washington, DC. Telephone: (202) 588-7800.

Web Site: www.britishembassy.ie

United Kingdom

Tourist Stay: Contact embassy.

Passport/Residency: Certain businesspeople and investors who make a substantial investment can get permanent residency which is good for four years and can lead to naturalization. As for retirees, the United Kingdom is an attractive place to live, and, if you are over age 59 and have a minimum annual income of 25,000 sterling pounds with "close U.K. ties," you can get permanent residency after four years residence, a stepping-stone to full U.K. citizenship.

Taxes: High taxes, like those in the United States. With recent developments in the loss of confidentiality in financial matters, and the aggressive attitude of the English taxman who is going after offshore depositors and suspected tax dodgers with a vengeance, England would not be the best jurisdiction for business, investing, and immigration purposes. As English businesspeople are again exiting the country, it is unlikely you will want to take them up on becoming a "business-investor" or "investor" for the sake of eventually becoming a U.K. citizen. Many are going to Monte Carlo today. London might make a good business base for certain purposes, and by incorporating an English company and having a communication facility there, you could have a first-class presence while operating it unprofitably, an extension of your offshore operation, and letting the real flow of income and profits rest elsewhere, namely in a low- or no-tax haven. There is a special status exemption worth noting: Citizens of certain nations, and lawyers, writers, and artists from other countries are encouraged to do business and seek residency without the requirement of investment and employment.

Embassy: Washington, DC. Telephone: (202) 588-7800.

Web Site: www.britishembassy.ie

Uruguay

Tourist Stay: Visa is not required for tourist or business stay up to 90 days.

Passport/Residency: This country has been a good haven for expatriates and a fairly easy one in which to obtain permanent residency that leads to naturalization in three years. The permanent residency process takes approximately 30 days. The Uruguay passport is good throughout countries that are party to the Mercosur Agreement. Proven financial self-support is required.

Taxes: No personal income tax. No currency controls. Passive foreign-source income exempt for foreign nationals. There are tax-free zones for establishing or relocating a business.

Embassy: Washington, DC. Telephone: (202) 331-4219.

Web Site: www.uruwashi.org

MORE COUNTRIES TO INVESTIGATE

Antigua and Barbuda

Tourist Stay: Up to six months with a visa.

Embassy: Washington, DC. Telephone: (202) 362-5122/5166/5211.

Anguilla, W.I. (British)

Tourist Stay: Up to three months with passport.
Embassy: Washington, DC. Telephone: (202) 588-7800.
Web Site: www.britishembassy.com

Aruba

Tourist Stay: Visa not required for tourist/business stay up to 90 days.
Embassy: Washington, DC. Telephone: (202) 244-5300.
Web Site: www.netherlands-embassy.org

Australia

Tourist Stay: With visa, up to three months.
Embassy: Toll free in the U.S. (888) 990-8888.
Web Site: www.austemb.org

Bahrain

Tourist Stay: Single entry visa valid for two weeks.
Embassy: Washington, DC. Telephone: (202) 342-1111.
Web Site: www.bahrainembassy.org

Barbados

Tourist Stay: Visa not required for stay up to six months.
Embassy: Washington, DC. Telephone: (202) 939-9200.
Web Site: http://bridgetown.usembassy.gov

Belgium

Tourist Stay: Visa not required for stay up to 30 days.
Embassy: Washington, DC. Telephone: (202) 333-6900.
Web Site: www.diplobel.us

Bermuda

Tourist Stay: Visa not required for tourist stay up to three months.
Embassy: Washington, DC. Telephone: (202) 588-7800.
Web Site: www.immigration.gov.bm

Brunei

Tourist Stay: Visa not required for tourist/business stay up to 90 days.
Embassy: Washington, DC. Telephone: (202) 237-1838.
Web Site: www.bruneiembassy.org

Bulgaria

Tourist Stay: Visa not required for stay up to 30 days.
Embassy: Washington, DC. Telephone: (202) 387-7969/387-0174.
Web Site: www.bulgaria-embassy.org

Cape Verde

Tourist Stay: Visa required. Contact embassy.
Web Site: www.virtualcapeverde.net

Cayman Islands, W.I. (British)

Tourist Stay: Up to three months with passport.
Embassy: Washington, DC. Telephone: (202) 588-7800.
Web Site: www.britishembassy.ie

Centa and Melilla (Spain)

Tourist Stay: Contact embassy.
Embassy: Washington, DC. Telephone: (202) 728-2330.
Web Site: http://madrid.usembassy.gov
Note: Two interesting Spanish enclaves on Moroccan Mediterranean coast where taxes are about half of those in Spain.

Cook Islands

Tourist Stay: Visa not required for visit up to 31 days.
Embassy: Honolulu, HI. Telephone: (808) 847-6377.

Cyprus

Tourist Stay: Visa not required for tourist/business stay up to three months.
Embassy: Washington, DC. Telephone: (202) 462-5772.
Web Site: www.cyprusembassy.net

Denmark

Tourist Stay: Visa not required for stay up to 90 days.
Embassy: Washington, DC. Telephone: (202) 234-4300.
Web Site: www.denmark.org

Dubai, U.A.E.

Tourist Stay: Visa not required for stay up to 30 days.
Embassy: Washington, DC. Telephone: (202) 243-2400.
Web Site: www.UAEembassy.org

Fiji

Tourist Stay: Visa not required for stay up to four months.
Embassy: Washington, DC. Telephone: (202) 337-8320.
Web Site: www.fijiembassy.org

Finland

Tourist Stay: Tourist/business visa not required for stay up to 90 days.
Embassy: Washington, DC. Telephone: (202) 298-5800.
Web Site: www.finland.org

France

Tourist Stay: Visa not required for tourist/business stay up to 90 days.
Embassy: Washington, DC. Telephone: (202) 944-6200.
Web Site: www.info-france-usa.org

Germany

Tourist Stay: Tourist/business visa not required for a stay up to 90 days.
Embassy: Washington, DC. Telephone: (202) 298-4393.
Web Site: www.germany-info.org

Gibraltar

Tourist Stay: Visa not required for tourist stay up to 90 days.
Embassy: Washington, DC. Telephone: (202) 588-7800.
Web Site: www.germany-info.org

Grenada

Tourist Stay: Need proof of citizenship. Visa not required for tourist stay up to three months.
Embassy: Washington, DC. Telephone: (202) 265-2561.
Web Site: www.grenadaembassyusa.org

Greece

Tourist Stay: Visa not required for tourist/business stay up to 90 days.
Embassy: Washington, DC. Telephone: (202) 939-1333.
Web Site: www.greekembassy.org

Honduras

Tourist Stay: Visa not required for stay up to 90 days.
Embassy: Washington, DC. Telephone: (202) 737-2972/78.
Web Site: www.hondurasemb.org

Hungary

Tourist Stay: Visa not required for stay up to 90 days.
Embassy: Washington, DC. Telephone: (202) 362-6730.
Web Site: www.hungaryemb.org

Iceland

Tourist Stay: Visa not required for stay up to 90 days.
Embassy: Washington, DC. Telephone: (202) 265-6653/5.
Web Site: www.iceland.org/us or www.utl.is

India

Tourist Stay: Passport and visa required. Contact Indian embassy.
Embassy: Washington, DC. Telephone: (202) 939-9806/9899.
Web Site: http://newdelhi.usembassy.gov

Israel

Tourist Stay: Visa not required for tourist or business stay up to 90 days.
Embassy: Washington, DC. Telephone: (202) 364-5527.

Jamaica

Tourist Stay: Proof of citizenship. Contact Jamaican embassy.
Embassy: Washington, DC. Telephone: (202) 452-0660.
Web Site: www.congenjamaica-ny.org

Japan

Tourist Stay: Visa not required for tourist or business stay up to 90 days.
Embassy: Washington, DC. (202) 238-6800.
Web Site: www.us.emb-japan.go.jp

Liechtenstein

Tourist Stay: Visa not required for tourist or business stay up to 90 days.
Embassy: Washington, DC. Telephone: (202) 215-0460.
Web Site: www.swissembassy.org

Luxembourg

Tourist Stay: Visa not required for tourist or business stay up to 90 days.
Embassy: Washington, DC. Telephone: (202) 265-4171.
Web Site: http://luxembourg.usembassy.gov

Malaysia

Tourist Stay: Visa not required for stay up to three months, extendable for an additional two months.
Embassy: Washington, DC. Telephone: (202) 328-2700.
Web Site: http://malaysia.usembassy.gov

Mauritius

Tourist Stay: Visa are issued at port of entry. Contact Mauritius embassy.
Embassy: Washington, DC. Telephone: (202) 244-1491/2.
Web Site: http://mauritius.usembassy.gov

Mexico

Tourist Stay: Proof of citizenship. Tourist card required; valid for three months for a single entry up to 180 days.
Embassy: Washington, DC. Telephone: (202) 736-1000.
Web Site: www.embassyofmexico.org

The Netherlands Antilles

Tourist Stay: Proof of citizenship. Visa not required for tourist or business stay up to 90 days.
Embassy: Washington, DC. Telephone: (202) 244-5300.
Web Site: www.netherlands-embassy.org

New Zealand

Tourist Stay: Visa not required for tourist or business stay up to 30 days.
Embassy: Washington, DC. Telephone: (202) 328-4800.
Web Site: www.nzembassy.com/usa

Nicaragua

Tourist Stay: Passport required and no visa for a stay up to 30 days. A tourist card is required and is valid for 30 to 90 days.
Embassy: Washington, DC. Telephone: (202) 939-6531.
Web Site: http://managua.usembassy.gov/wwwhemba.htm

Norfolk Islands

Tourist Stay: Visa issued for up to 30 days, extendable. Contact Australian embassy.
Embassy: Washington, DC. Telephone: (202) 797-3000.
Web Site: www.austemb.org or www.pitcairners.org

Norway

Tourist Stay: Visa not required for stay up to 90 days.
Embassy: Washington, DC. Telephone: (202) 333-6000.
Web Site: www.norway.org

Pakistan

Tourist Stay: Obtain visa before arrival. Contact Pakistan embassy.
Embassy: Washington, DC. Telephone: (202) 243-6500.
Web Site: www.embassyofpakistan.org

Paraguay

Tourist Stay: Passport and visa required. Contact embassy.
Embassy: Washington, DC. Telephone: (202) 483-6960.
Web Site: http://paraguay.usembassy.gov

Peru

Tourist Stay: Visa not required for tourist stay up to 90 days, extendable.
Embassy: Washington, DC. Telephone: (202) 462-1081/4/5.
Web Site: www.consuladoperu.com or www.peruvianembassy.us

Saint Lucia

Tourist Stay: Passport and visa required. Contact St. Lucia embassy.
Embassy: Washington, DC. Telephone: (202) 364-6792.

Saint Martin (French)/St. Marteen (Dutch), W.I.

Tourist Stay: Visa not required for tourist/business stay up to 90 days.
Embassy: Washington, DC. (202) 944-6000.
Web Site: www.info-france-usa.org

Saint Vincent and the Grenadines

Tourist Stay: Proof of citizenship for stay up to six months.
Embassy: Washington, DC. Telephone: (202) 364-6730.

Samoa

Tourist Stay: Visa not required for stay up to 60 days.
Embassy: New York, NY. Telephone: (212) 599-6196.

San Marino (Italy)

Tourist Stay: Visa not required for tourist stay up to 90 days.
Embassy: Washington, DC. Telephone: (202) 223-3517.

Seychelles

Tourist Stay: Visa issued on arrival for one month, extendable up to one year.
Embassy: New York, NY. Telephone: (212) 972-1785.

Singapore

Tourist Stay: Visa not required for tourist or business stay, length determined at the discretion of immigration officer, but normally 30 days.
Embassy: Washington, DC. Telephone: (202) 537-3100.
Web Site: www.mfa.gov.sg/washington

Spain

Tourist Stay: Visa not required for tourist or business stay up to 90 days.
Embassy: Washington, DC. Telephone: (202) 452-0100 or (202) 728-2330.
Web Site: http://madrid.usembassy.gov

Sweden

Tourist Stay: Visa not required for stay up to 90 days.
Embassy: Washington, DC. Telephone: (202) 467-2600.
Web Site: www.swedenny.com

Thailand

Tourist Stay: Visa not required for tourist or business stay up to 90 days.
Embassy: Washington, DC. Telephone: (202) 944-3600.
Web Site: www.thaiembdc.org

Trinidad and Tobago

Tourist Stay: Visa not required for tourist or business stay up to 90 days.
Embassy: Washington, DC. Telephone: (202) 467-6490.
Web Site: http://trinidad.usembassy.gov

Turkey

Tourist Stay: Visas can be obtained at Turkish border crossings for tourist/business stay up to three months.
Embassy: Washington, DC. Telephone: (202) 612-6740/41.
Web Site: www.turkishembassy.org

Vanuatu

Tourist Stay: Visa not required for stay up to 30 days.
Embassy: New York, NY. Telephone: (212) 593-0144 or 0215.

Vietnam

Tourist Stay: Passport and visa required. Contact Vietnam embassy.
Embassy: Washington, DC. Telephone: (202) 861-2293.
Web Site: www.vietnamembassy-usa.org

Virgin Islands, British

Tourist Stay: Proof of citizenship for tourist stay up to six months.
Embassy: Washington, DC. Telephone: (202) 588-7800.
Web Site: www.britain-info.org

West Indies, British

Tourist Stay: Tourist stay up to three months with passport.
Embassy: Washington, DC. Telephone: (202) 588-7800.
Web Site: www.britishembassy.ie

West Indies, French

Tourist Stay: Visa not required for tourist or business stay up to 90 days.
Embassy: Washington, DC. Telephone: (202) 944-6000.
Web Site: www.info-france-usa.org

TRAVEL DESTINATIONS

Most countries allow travelers to stay in their country for a short period as a guest, for business or pleasure, often without the requirement of a visa. The length of stay varies by country and whether the trip is for business or pleasure. A typical length of stay is three months, but it can be as long as six or eight months, or as short as one month.

Besides the appropriate required travel documents, you may need to produce a return plane ticket, meet health requirements, such as immunizations, AIDS/HIV testing, and so on, and be able to show proof of financial support to stay the intended length.

Foreign entry requirements are imposed by each country and can be readily obtained by contacting the United States Department of State in Washington, DC, along with embassy contact information. Their web site is www.travel.state.gov for more information.

A worthwhile guide for frequent travelers is the Travel Information Manual (TIM) for $35. It gives foreign entry requirements for all countries. TIM, PO Box 902, NL-2130EA Hoofdorp, Netherlands. Web site: www.iata.og/tim/index.

Before leaving the United States, double-check the requirements for re-entry as requirements may change. Contact the National Passport Information Center at toll free (877) 487-2778 for more information.

All U.S. citizens returning from the Caribbean, Bermuda, Panama, Canada, Mexico, Central America, or South America will be required to have a valid U.S. passport or "other secure document" to re-enter the United States, effective as follows:

- As of December 31, 2006, this requirement applies to all air and sea travel to and from these departure points.
- As of December 31, 2007, this requirement will be extended to all land border crossings as well as air and sea travel.

The plan is for the preceding to be in full effect by January 1, 2008.

OFFSHORE READING

Forbidden Knowledge by Robert E. Bauman, JD. Sovereign Society Ltd. 2004. A wealth of offshore information from reliable authorities.

How to Bank, Invest and Do Business: Offshore and Tax Free by Hoyt L. Barber. McGraw-Hill, Business and Professional Trade Division, New York. Nine printings, 1993 to 2002.

Lawsuit Proof: Protecting Your Assets from Lawsuit and Claims by Robert J. Mintz and James J. Rubens. Lawtech Publishing, San Juan Capistrano, CA. 1995.

The Offshore Money Book by Arnold Cornez, JD. Contemporary Books, Chicago. 2000.

The Passport Book: The Complete Guide to Offshore Residency, Dual Citizenships and Second Passports by Robert E. Bauman, JD. Sovereign Society Ltd. 2004.

Secrets of Swiss Banking: An Owner's Manual to Quietly Building a Fortune by Hoyt Barber. Forthcoming book scheduled for release in 2007. Visit www.hoytbarber.com for further information.

Tax Havens of the World, 8th ed., by Thomas P. Azzara. $90. New Providence Press, 2003. PO Box CB-11552, Nassau, Bahamas. Telephone/Fax: (242) 327-7359. http://www.bahamasbahamas.com. The title is the same, but no relation to the Walter and Dorothy Diamond reference work mentioned elsewhere.

Where to Stash Your Cash . . . Legally by Robert E. Bauman, JD. The Sovereign Society Inc. 2004.

OFFSHORE REFERENCE WORKS

The following are excellent works for professionals and serious international investors:

International Trust Laws and Analysis. Warren, Gorham & Lamart, Boston, MA. Toll free: (800) 431-9025, ext. 3. Web site: www.wgl.com.

MICROPAL Guide to Offshore Investment Funds. International Offshore Publishing Ltd., PO Box 549, Les Sablons, St. Peters, Guernsey, Channel Islands, United Kingdom. Telephone: (44) 1481-66759. Fax: (44) 1481-66758.

Offshore Planning by Mary Simon, LLM (Taxation), JD (Law), BA (economics). Specialty Technical Publishers. 2005. A professional guide on the subjects of tax havens, asset protection, business opportunities, and capital preservation. Annual subscription. 1300A Boblett Street, Blaine, WA 98230. E-mail: orders@stpub.com. Web site: http://www.stpub.com. Telephone: (604) 983-3434. Fax: (604) 983-3445.

Practical International Tax Planning by Marshall Langer. Practicing Law Institute, Manhattan, NY. (Periodically updated).

Tax Havens and Their Uses. Economist Intelligence Unit, 15 Regent Street, London 8W1Y 4LR U.K. Telephone: 44 (207) 830-1007.

Tax Havens of the World by Walter and Dorothy Diamond. Mathew Bender & Co. A three-volume set, published annually and updated periodically, for international tax planning professionals written by "The Dean of Offshore." Toll free (800) 833-9844. www.bender.com.

NEWSLETTERS

Adrian Day's Global Analyst. PO Box 6644, Annapolis, MD 21401. Telephone: (410) 224-8885. Fax: (410) 224-8229.

Commodity Trend Alert. Edited by Eric Roseman. 5 Catherine Street, Waterford, Ireland. Telephone: (888) 358-8125. Fax: (410) 230-1269. Web site: www.commoditytrendalert.com.

The Daily Reckoning. Edited by Bill Bonner. Worthwhile newsletter. Free e-mail subscription. Web site: www.dailyreckoning.com.

Expat Investor. Monthly. Web site: www.expatinvestor.com.

Financial Privacy Report. Edited by Michael H. Ketcher. PO Box 1277, Burnsville, MN 55337. Telephone: (612) 895-8757. Fax: (612) 895-5526. E-mail: ketcher@ix.netcom.com.

Freedom Network News. Edited by Vincent H. Miller. International Society for Individual Liberty, 1800 Market Street, San Francisco, CA 94102. Telephone: (415) 864-0952. Fax: (415) 864-7506. Web site: www.free-market.net.

Global Asset Protection and *Offshore Tax Strategies.* E-newsletters edited by Vernon K. Jacobs, CPA and Tax Advisor, with Richard Duke. E-mail: Jacobs@offshorepress.com. Web site: www.offshorepress.com.

Global Mutual Fund Investor. Monthly. Edited by Eric Roseman. E.N.R. Asset Management Inc., 2 Westmount Square, Suite 1802, Westmount, Quebec H3Z 2S4, Canada. Telephone: Toll free: (877) 989-8027 (United States and Canada). E-mail: enr@qc.aibn.com. Web site: www.eas.ca.

International Harry Schultz Newsletter. Edited by Harry Schultz. PO Box 622, CH1001, Lausanne, Switzerland. Web site: www.hsletter.com.

International Speculator. Edited by Douglas Casey, investment author. PO Box 8978, Aspen, CO 81611. Telephone: (970) 923-2062. Fax: (970) 923-2064. Web site: www.internationalspeculator.com. Investment advisory service covering precious metals, commodities, stocks and real estate.

Money Laundering Alert. Alert Global Media Inc., 1100 Brickell Avenue, #601, PO Box 11390, Miami, FL 33101-1390. Telephone: (305) 530-0500. Fax: (305) 530-9434. Web site: www.moneylaundering.com.

The Money Trader. Edited by Kathy Lien and Boris Schlossberg. The Sovereign Society. Make money in the FX Spot Market trading currencies with solid advice from these experienced traders. Web site: www.money-trader.com.

Offshore Dossier: Your Passport to the World's Last Frontiers of Personal and Financial Freedom. Hoyt L. Barber. Available through Barber Financial Advisors. Web site: www.BarberFinancialAdvisors.com.

Offshore Financial News and Commentary. Ron Holland, Geneva, Switzerland. Toll free (800) 891-8332.

Offshore Investment. Edited by Charles A. Cain. Offshore Institute, 62 Brompton Road, Knightsbridge, London SW3 1BW United Kingdom. Telephone: 44 (171) 225-0550. Fax: 44 (171) 584-1093. Web site: www.offshoreinvestment.com/offshore.

Offshore Opportunities Letter. Monthly. Edited by Nicholas Pullen. E-mail: prometheus.press@virgin.net.

Ruff Times. Edited by investment author Howard Ruff. E-mail: service@rufftimes.com.

Select Information Exchange. A financial newsletter marketing company. Special combination offers. Request their free catalog. SIE, 244 W. 54th Street, New York, NY 10019. Toll free: (800) 743-9346. Web site: www.stockfocus.com.

The Sovereign Individual. Edited by Sean Broderick. 5 Catherine Street, Waterford, Ireland. Telephone: (888) 358-8125. Fax: (410) 230-1269. E-mail: info@thesovereignsociety.com. Web site: www.sovereignsociety.com.

Sovereign Society Offshore A-Letter. Excellent free weekly e-mail newsletter covering offshore developments, personal liberty, and wealth protection. Edited by Robert E. Bauman, JD. Web site: www.sovereignsociety.com.

The Stealth Investor: An Insider's Investment Newsletter. Edited by savvy investment advisor and best-selling author John Pugsley, Chairman of the Sovereign Society. Web site: www.stealthinvestor.com.

Strategic Investment. Edited by Jim Davidson. 108 N. Alfred Street, #200, Alexandria, VA 22314. Telephone: (703) 836-8250. Fax: (703) 836-4061. Web site: www.strategicinvestment.com.

Swiss Perspective. Edited by Rosanna Arguella. JML Swiss Investment Counsellors, Germaniastrasse 55, Zurich 08033, Switzerland. Telephone: 41 (1) 360-1800. Fax: 41 (1) 361-4074. Web site: www.jml.ch.

Tax Haven Reporter. Edited by Thomas P. Azzara. New Providence Press, PO Box CB-11552, Nassau, Bahamas. T/F (242) 327-7359. E-mail: taxman @batelnet.bs. Web site: http://www.bahamasbahamas.com.

TravLtips. Monthly. Cruise and Freight Travel Association, PO Box 580218, Flushing, NY 11358. E-mail: info@travltips.com. $25 per year, $35 for two years. Alternative cruising deals and information on worldwide travel opportunities.

World Reports. Edited by Gary Scott, international investment authority/ economist/investment author and fellow novelist. International Service Center, PO Box 157, Lansing, NC 28643. Fax: (336) 384-1577. E-mail: info@garyscott.com. Web site: www.garyscott.com.

TRAVEL BOOKS

The World's Most Dangerous Places, 4th ed., by Robert Young Pelton. Harper-Collins, New York. 2000. The title speaks for itself, by an author who has seen it all. Offbeat and entertaining.

TRAVEL BOOKSTORES AND MAP DEALERS

Map Marketing, 4A Hatherleigh Industrial Estate, Holsworthy Road, Hatherleigh Devon EX20 3LP United Kingdom. Telephone: (44) 8705-862013. Fax: (44) 8701-200-006. Web site: www.mapmarketing.com. Over 500 maps from which to choose.

The Map Shop, 15 High Street, Upton upon Severn, Worcestershire WR8 OH5 United Kingdom. Telephone: (44) 1684-593146. Fax: (44) 1684-594559. Web site: www.themapshop.co.uk. E-mail: themapshop @btInternet.com. Maps and travel guide books.

The Map Shop, Greenville, SC. Toll free (888) 571-6277. Web site: www.the mapshop.com. Maps, globes, more. No connection to the Map Shop in England.

The Travel Bookshop, 13–15 Blenheim Crescent, Notting Hill, London W11 2EE United Kingdom. Telephone: 44 (20) 7229-5260. Fax: 44 (20) 7243-1552. Web site: www.thetravelbookshop.com. Travel books.

TRAVEL INFORMATION

Information Please. Country information. Web site: www.infoplease.com /countries.html.

Tourism Offices Worldwide Directory. To locate government tourist offices, convention bureaus, chambers of commerce, and other organizations by country. Web site: www.towd.com.

Travel Information and Advisories. U.S. State Dept., Washington, DC. Web site: http://travel.state.gov.

Travel Information and Assistance. Traveler's Aid International, 1612 K Street, Suite 206, Washington, DC 20006. Telephone: (202) 546-1127. Web site: www.travelersaid.org. If stranded, in crises, or when in need of information, go to e-help@travelersaid.org.

Travel Information Manual (TIM). TIM, PO Box 902, NL-2130EA Hoofdorp, Netherlands. Monthly publication. Telephone: 31 (0) 20-316-3714. Fax: 31 (0) 20-316-3801. Web site: www.iata.org/tim/index. Single copy U.S. $35. Annual subscription U.S. $166 per year. Excellent travel reference guide with foreign entry requirements for all countries.

Travel Tips. Lonely Planet. Web site: http://www.lonelyplanet.com.

FINANCIAL INFORMATION AND BUSINESS OPPORTUNITIES

BusinessWeek International magazine. McGraw-Hill, New York. Telephone: (212) 512-3867. Fax: (212) 512-6556. Web site: www.businessweek.com.

FundsInsite. Free access to 13,500 funds online. Brought to you by the International Herald Tribune and developed in association with Standard & Poor's. Visit www.iht.com/funds.

Economist magazine. New York. Telephone: (212) 541-5730. London. Telephone: 44 (171) 830-7000. Fax: 44 (171) 839-2968. Web site: www.economist.com.

Financial Times. Daily English financial and business newspaper. FT Publications, New York. Toll free (800) 568-7265. London 44 (171) 873-3000. Fax: 44 (171) 831-9136. Web site: www.ft.com.

Investment Data. Infodat. Web site: www.infodat.com.

Offshore Business Opportunities. Usernet Newsgroup. Alt.business.offshore.

Offshore Dossier newsletter. "Your Passport to the World's Last Frontiers in Personal and Financial Freedom." Offshore Investment, Financial, and Business Opportunities. Hoyt L. Barber. Available six times a year through Barber Financial Advisors, Vancouver, BC, Canada. U.S. $149 a year. Web site: www.BarberFinancialAdvisors.com.

Standard & Poor's Guide to Offshore Investment Funds. Lists over 6,800 funds and in-depth surveys of the top 350 performing investments. Go to http://www.funds-sp.com/home.aspx and while registering under database of choice, select "Offshore."

South China Morning Post. Daily English newspaper. Hong Kong. Telephone: (852) 2680-8661. Fax: (852) 2680-8688. U.K. Telephone: 44 (171) 587-3683. Web site: www.scmp.com.

Western Investor. 501-1155 W. Pender Street, Vancouver, BC. V6E 2P4 Canada. Telephone: (604) 669-8500. Fax: (604) 669-2154. E-mail: subscribe @western investor.com. Web site: www.westerninvestor.com. Monthly tabloid covering commercial real estate, franchises, and business opportunities in Western Canada.

Wall Street Journal. Daily U.S. financial and business newspaper. United States, European and Asian editions. Palo Alto, CA. Web site: www.wsj.com.

BANK RESOURCES

Bank Web Sites Worldwide. Web site: www.qualisteam.com.

Thomas Bank Directory, World Bank Directory (edition), Accuity Solutions, 4709 W. Gold Road, Suite 600, Skokie, IL 60076-1253. Telephone: (847) 676-9600. Fax: (847) 933-8101. E-mail: custserv@AccuitySolutions.com. Web site: www.accuitysolutions.com.

To verify the financial standing of a bank you are interested in doing business with, visit www.fitchratings.com.

ANTISURVEILLANCE AND PRIVACY SOURCES

In the spirit of keeping up with the opposition, here are some fun materials and contacts for keeping your privacy:

The Covert Catalog by Lee Lapin. 1999. Intelligence Incorporated, 3555 S. El Camino Real, San Mateo, CA 94403. The ultimate guide to surveillance, antisurveillance, covert entry, and investigative equipment suppliers.

Eye Spy magazine. The international intelligence magazine. Stay abreast of the activities of the latest terror cells, the intelligence agencies of the world, surveillance and counterespionage tactics and developments, and more. A U.S. subscription to this slick monthly is U.S. $48. In the United States, call Toll free (877) 309-9243, in England call (44) 01756-770199. E-mail: editor@eyespymag.com. Web site: www.eyespymag.com.

The Spy Store. They claim to be the world's largest spy equipment supplier at the lowest prices. The Spy Store Inc., 12128 N. Division Street, Suite 155, Spokane, WA 99218. Telephone: (509) 238-5094. Fax: (509) 238-5124. E-mail: info@thespystore.com.

Underground Database. 1993. Index Publishing Group, 3368 Govenor Drive, Suite 273F, San Diego, CA 92122. A covert little manual of more resources, suppliers, and publishers of grey market goodies.

The Whole Spy Catalog by Lee Lapin. 1995. Intelligence Incorporated. A resource encyclopedia on all things for spying and counterspying.

BOOKS OF INTEREST

Here are some good books about the powers behind-the-scenes that are affecting our daily lives and liberties:

America's Secret Establishment: An Introduction to the Order of Skull and Bones by Antony C. Sutton. Trine Day. 2002. PO Box 577, Walterville, OR 97489. This book explores the secret order of which the Bush family are members.

Body of Secrets by James Bamford. Doubleday, New York. 2001. More on the secretive National Security Agency (NSA).

The Case against the Global Economy. Edited by Jerry Mander and Edward Goldsmith. Sierra Book Club Books, San Francisco, CA. 1996.

The Puzzle Palace by James Bamford. Penquin Group, New York. 1983. Inside look at the secretive National Security Agency (NSA).

Rule by Secrecy by Jim Marrs. HarperCollins, New York. 2001. This is a must read.

The Secret History of the CIA by Joseph J. Trento. Prima Publishing, Roseville, CA. 2001. The title says it all.

The Secret Society Handbook by Michael Bradley. Barnes and Noble, New York. 2004. Your pocket guide to secret societies. A nice overview of many secret societies influencing the world today.

The Swiss Banks by T. R. Fehrenbach. McGraw-Hill, New York. 1966. Enlightening reading on the history of Swiss banking.

Books on Freedom and Privacy

Hiding Your Money by Jerome Schneider. Prima Publishing, Roseville, CA. 2000. Ways to squirrel your valuables and money away from all predators.

How I Found Freedom in an Unfree World by Harry Browne. Avon Books, New York. 1974. The ideas still apply. Think out of the box.

Mark Skousen's Complete Guide to Financial Privacy. Alexandria House Books, 1979. 901 N. Washington, Alexandria, VA 22314. Somewhat outdated, but areas covered are still areas of concern today.

My Country Is the World by Garry Davis. G.P. Putnam's Sons, New York. 1961. The author is founder of World Service Authority and has an interesting personal story of individual sovereignty.

No Place to Hide by Robert O'Harrow Jr. Free Press, New York. 2005/2006. The dark side of the Digital Age.

The Sovereign Individual by James Dale Davidson and Lord William Rees-Mogg. Simon & Schuster, New York. 1997. Learn why citizens of high-tax countries are leaving in record numbers.

Unwarranted Intrusions: The Case against Government Intervention in the Marketplace by Martin Fridson. John Wiley & Sons, Hoboken, NJ. 2006. Web site: www.wiley.com.

Your House Is under Arrest by Brenda Grantland, President of Forfeiture Endangers American Rights (FEAR). Visit www.fear.org.

Here are a couple books that will give you an insight into international crime and money laundering today:

Illicit by Moises Naim, editor of Foreign Policy. Doubleday, New York. 2005. About the international black market.

The Merger by Jeffrey Robinson. Overlook Press, Woodstock, NY. 2000. Mr. Robinson, also author of *The Laundreymen,* explores the expanding international crime scene and its growing consolidation.

The Secret Money Market by Ingo Walter. Harper & Row, New York. 1990. Mr. Walter has made a science of the subjects of tax evasion, financial fraud, insider trading, money laundering, and capital flight.

Investment and Economic Books

The Coming Collapse of the Dollar and How to Profit from It: Make a Fortune by Investing in Gold and Other Hard Assets by James Turk and John Rubino. Doubleday, New York. 2004. Visit www.dollarcollapse.com.

Empire of Debt by Bill Bonner and Addison Wiggin. John Wiley & Sons, Hoboken, NJ. 2006. Visit www.dollarcollapse.com.

Financial Reckoning Day: Surviving the Soft Depression of the 21st Century by Bill Bonner and Addison Wiggin. John Wiley & Sons, Hoboken, NJ. A *Wall Street Journal* best seller.

International Real Estate Handbook by Christian H. Kalin. John Wiley & Sons, Customer Service Department, 1 Oldlands Way, Bognor Regis, West Sussex PO 22 9SA England, U.K. Telephone: (44) 1243-843294. Fax: (44) 1243-843296. E-mail: cs-books@wiley.co. Web site: www.wiley.com. U.S. $199.

Switzerland Business & Investment Handbook by Christian H. Kalin. Orell Fusseli Verlag AG. England, John Wiley & Sons. 2005. U.S. $215. Available from Orell Fusseli Verlag AG, Auslieferung, BD Bucherdienst AG, Kobiboden, Switzerland. Telephone: 41 (0) 55-418-89-89, Fax: 41 (0) 55-418-89-19. E-mail: info@buecherdienst.ch. Web site: www.ofv.ch. U.S. $215 or visit www.wiley.com.

PUBLISHERS OF UNUSUAL BOOKS AND HARD-TO-FIND INFORMATION

Eden Press, PO Box 8410, Fountain Valley, CA 92708. Toll free (800) 338-8484. Fax: (714) 556-0721. Web site: www.EdenPress.com. Contact them for a free copy of their Privacy Catalog. Publishers and sellers of information you won't find elsewhere, including two useful directories: *The Eden Directory of Private Mail Drops in the U.S. and 90 Foreign Countries,* and *The Worldwide Maildrop Guide.*

Laissez Faire Books, 942 Howard Street, San Francisco, CA 94103. Web site: www.lfb.com. Free catalog of good books.

Scope International Ltd., Forestside House, Rowlands Castle, Hants PO9 6EE, United Kingdom. Offshore books and information.

PERIODICALS

International Herald Tribune. Excellent daily international English newspaper. Web site: www.iht.com. Recommended for international news, travel, entertainment, business, investments, more. Expats and those considering moving abroad would benefit from subscribing. Excellent journalism and good classifieds. Editorial board in Paris. Published in New York. Owned by the New York Times.

The *New Yorker* magazine has good coverage and thought-provoking articles on culture and current events. www.newyorker.com.

REAL ESTATE

Escape Artist. Web site: www.escapeartist.com.

International Living. Excellent source for real estate opportunities and information to prospective expatriates. Subscribe to their free e-mail postcards. Better yet, become a member. Web site: www.internationalliving.com.

Private Islands. Two brokers specializing in islands for sale around the world are: Morrison's Private Islands. E-mail: privateislands@yahoo.com and Vladi Private Islands. Web site: www.vladi.de.

Real Estate Worldwide. Visit www.LandandFarm.com. Also publishers of Rural Property Bulletin. Both are excellent sources for commercial, residential, acreage, country, and ranch properties.

Mr. Lief Simon. Global Real Estate Investor. Web site: www.globalrealestateinvestor.com. E-mail: Lsimon@InternationalLiving.com.

EXPAT INFORMATION

American Automobile Association (AAA). Web site: www.aaa.com/vacation/idp.html.

Expat Exchange. Information on living and working overseas. Web site: www.expatexchange.com.

Escape Artist. Living overseas, international real estate, overseas jobs, and expatriate resources. Web site: www.escapeartist.com.

Expat Network. Helpful information on overseas jobs, finance, shopping, health, travel, and more. Web site: www.expatnetwork.co.uk.

International Country Risk Guide. Edited by Tom Sealy. Political Risk Services IBC United States Publications Inc., PO Box 6482, Syracuse, NY 13217-6482. Telephone: (315) 472-1224. Fax: (315) 472-1235. Web site: www.prsgroup.com/icrg/riskdata.html.

International Living. Good source of foreign real estate opportunities and other information of interest to those considering expatriating. Web site: www.internationalliving.com. Subscribe to their free e-mail postcards. Membership recommended.

Job Search Overseas. PO Box 35, Fulmouth, Cornwall, TR11 3UB U.K. Telephone: (44) 872-870070. Fax: (44) 872-870071.

Live Abroad. Network for Living Abroad. Linking expats past, present, and future. Web site: www.liveabroad.com.

Offshore Citizen. Edited by Michael E. Addison, Promotions Plus, PO Box 337, Guelles Road, St. Peter Port, Guernsey, Channel Islands, U.K. Telephone: (44) 1481-66297. Fax: (44) 1481-66398. Web site: www.offcit.com.

Offshore Dossier: Your Passport to the World's Last Frontiers of Personal and Financial Freedom. Hoyt L. Barber. An international newsletter published six times a year available through Barber Financial Advisors, 355 Burrard Street, Suite 1000, Vancouver, BC V6C 2G8. Canada. U.S. $149 per year. Web site: www.BarberFinancialAdvisors.com.

Overseas Job Network. Premium House, Skoreham Airport, Sussex, BN43 5FF U.K. Telephone: (44) 1273-440220/440229. Web site: www.overseasjobs.com. Publishers of Overseas Employment Newsletter.

Transitions Abroad magazine. Box 3000, Danville, NJ 07834. Telephone: (413) 256-3414. Fax: (413) 256-0373. Web site: www.transabroad.com.

EXPAT BOOKS

An American's Guide to Living Abroad by Christopher Weber. Living Abroad Publishing, New York. Telephone: (212) 941-9602. Fax: (212) 941-9690.

Escape from America by Roger Gallo. Manhattan Loft Publishing, Portland, OR. 1997. Toll free: (888) 314-1592.

Tips & Traps of Going Global by Jon W. Golding. Sterling Westminster International Ltd., 178 Brompton Road, London SW3 1HQ U.K. Telephone: (44) 171-5813551. Fax: (44) 171-581-3671.

USA Citizens Abroad Handbook. USA Today Books, Washington, DC. 1988. Telephone: (703) 276-5978.

RETIREMENT RESOURCES

American Association of Retired Persons, 601 E Street, NW, Washington, DC 20049. Toll free: (800) 424-3410.

Elderhostel. Web site: www.elderhostel.org.

HEALTH INSURANCE FOR EXPATRIATES AND TRAVELERS

AARP Health Care Options. Toll free (800) 245-1212, operator 36.

Access America. Toll free (800) 955-4002.

American Express Travel Protection Plan. Toll free (800) 234-0375.

International SOS Assistance. Toll free (800) 523-6586.

Medex. Toll free (800) 537-2029.

Travel Assistance International. Toll free (800) 821-2828.

Travel Insured International. Toll free (800) 243-3174.

TravMed International Traveler's Assistance Association. Toll free (800) 732-5309.

Universal Travel Protection Insurance. Web site: www.noelgroup.com.

ORGANIZATIONS

The Cato Institute, 1000 Massachusetts Avenue, NW, Washington, DC 20001-5403. Telephone: (202) 842-0200. Fax: (202) 842-3490. Promotes limited government, individual liberty, free markets, and peace. Web site: www.cato.org. Also publishers of books on these themes.

Downsize DC.org Inc., a nonprofit educational organization co-founded by Harry Browne and Jim Babka. Visit their web site at http://www.DownsizeDC.org for more information on their ideas for promoting individual liberty, personal responsibility, free markets and small government. I wish them much success!

Forfeiture Endangers American Rights (FEAR). Web site: www.fear.org. Discover how government today is confiscating private property and assets, without due process of law, in the name of crime.

Freedom House. A country's freedom level ranked according to the Freedom Rating. Web site: www.freedomhouse.org

The Heritage Foundation and the Center for Freedom and Prosperity. Visit their web site at www.freedomandprosperity.com. They are waging an effective and ongoing counterattack against the OECD.

International Money Laundering Information Network (IMoIDN). Web site: www.imolin.org.

International Society for Individual Liberty, 836-B Southampton Road, #299, Benicia, CA 94510. Telephone: (707) 746-8796. Fax: (707) 746-8797. E-mail: isil@isil.org. Web site: www.isil.org.

The Society for Trust and Estate Practitioners. Web site: www.step.org.

The Sovereign Society, 5 Catherine Street, Waterford, Ireland. Telephone: (353) 51-844068. Fax: (353) 51-304561. E-mail: info@sovereignsociety.com. Web site: www.sovereignsociety.com. Investment author, John A. Pugsley, Chairman. Membership recommended.

World Service Authority. Headquartered in Washington, DC. Founded by Garry Davis. They issue their own passport and travel documents, which have received *de jure* and *de facto* recognition from over 150 countries since 1948. They are commonly used for emergency purposes and to assist refugees. Web site: www.worldservice.org.

GOVERNMENT WEB SITES

Background Notes. Information by country. U.S. State Dept., Washington, DC. Web site: www.state.gov/r/pa/ei/bgn.

CIA World Factbook. Country information. Central Intelligence Agency (CIA), Washington, DC. Web site: www.cia.gov/cia/publications/factbook.

Financial Action Task Force (FATF). Web site: www.fatf.org.

Financial Crimes Enforcement Network (FINCEN). Web site: www.fincen.gov.

Human Development Report. United Nations, New York, NY. Web site: www.hdr.undp.org.

National Passport Information Center. Toll free (888) 362-8668.

Organization for Economic Co-operation and Development (OECD). Web site: www.oecd.org.

U.S. Center for Disease Control and Prevention, Atlanta, GA. Toll free (877) FYI-TRIP or (877) 394-8747. Web site: www.edu.gov/travel Health advisories worldwide.

U.S. Customs. Contact them to determine what they consider to be a "negotiable instrument" before traveling. Toll free (800) 232-5378.

U.S. Government Publications Currently Available. Web site: www.bdtax.net/english/publications.htm. The U.S. Government's Explanation of International Taxation.

Visa Information Telephone: Numbers. U.S. State Dept., Washington, DC. Web site: http://travel.state.gov

Internal Revenue Service (IRS). Lots of tax information, publications and forms. Web site: www.irs.gov.

Travel Information Services. Web site: www.state.gov.

FINANCIAL AND INVESTMENT SERVICES

Visit these companies and explore their many valuable financial and investment services:

International Wire Transfers, Currency Conversion Services, Foreign Exchange, Precious Metals Certificate Programs, Bullion, Coins, and Bars

Asset Strategies International Inc., 1700 Rockville Pike, Suite 400, Rockville, MD 20852-1631. Toll free (800) 831-0007 or (301) 881-8600. Fax: (301) 881-1936. Web site: www.assetstrategies.com. Mr. Michael Checkan, President. E-mail: rcheckan@assetstrategies.com.

Investment Rarities Incorporated, James Cook, President, 7850 Metro Parkway, Minneapolis, MN 55425. Toll free (800) 328-1860. Web site: www.investmentrarities.com. Reputable, customer-oriented precious metals dealer since the 1970s. Jim is a fellow novelist.

Currency Exchange, International Wires, Foreign Drafts, Traveler's Checks, International Receipt of Funds, Forward Contracts, Coin Sets and Precious Metals, Risk Management

Custom House. Web site: www.customhouse.com or their affiliate XEtrade at www.xe.com/fx.

Gold-Backed Electronic Currencies

Alternative to using the federal banking system—and, your money is backed by gold, not worthless government promissory notes. For more information and to set up a free account in minutes, visit www.BarberFinancialAdvisors.com for more information.

Precious Metals Certificates

Perth Mint Certificate Program. To obtain more information, or to purchase a certificate, contact: Asset Strategies International Inc., 1700 Rockville Pike, Suite 400, Rockville, MD 20852-1631. Toll free (800) 831-0007. Telephone: (301) 881-8600. Fax: (301) 881-1936. E-mail: assetsi@assetstrategies.com. Web site: www.assetstrategies.com.

Offshore Physical Storage Facility

Via Mat Management AG. Head Office: Obstgartenstrasse 27, PO Box 635, CH-8302 Kloten, Switzerland. Telephone: 41 (44) 804-92-92. Fax: 41 (44) 804-92-93. E-mail: info@viamat.com. Web site: www.viamat.com.

Safes Fidelity SA, 6, place Chevelu, CH-1211 Geneva 1, Switzerland. Telephone: 41 (22) 731-78-90.

Fixed and Variable Annuities

Mr. Colin Bowen, Isle of Man Assurance Ltd., IOMA House, Hope Street, Douglas, Isle of Man IM1 1AP U.K. Telephone: 44 (1) 62-468-1200. Fax: 44 (1) 62-468-1397.

Fixed, Variable, and Private Annuities, Endowments, Portfolio Bonds, Life Insurance, Bank Accounts, Portfolio Managers, Asset Protection Techniques

Mr. Marc Sola, NMG International Financial Services Ltd., Goethestrasse 22, 8001 Zurich, Switzerland. Telephone: 41 (1) 266-21-41. Fax: 41 (1) 266-21-49. E-mail: marcsola@nmg-ifs.com. Web site: www.swissinvesting.com/nmg.

Isle of Man Trusts, Asset Protection, Tax Reduction Strategies for Americans and Hybrid Companies

Mr. Charles Cain, Director, Skye Fiduciary Consultants, Skyefid Limited, 2 Water Street, Ramsey, Isle of Man IM8 1JP British Isles, U.K. Telephone: (44) 1624-811611. Fax: (44) 1624-816645. E-mail: mail@skyefid.com. Web site: www.skyefid.com.

International Asset Management, Domestic and Global Tax Planning Services

Ms. Mary Simon, Attorney-at-Law and Tax Specialist. Mr. William Vigal, International Business Specialist. Vigal & Simon, Inc. One Union Square Building 600 University, Suite 2401, Seattle, WA 98101. Telephone: (206) 728-5150. Fax: (206) 728-5140. Web site: www.vigalsimon.com.

Asset Management for High Net Worth Individuals. Unique Strategies Utilizing Offshore Insurance Structures

Mr. Richard Colombik, International Tax Associates, 1111 Plaza Drive, Suite 430, Schaumburg, IL 60173. Telephone: (847) 619-5700. Fax: (847) 619-0971. E-mail: rcolombik@colombik.com.

Wealth Management

Mr. John Bujouves, President, Bayshore Asset Management Inc., Royal Bank Plaza, South Tower, Box 163, 200 Bay Street, Toronto, Ontario M5J 2J4. Toll free (866) 991-9982. Fax: (866) 566-4619. Web site: www.bayshorecapital.com.

Independent Portfolio Management and Swiss Banking

Mr. Adrian Hartmann/Mr. Robert Vrijhof, Weber Hartmann Vrijhof & Partners Ltd., Zurichatrasse 110B, CH-8134 Adilswil, Switzerland. Telephone: 41 (1) 709-11-15. Fax: 41 (1) 709-11-13. Minimum opening portfolio $250,000.

Swiss Personal Portfolio Management

Mrs. Daniela Casadei, Bank Julius Baer & Co., Bahnhofstrasse 36, CH-8010 Zurich, Switzerland. Telephone: 41 (58) 888-58-42. Fax: 41 (58) 888-50-23. Web site: www.juliusbaer.com. Minimum opening portfolio $500,000.

Shahab Malek-Abhari, Wealth Manager, Anker Bank Lausanne, Private Banking, Avenue de la Gare, 50, CH-1001 Lausanne, Switzerland. Telephone: 41 (0) 21-321-07-07. Fax: 41 (0) 21-321-07-98. Direct: 41 (0) 21-321-07-33. E-mail: shahabeddin.malek-abhari@ankerbank.ch. Investment Management. Minimum to establish a portfolio is U.S. $200,000. A personal visit is required.

Swiss Investment Advisor Handling Swiss Annuities, Swiss Asset Protection Certificate, Swiss Life Insurance, Swiss Portfolio Bonds, and More

Mr. Jurg M. Lattmann, JML Jurg M. Lattmann AG, Baaerstrasse 53, 6304 Zug, Switzerland. Telephone: 41 (1) 726-55-55/00. Fax: 41 (1) 726-55-90. E-mail: info@jml.ch. Web site: www.jml.ch.

Swiss Annuities

Mr. Darrell Aviss, Managing Director, SwissGuard International, GmbH, Bahnhofstrasse 52, CH-8001 Zurich, Switzerland. Telephone: 41 (1) 214-62-47. Fax: 41 (1) 214-65-19. E-mail: info@swiss-annuity.com. Web site: www.swiss-annuity.com. Toll free from the United States 1 (800) 796-7496.

Offshore Brokerage Services

Trading online in stocks, bonds, CFDs, futures, Forex, Forex funds options as well as asset management, mutual funds, asset protection, structured notes, tax-free investing—I will provide you with a personal introduction to a top-flight offshore brokerage firm where you can establish an account quickly for personal use or on behalf of your offshore corporation. Simply e-mail to my attention at BarberFinancial @hotmail.com. with your name, address, telephone and fax numbers, and your e-mail address for a prompt reply.

Global Mutual Funds

Mr. Eric Roseman, ENR Asset Management, 2 Westmount Square, Suite 1802, Quebec H3Z 2S4, Canada. Telephone: (514) 989-8027. Fax: (514) 989-7060. E-mail: enr@qc.aibn.com.

Global Markets

Mr. Neil J. George Jr., Leeb Brokerage Services, 500 Fifth Avenue, Suite 3120, New York, NY 10110. Telephone: (212) 246-3696. E-mail: njgeorge@ leeb.net.

Eurodollar Bonds

Mr. Thomas P. Azzara, Offshore Tax and Estate Planners, PO Box CB 11552, Nassau, Bahamas. Telephone: Fax: (242) 327-7359. E-mail: taxman@batelnet.bs. Web site: www.bahamasbahamas.com.

International Financial Services

Dr. Erich Stoeger, PO Box 4, A1191 Vienna, Austria. Telephone: 43 (1) 367-53-53. Fax: 43 (1) 367-53-54. E-mail: dr.stoeger@gmx.at.

Tax Haven Incorporations, Company Management, Asset Protection, Offshore Bank Accounts, Credit and Debit Cards, and the Offshore Evaluation Service

Barber Financial Advisors, 355 Burrard Street, Suite 1000, Vancouver, BC. V6C 2G8 Canada. Telephone: (604) 608-6177. Fax: (604) 608-2984. E-mail: info@BarberFinancialAdvisors.com. Web site: www .BarberFinancialAdvisors.com.

IMMIGRATION SERVICES

Saint Kitts and Nevis and Dominica Economic Citizenship Programs and Residency in Other Countries

Henley & Partners Inc., PO Box 481, 3 Church Street, Basseterre, St. Kitts, West Indies. Telephone: (869) 465-1711. Fax: (869) 465-1004. E-mail: Caribbean-office@henleyglobal.com. Web site: www.henleyglobal.com.

Henley & Partners Inc., 10 Castle Street, Commonwealth of Dominica. Telephone: (767) 449-98-00. Fax: (767) 449-97-77. E-mail:dominica-office@henleyglobal.com. Web site: www.henleyglobal.com.

Panama Immigration for Retirement or Employment

Mr. Oliver Munoz, Quijano & Associates, Attorneys-at-Law, Salduba Bldg., 3rd Floor, PO Box 0816-02884, Panama, Republic of Panama. Telephone: (507) 269-2641 or (507) 269-2743. Fax: (507) 269-2591 or (507) 263-8079. E-mail: quijano@quijano.com. Web site: www.quijano.com.

Canadian Citizenship/Residency and Offshore Strategists

Mr. David S. Lesperance, Barrister and Solicitor, 84 King Street West, Suite 202, Dundas, Ontario L9H 1T9 Canada. Telephone: (905) 627-3037. Fax: (905) 627-9868. E-mail: DSL@globalrelocate.com. Web site: www.globalrelocate.com.

Mr. David Melnik, QC, 350 Lonsdale Road, Suite 311, Toronto, Ontario M5P 1R6 Canada. Telephone: (416) 488-7918. Fax: (905) 877-7751. E-mail: dm1976cp@netcom.ca.

For additional immigration services for these and other countries, refer to the contacts in "Part Three: Today's Tax Havens" and the Appendix.

TAX PROBLEMS

I personally recommend Mr. Donald W. "Mac" MacPherson, Attorney-at-Law and author. Mac is a former Green Beret and graduate of West Point Academy. He specializes in tax law, tax/bankruptcy, offshore/tax shelters, criminal defense, civil litigation, and evaluations, with emphasis on trials and appeals. The MacPherson Group Attorneys is a nationwide network of expert lawyers. Contact him toll free at 1 (800) BeatIRS. Telephone: (800) 232-8477, (623) 209-2003. His offices are located at 7508 N. 59th Avenue, Glendale, AZ 85301. Web site: www.beatirs.com.

WORLDWIDE SERVICED OFFICES

HQ Business Offices. Affiliated with Regus. Web site: www.hq.com. Toll free (800) 956-9543. Regus. Web site: www.regus.com. Toll free (888) 271-4615. 750 locations worldwide.

Instant Offices Ltd. Web site: www.instant-offices.com. Toll free (866) 918-4640. 5000 locations worldwide.

World Office Network, 29 Harley Street, London W1G 9QR U.K. Telephone: 44 (207) 255-2557. Fax: 44 (207) 637-0419. E-mail: info@worldofficenetwork.com. Web site: www.worldofficenetwork.com. 26 locations.

GLOBAL MAIL DROPS

Web site: www.escapeartist.com/global/maildrops.htm.

INTERNATIONAL ENGLISH LANGUAGE NEWSPAPERS

Links to newspapers worldwide published in English or with English editions. Good source for local, national, business, news, jobs, business opportunities, real estate, and more. Web site: www.thebigpicture.co.uk/news.

News Links. More than eighteen thousand newspapers and other news services worldwide. Web site: www.abyzNewsLinks.com.

The Paper Boy. Over six thousand newspapers online worldwide. Web site: www.paperboy.com.

ONLINE RESOURCES

Financial Times World Reference Desk. Country information and statistics. Web site: www.dk.com/world-deskreference.

Information by Country. Usernet newsgroup(s)—soc.culture.(name of country).

International Calling Codes. Country and city codes. Web site: www.the-acr.com/codes/cntrycd.htm.

Offshore Tax Information. Web site: www.cifa.an.

Reference Desk. Great site with hundreds of links to every imaginable information source. Web site: www.refdesk.com.

GOVERNMENT PUBLICATIONS

Organisations for Economic Cooperation and Development (OECD). Web site: www.oecdbookshop.org.

United Nations (UN) Publications. Web site: www.UN.org.

OFFSHORE DOSSIER

Offshore Dossier: Your Passport to the World's Last Frontiers of Personal and Financial Freedom. Hoyt L. Barber. Available six times a year through Barber

Financial Advisors, 355 Burrard Street, Suite 1000, Vancouver, BC V6C 2G8 Canada. U.S. $149 a year. E-mail address required for subscription. Web site: www.BarberFinancialAdvisors.com. The best way to stay on top of the subjects covered by this book, including critical new offerings and changes in the areas of offshore and Swiss banks, banking services, offshore business and e-commerce, lucrative and safe investments, financial and investment strategies, offshore tax angles, asset protection, tax haven countries, offshore citizenship programs and permanent residency, expatriating, money laundering, foreign business opportunities, offshore and foreign real estate, and Hoyt Barber's T-7 rating of tax havens. Complete with sources and contact information. Free e-mail alert service of any breaking developments that would be of interest to readers or have a potential effect on them.

OFFSHORE EVALUATION SERVICE

The Offshore Evaluation Service (OES) is provided by Barber Financial Advisors as an efficient and economical means of providing reliable offshore information and recommendations for readers seeking offshore financial sources and professionals. We evaluate the reader's current situation, needs, and interest in going offshore based on information provided and then furnish appropriate qualified contacts, referrals, and recommendations to achieve their goals.

The service covers banks and banking services; investments; financial, tax, and estate planning; asset protection; offshore citizenship programs; offshore business and e-commerce; tax havens; professionals and more. OES is an excellent shortcut through the myriad information and sources put forth in the field, much of which is inaccurate or unreliable, and put you in immediate contact with the right information and reputable professionals and institutions. For more information, visit www.BarberFinancialAdvisors.com.

OFFSHORE FINANCIAL SERVICES

Barber Financial Advisors, Vancouver, BC, provides tax haven incorporations, company management, asset protection, offshore bank accounts, prepaid Visa cards, offshore credit cards, gold-backed electronic currency accounts, offshore brokerage services, and in conjunction with others, professional and financial specialists, and provision of other offshore services worldwide. Specializing in the T-7 tax havens. Visit their web site at www.BarberFinancialAdvisors.com.

APPENDIX

IMPORTANT INVESTMENT, BUSINESS, AND LEGAL ADVISORS: CONTACTS IN NON-TAX HAVEN COUNTRIES

CANADA

Hoyt L. Barber
President
Barber Financial Advisors
355 Burrard Street, Suite 1000
Vancouver, BC V6C 2G8
Telephone: (604) 608-6177
Fax: (604) 608-2984 or (604) 608-6163
E-mail: Info@BarberFinancialAdvisors.com,
BarberFinancial@hotmail.com
Web site: www.BarberFinancialAdvisors.com
Tax Haven Incorporations/Company Management/Asset Protection/
Offshore Bank Accounts/Credit and Debit Cards/and the Offshore
Evaluation Service

Bayshore Wealth Management Corporation
BCE Place, Bay Wellington Tower
181 Bay Street, Suite 2800
Toronto, ON M5J 2T3
Telephone: (416) 642-2274
Fax: (416) 214-0919
E-mail: john@bayshorecapital.com
Web site: www.bayshorecapital.com
Asset Management/Private Banking/International Estate and
Tax Planning

B. G. Bergh Law Corporation
PO Box 638
Salmon Arm, BC V1E 4N7
Telephone: (250) 832-8084
Fax: (250) 832-5303
E-mail: law@bergh.bc.ca
International Estate Planning

The Corporate Group
357 Bay Street #900
Toronto, ON, M5H 2T7
Telephone: (416) 362-9949
Fax: (416) 369-0129
Offshore Incorporations/Trusts/International Tax Planning

David Lesperance, Barrister & Solicitor
c/o Global Relocation Consultants S.A.
84 King Street West, Suite 202
Dundas, Ontario L9H 1T9
Telephone: (905) 627-3037
Fax: (905) 627-9868
E-mail: DSL@globalrelocate.com
Web site: www.globalrelocate.com
Canadian Immigration/Offshore Financial Advisor

David Melnik, QC
350 Lonsdale Road, Suite 311
Toronto, Ontario M5P 1R6
Telephone: (416) 488-7918
Fax: (905) 877-7751
E-mail: dm1976cp@netcom.ca
Assistant: Carol Bruce
Telephone: (905) 877-3156
Canadian Immigration/Offshore Financial Advisors

Derek Sambrook
Trust Services Ltd.
Balboa Plaza, Suite 522
Avenida Balboa, Panama, Republic of Panama
Mailing address: Apartado 0832-1630, World Trade Center
Panama, Republic of Panama
Telephone: (507) 269-2438
Fax: (507) 269-4922
E-mail: Sambrook@trustserv.com

Web site: www.trustserv.com
Offshore Immigration Trusts for Canadian Immigration/Trust and Estate Planning and Management of Offshore Financial Institutions

Eric Roseman
President
Emerald Analytical Services Inc.
Two Westmount Square, Suite 1802
Westmount, PQ H3Z 2S4
Toll free: (877) 989-8027
Telephone: (514) 989-8027
Fax: (514) 989-7060
E-mail: enr@qc.aibn.com
Web site: www.eas.ca
Global Asset Allocation/Portfolio Management

Globacor Consultants Corporation
c/o 66 Kingsway Crescent
Toronto, ON, M8X 2R6
Telephone: (416) 214-6800
Fax: (416) 207-8502
E-mail: globacor@consultant.com
Establishment and Management of Offshore Financial Institutions

H. Arnold Sherman Professional Corporation
Suite 805, 808 Fourth Avenue SW
Calgary, AB, T2P 3E8
Telephone: (403) 269-8833
Fax: (403) 269-8921
E-mail: arnoldsherman@telus.net
International Tax Planning

Hendler, Douglas
Aylesworth Thompson Phelan O'Brien LLP
Ernst & Young Tower, Toronto-Dominion Center
PO Box 124, 18th Floor, 222 Bay Street
Toronto, ON M5K 1H1
Telephone: (416) 777-4024
Fax: (416) 865-0101
Asset Protection/Estate Planning

H.O. Financial Services Inc.
1067 Yonge Street
Toronto, ON, M4W 2L2

Telephone: (416) 925-5504
Fax: (416) 925-8192
Financial Planning for High Net Worth Individuals

Holmes Greenslade, Barristers & Solicitors
1880-1066, W. Hastings Street
Vancouver, BC, V6E 3X1
Telephone: (604) 688-7861
Fax: (604) 688-0426
Offshore and Financial Law Firm

Law Offices of Gordon L. Jacobs
73 Mutual Street
Toronto, ON, M5B 2A9
Telephone: (416) 981-0901
Fax: (416) 981-0993
International Wealth Preservation

PricewaterhouseCoopers LLP
3100, 111 Fifth Avenue SW
Calgary, AB, T2T 5L3
Telephone: (403) 509-7584
Fax: (403) 781-1825
Offshore Financial and Accounting Advisors

Prime Quadrant
18 Dewbourne Avenue
Toronto, ON, M5P 124
Telephone: (416) 822-4554
Fax: (416) 352-6116
E-mail: ianros@primequad.com
Web site: www.primequad.com
International Financial Planning

Shibaev Enterprises
7111 Appleby Line
Milton, ON, L9T 2Yl
Telephone: (416) 605-3541
Fax: (905) 875-0910
E-mail: sshibaev@wwdb.org
International Financial Planning

UNITED KINGDOM

ADM Investor Services International Limited
10th Floor, Temple Court
11 Queen Victoria Street
London EC4N 4TJ
Telephone: 44 (020) 7390-2952
Fax: 44 (020) 7294-0229
E-mail: eddie.tofpik@admisi.com
Web site: www.admisi.com
Serving Investors Around the Clock Worldwide in Foreign Exchange, Commodities, Equities, and Options

Albany Systems Group
Wellington Building
28–32 Wellington Road
London NW8 9SP
Telephone: 44 (020) 7483-9275
Fax: 44 (020) 7483-9276
E-mail: info@albany-systems.com
Web site: www.albany-systems.com
International Tax Planning

Appleby Spurling & Kempe
2nd Floor, 1 Royal Exchange Buildings
London EC3V 3LF
Telephone: 44 (020) 7283-6061
Fax: 44 (020) 7469-0540
E-mail: london@ask.bm
Legal Services in Financing, Partnerships, Trusts, E-Commerce, Offshore

Atteys
Regent House, 50 Moorgate Street
Rotherham
South Yorkshire S602EY
Telephone: 44 (01709) 834200
Fax: 44 (01709) 830808
Incorporation/Individual Tax Emigration

B.C. Business Centrum Limited
788–790 Finchley Road
London NW11 7TJ

Telephone: 44 (020) 8201-8998
Fax: 44 (020) 8201-9448
E-mail: bc@centrum-uk.com
Web site: www.centrum-uk.com
Incorporation/Management/U.K. and Offshore

BDO Stoy Hayward
Emerald House, East Street
Epsom, Surrey, KT17 1HS
Telephone: 44 (01372) 734300
Fax: 44 (01372) 734301
E-mail: andy.wells@bdo.co.uk.com
Consultant on Tax Aspects of Expatriation

Beder-Harrison & Co.
78 Marylebone Lane
London W1U 2PT
Telephone: 44 (020) 7486-3660
Fax: 44 (020) 7486-3860
U.K. Immigration

Belgravia Group International
L7 Tower 42
25 Old Broad Street
London EC2N 1HN
Telephone: 44 (020) 7877-4004
Fax: 44 (020) 7877-0708
E-mail: peter@belgravia-group.com
International Financial Planning

The Bonalbo Group
Suite 38/40, London Fruit Exchange, Brushfield Street
London, E1 6EU
Telephone: 44 (020) 7247-2825
Fax: 44 (020) 7247-8052
E-mail: uk@bonalbo.com
Offshore Incorporations/Management/Trusts/Tax and Accounting

Boodle Hatfield
61 Brook Street
London W1K 4BL
Telephone: 44 (020) 7629-7411
Fax: 44 (020) 7629-2621

E-mail: law@boodlehatfield.com
Web site: www.boodlehatfield.com
Offshore Trust Specialist

Campbell Hooper
35 Old Queen Street
London, SW1H 9JD
Telephone: 44 (020) 7222-9070
Fax: 44 (020) 7222-5591
E-mail: alexcuppage@campbellhooper.com
Web site: www.campbellhooper.com
Legal and Tax Advice

Charles Cain
Skye Fiduciary Consultants
Skydid Limited
2 Water Street
Ramsey, Isle of Man IM8 1JP, British Isles
Telephone: 44 (1624) 811611
Fax: 44 (1624) 816645
E-mail: mail@skyefid.com
Web site: www.skyefid.com
Isle of Man Trusts/Hybrid Companies/Strategies for U.S. Persons

Charts (Chartered Accountants)
17–19 Church Road
Northfield, Birmingham, B31 2JZ
Telephone: 44 (0121) 477-3533
Fax: 44 (0121) 476-3925
E-mail: mbrown@chartax.com
International Accountants/Tax Advisors

Citroen Wells
Devonshire House, 1 Devonshire Street
London, W1W 5DR
Telephone: 44 (020) 7304-2000
Fax: 44 (020) 7304-2020
E-mail: cw@citroenwells.co.uk
Web site: www.citroenwells.co.uk
Offshore Company and Trust Administration/International Tax Planning

Colin Bowen
Isle of Man Assurance Ltd.

IOMA House, Hope Street
Douglas, Isle of Man IM1 1AP
Telephone: 44 (1) 62-468-1200
Fax: 44 (1) 62-468-1397
Fixed and Variable Annuities

Compass Group International
64 Knightsbridge
London SW1X 7JF
Telephone: 44 (20) 7590-9600
Fax: 44 (20) 7590-9601
E-mail: info@compassgroupintl.com
Web site: www.compassgroupintl.com
Asset Management

Creaseys Tax Consulting
12 Lonsdale Gardens, Tunbridge Wells
Kent TN4 9QU
Telephone: 44 (01892) 546-546
Fax: 44 (01892) 542-622
E-mail: tax advice@creaseys.co.uk
International Taxation Specialists

Credo Management Services Limited
3rd Floor, 33 Margaret Street
London, W1G 0JD
Telephone: 44 (020) 7291-3200
Fax: 44 (020) 7291-3290
E-mail: power@credogroup.com
Swiss Incorporations/Management/Trusts

Crown Dewhurst LLP
51 Lafone Street
London, SE1 2LX
Telephone: 44 (020) 7403-0787
Fax: 44 (020) 7403-6693
E-mail: info@chowndewhurst.com
International Tax and Financial Planning

David Tweedie Associates
Darnley House, 31 Oxberry Avenue
London, SW6 5SP

Tel/Fax: 44 (020) 7736-5644
E-mail: dtweedie41@aol.com
English Lawyers

Farrer & Co.
66 Lincoln's Inn Fields
London WC2A 3LH
Telephone: 44 (020) 7242-2022
Fax: 44 (020) 7242-9899
E-mail: enquiries@farrer.co.uk
Web site: www.farrer.co.uk
U.K. and Offshore Trusts/Tax Advice

Farrington Webb
12A Marlborough Place
Brighton, BN1 1WN
Telephone: 44 (01273) 600-311
Fax: 44 (01273) 687037
Trusts/Wills/U.K. Inheritance Tax Planning

Fladgate Fielder
25 North Row
London, W1K 6DJ
Telephone: 44 (020) 7323-4747
Fax: 44 (020) 7629-4414
E-mail: amckenzie@fladgate.com
Legal Advice on U.K. and Offshore Tax, Trust, and Other Structures

Francis Jordan and Co.
3 Limpsfield Road
South Croydon, CR2 9LA
Telephone: 44 (0870) 443-8212
Fax: 44 (0870) 443-8213
E-mail: info@francisjordan.co.uk
Incorporation/Tax Services/Accounting

Global Fund Analysis
Fortune House, 7 Stratton Street
Mayfair, London, W1J 8LE
Telephone: 44 (020) 7355-2000
Fax: 44 (020) 7355-2300
E-mail: info@globalfundanalysis.com
Offshore Investment Advice

Goldsworth, John, LLB, LLM
The Mill Office
Wendens Ambo
Saffron Walden, Essex
Nr Cambridge CB11 4JX
Telephone: 44 (1799) 541152
Fax: 44 (1799) 541972
E-mail: trusts@dial.pipex.com
or
Goldsworth Chambers, 1st Floor South
10/11 Gray's Inn Square
London WC1R 5JD
Telephone: 44 (020) 7405-7117
Fax: 44 (020) 7831-8308
E-mail: trust@dial.pipex.com
A Principal of Compass Asset Management

Gray's Inn Tax Chambers
Gray's Inn Chambers, Gray's Inn
London, WC1R 5JA
Telephone: 44 (020) 7242-2642
Fax: 44 (020) 7831-9017
E-mail: grundy@itpa.org
International Tax Advice

Herbert Smith
Exchange House, Primrose Street
London, EC2A 2HS
Telephone: 44 (020) 7374-8000
Fax: 44 (020) 7374-0888
U.K. and Offshore Tax Advice

Immigration Advisory Service
190 Great Dover Street
London, SEE 4YB
Telephone: 44 (020) 7357-7511
Fax: 44 (020) 7403-5857
Web site: www.iasuk.org
Securing U.K. Residence Status

International Company Formations Ltd.
International House
31 Church Road

Hendon, London, NW4 4EB
Telephone: 44 (020) 8202-2333
Fax: 44 (020) 8202-2777
E-mail: accessco@btclick.com
Incorporation/Management/U.K. and Offshore

International Law Systems Limited
3rd Floor, 45–47 Cornhill
London, EC3V 3PD
Telephone: 44 (020) 7623-2288
Fax: 44 (020) 7623-2299
E-mail: ilslondon@ils-world.com
Web site: www.ils-world.com
Offshore Incorporations and Management

International Registries (U.K.) Ltd.
Northumbrian House, 2nd Floor
14 Devonshire Square
London, EC2M 4YT
Telephone: 44 (020) 7247-8782
Fax: 44 (020) 7247-8771
E-mail: London@register-iri.com
Incorporation/Management/Maritime Services

International Tax Solutions
105 Baker Street
London, W1U 6NY
Telephone: 44 (020) 7487-3493
Fax: 44 (020) 7935-5087
E-mail: info@internationaltaxsolutions.com
Expatriate Tax and Financial Services

Intertrust (U.K.) Limited
No. 2 Babmaes Street
London, SW1Y 6NT
Telephone: 44 (020) 7930-7111
Fax: 44 (020) 7930-7444
E-mail: paolodifilippo@intertrustgroup.com
International Trust Services

Intrust Ltd.
38 Wigmore Street
London, W1O 2HA

Telephone: 44 (020) 7467-4000
Fax: 44 (020) 7467-4081
Offshore Incorporations/Management/International Tax Planning

James McNeile, Solicitor
Farrer & Co
66 Lincoln's Inn Fields
London, WC2A 3LH
Telephone: 44 (020) 7242-2022
Fax: 44 (020) 7242-9899
E-mail: enquiries@farrer.co.uk
U.K. Residency and Taxation

Jeffreys Henry
Finsgate, 5/7 Cranwood Street
London, EC1V 9EE
Telephone: 44 (020) 7309-2222
Fax: 44 (020) 7309-2309
E-mail: adb@jeffreyshenry.com
Offshore Incorporations and Financial Strategies

John Sturgeon, JD
Telephone: 44 (1624) 617050
Fax: 44 (1624) 617051
E-mail: Dakota@enterprise.net
U.S. Attorney/Offshore Assistance

Jordans Limited
21 St. Thomas Street
Bristol, BS1 6JS
Telephone: 44 (0117) 923-0600
Fax: 44 (0117) 923-0063
E-mail: international@jordans.co.uk
Web site: www.jordans.uk.com
Incorporation/Management/Trusts/Accounting/United Kingdom and Offshore

Lawrence Graham
190 Strand
London, WC2R 1JN
Telephone: 44 (020) 7379-0000
Fax: 44 (020) 7379-6854
E-mail: info@lawgram.com

Web site: www.lawgram.com
Wealth Preservation/Trusts/Tax Advice

Mary Tait, Investment Manager
Lorne House Trust Limited
Lorne House, Castletown, Isle of Man, British Isles IM9 1AZ
Telephone: 44 (0) 1624-822952
E-mail: general@lorne-house.com
Web site: www.lorne-house.com
Founded in 1982 by Ronald Buchanan
Investment Management/Trust and Corporate Services

Macfarlanes
10 Norwich Street
London, EC4A 1BD
Telephone: 44 (020) 7831-9222
Fax: 44 (020) 7831-9607
E-mail: john.rhodes@macfarlanes.com
Wealth Preservation Strategies

Maitland International (Maitland & Co., Consulting Division)
5th Floor, 44–48 Dover Street
London, W1S 4NX
Telephone: 44 (020) 7344-7500
Fax: 44 (020) 7344-7555
E-mail: London@maitlandco.com
Web site: www.maitlandgroup.com
International Accounting Services

Marshall J. Langer, JD
c/o Shutts & Bowen
43 Upper Grosvenor Street
London W1X 9PG
Telephone: 44 (171) 493-4840
Fax: 44 (171) 493-4299
E-mail: mjlanger@aol.com
International Tax Specialist

Mayer, Brown, Rowe & Maw
11 Pilgrim Street
London, EC4V 6RW
Telephone: 44 (020) 7248-4282
Fax: 44 (020) 7248-2009

E-mail: London@eu.mayerbrownrowe.com
International Corporate Finance/Legal

MeesPierson Intertrust Ltd.
2 Babmaes Street
London, SW1Y 6NT
Telephone: 44 (020) 7930-7111
Fax: 44 (020) 7930-7444
Private Banking and Trust Services

Mills & Reeve
Francis House, 3/7 Redwell Street
Norwich, Norfolk, NR2 4TJ
Telephone: 44 (01603) 660155
Fax: 44 (01603) 633027
Offshore Tax Planning

Moore Stephens
St. Paul's House, Warwick Lane
London, EC4P 4BN
Telephone: 44 (020) 7334-9191
Fax: 44 (020) 7248-3408
E-mail: postmaster@moorestephens.com
International Tax Planning for the Wealthy

Morgan & Morgan
20–22 Queen Street, Meadows House
Mayfair, London, W1J 5PR
Telephone: 44 (020) 7493-1978
Fax: 44 (020) 7493-1979
E-mail: London@morimor.com.
Offshore Incorporations/Management/Fiduciary/Tax Strategies

Morton Fisher
5 Center Court, Vine Lane
Halesowen, West Midlands, B63 3EB
Telephone: 44 (0121) 550-0777
Fax: 44 (0121) 550-6888
E-mail: alan.neal@mfsolicitors.com
Offshore Trusts/Legal Specialists in Taxation and Finance

Mundays
Cedar House
78 Portsmouth Road

Cobham, Surrey, KT11 1AN
Telephone: 44 (01932) 590500
Fax: 44 (01932) 590220
E-mail: hub@mundays.co.uk
Comprehensive Corporate & Commercial Law/Private Wealth Preservation

Newton Investment Management
71 Queen Victoria Street
London, EC4V 4DR
Telephone: 44 (020) 7332-9000
Fax: 44 (020) 7332-5532
Global Discretionary Wealth Management

Nicholson Graham & Jones
110 Cannon Street
London, EC4N 6AR
Telephone: 44 (020) 7648-9000
Fax: 44 (020) 7648-9001
E-mail: info@ngj.co.uk
Web site: www.ngj.co.uk
U.K. and International Tax Planning

Paris Smith & Randall
Number 1 London Road
Southampton, SO15 2AE
Telephone: 44 (023) 8048-2482
Fax: 44 (023) 8063-1835
Offshore Trusts/Offshore Investments

Pearse Trust International Limited
4th Floor, Queens House
55–56 Lincoln's Inn Fields
London, WC2A 3LJ
Telephone: 44 (020) 7421-7733
Fax: 44 (020) 7421-7711
E-mail: info@pearse-trustint.com
Web site: www.pearse-trust.ie
U.K. and Offshore Incorporations/Trusts

Penningtons
Bucklersbury House
83 Cannon Street
London, EC4N 8PE

Telephone: 44 (020) 7457-3000
Fax: 44 (020) 7457-3240
U.K. and Offshore Trusts/Tax Advice

Pinsent Curtis Biddle
3 Colmore Circus
Birmingham, B4 6BH
Telephone: 44 (0121) 200-1050
Fax: 44 (0121) 626-1046
E-mail: stephen.pallister@pinsents.com
International Tax Planning/Offshore Investments

PricewaterhouseCoopers
1 Embankment Place
London, WC2N 6RH
Telephone: 44 (020) 7804-5260
Fax: 44 (020) 7804-2299
E-mail: peter.cussons@uk.pwcglobal.com
International Tax and Legal Advisors

Proform Offshore Limited
Thurston House, 80 Lincoln Road
Peterborough, PE1 2SN
Telephone: 44 (01733) 763023
Fax: 44 (020) 7900-2523
E-mail: sales@proform.co.uk
Web site: www.proform.co.uk
Offshore Incorporations/Management

Radcliffes Le Brasseur
5 Great College Street, Westminster
London, SW1P 3SJ
Telephone: 44 (020) 7222-7040
Fax: 44 (020) 7222-6208
U.K. and Offshore Trusts Tax and Financial Planning

Rawlinson & Hunter
Eagle House, 110 Jermyn Street
London, SW1Y 6RH
Telephone: 44 (020) 7451-9000
Fax: 44 (020) 7451-9090
E-mail: james.kelly@rawlinson-hunter.com
U.K. and Offshore Tax and Financial Advice/Legal

Richard Kennedy Guelff
371 Wimbledon Park Road
London, SW19 6PE
Telephone: 44 (020) 8788-9282
Fax: 44 (020) 8789-2454
Offshore Trusts/Legal

Rooks Rider
Challoner House
19 Clerkenwell Close
London, EC1R ORR
Telephone: 44 (020) 7689-7000
Fax: 44 (020) 7689-7001
E-mail: lawyers@rooksrider.co.uk
Offshore Trusts/International Tax Planning

Sarasin Investment Management Limited
Sarasin House, 37–39 St. Andrew's Hill
London, EC4V 5DD
Telephone: 44 (020) 7236-3366
Fax: 44 (020) 7248-0173
International Investment Management

Schnecker Van Syk & Pearson
3rd Floor, Prince Rupert House
64 Queen Street
London, EC4R 1AD
Telephone: 44 (020) 7329-2600
Fax: 44 (020) 7329-2601
International Law Firm/Management and Financial Strategies

Sherman & Partners, Chartered Accountants
Suite 4, Harcourt House
19A Cavendish Square
London, W1M 9AD
Telephone: 44 (020) 7290-0100
Fax: 44 (020) 7290-0101
E-mail: steven@shermanandpartners.com
U.K. Tax Strategists

Simmons & Simmons
CityPoint, 1 Ropemaker Street
London, EC2Y 9SS

Telephone: 44 (020) 7628-2020
Fax: 44 (020) 7628-2070
International Tax and Legal Advisors

Somers Baker Prince Kurz
Premier House
45 Ealing Road
Wembley, Middlesex, HAO 4BA
Telephone: 44 (020) 8903-0337
Fax: 44 (020) 8795-2240
E-mail: support@sbpk.co.uk
Incorporation/Management/Offshore Structures/U.K. and Ireland

Sothebys, Tax & Heritage Department
34–35 New Bond Street
London, W1A 2AA
Telephone: 44 (020) 7293-5335
Fax: 44 (020) 7293-5965
E-mail: jamie.jowitt@sothebys.com
Art Experts

Sovereign Corporate & Fiscal Services Limited
40 Craven Street
London, WC2N 5NG
Telephone: 44 (020) 7389-0555
Fax: 44 (020) 7930-1151
E-mail: uk@sovereigngroup.com
Web site: www.sovereigngroup.com
Offshore Tax Strategies

Stephenson Harwood
One, St. Paul's Churchyard
London, EC4M 8SH
Telephone: 44 (020) 7329-4422
Fax: 44 (020) 7606-0822
E-mail: info@shlegal.com
Web site: www.shlegal.com
International Legal and Financial Services

Stikeman, Elliott
Dauntsey House
4B Fredericks Place
London, EC2R 8AB

Telephone: 44 (020) 7367-0150
Fax: 44 (020) 7367-0160
International Canadian Law Firm

Totalserve Management Limited
Queens House, 180 Tottenham Court Road
London, W1T 7PD
Telephone: 44 (020) 7907-1455
Fax: 44 (020) 7907-1456
E-mail: London@totalservecy.com
Web site: www.totalservecy.com
Incorporation/Management/Trusts/Fiduciary

Trident Trust Company (U.K.) Limited
7 Welbeck Street
London, W1G 9YE
Telephone: 44 (020) 7935-1503
Fax: 44 (020) 7935-7242
E-mail: uk@tridenttrust.com
Web site: www.tridenttrust.com
Offshore Incorporations/Trusts/Fund Structuring/Offices Worldwide

Turcan Connell
Princes Exchange, 1 Earl Grey Street
Edinburgh, EH3 9EE
Telephone: 44 (0131) 228-8111
Fax: 44 (0131) 228-8118
Offshore Tax Specialists

Union Bancaire Privee
26 St. James's Square
London, SW1Y 4JH
Telephone: 44 (020) 7369-1350
Fax: 44 (020) 7369-0460
Private Banking

Wedlake Bell
16 Bedford Street, Convent Garden
London, WC2E 9HF
Telephone: 44 (020) 7395-3000
Fax: 44 (020) 7836-9966
E-mail: legal@wedlakebell.com

Web site: www.wedlakebell.com
Offshore Legal Services

Withers
16 Old Bailey
London, EC4M 7EG
Telephone: 44 (020) 7597-6000
Fax: 44 (020) 7597-6543
Web site: www.withers.worldwide.com
International Estate Planning

Wright Vigar & Co.
15 Newland,
Lincoln, LN1 1XG
Telephone: 44 (01522) 531341
Fax: 44 (01522) 546286
E-mail: Richard@wrightvigar.co.uk
Offshore Companies/Offshore Trusts

Wrigleys
19 Cookridge Street
Leeds, LS2 3AG
Telephone: 44 (0113) 244-6100
Fax: 44 (0113) 244-6101
Offshore Trusts

UNITED STATES

AJ Robbins, PC
216 16th Street, Suite 600
Denver, CO 80202
Telephone: (303) 321-1281
Fax: (303) 321-1288
E-mail: aj@ajrobbins.com
International Tax Preparation

Allen, Atkin & Clarkson LLC
1240 E. 1000 So. #10
St. George, UT 84760
Telephone: (435) 673-7603
Fax: (435) 656-0809
E-mail: jratkin@infowest.com
Asset Protection and Tax Strategies

Altheimer & Gray
One Bush Street, Suite 1200
San Francisco, CA 94104
Telephone: (415) 262-8650
Fax: (415) 262-8601
E-mail: Taylorg@Altheimer.com
Wealth Management/Global Tax Strategies/International Business Law

Arnold S. Goldstein & Associates P.A.
384 S. Military Trail
Deerfield Beach, FL 33442
Telephone: (954) 420-4990
Fax: (954) 698-0057
E-mail: asgoldstein@asgoldstein.com.
Offshore and Onshore Asset Protection/Estate Planning

Asset Strategies International Inc.
1700 Rockville Pike, Suite 400
Rockville, MD 20852
Telephone: (301) 881-8600
Fax: (301) 881-1936
E-mail: mcheckan@assetstrategies.com
Web site: www.assetstrategies.com
Precious Metals/Foreign Exchange/International Wire Transfers

ATC Trustees—U.S. Representative Office,
Schiltkamp International Consultants Inc.
24 West 71st Street
New York, NY 10023-4201
Telephone: (212) 579-4700
Fax: (212) 579-4710
E-mail: arrien@schiltkamp.com
Comprehensive Offshore and Financial Trustee Services

The Bennett Law Firm
200 Crescent Court, Suite 1375
Dallas, TX 75201
Telephone: (214) 756-6315
Fax: (214) 853-5204
E-mail: jb@offshoreprotection.com
Offshore Asset Protection & Privacy Strategies

Berg & Duffy LLP
585 Stewart Avenue, Suite 540

Garden City, NY 11530
Telephone: (516) 228-0500
Fax: (516) 228-0350
E-mail: pjduffy@bergduffy.com
International Business Law

Capital Asset Management, LLC
27349 Jefferson Avenue, Suite 200
Temecula, CA 92590
Telephone: (909) 296-9945
Fax: (909) 296-9947
Offshore Companies and Trusts/Asset Protection/Mutual Funds

Capital Choice Inc.
7400 Carmel Executive Park #145
Charlotte, NC 28226
Telephone: (704) 542-5499
Fax: (704) 542-6925
E-mail: IFEP@mindspring.com
International Asset Protection Planning/Investment Advisors

Carnick & Company
675 Southpointe Court, Suite 102
PO Box 7
Colorado Springs, CO 80901-0007
Telephone: (719) 579-8000
Fax: (719) 579-8010
E-mail: craig@wealthadvisory.com
International Asset Protection

Chatsky, Michael, JD
Chatsky & Associates
4250 Executive Square, Suite 660
La Jolla, CA 92037
Telephone: (858) 638-4530
Fax: (858) 638-4535
E-mail: mgchatsky@aol.com
Offshore Legal Services

Citco Corporate Services Inc.
450 Lexinton Avenue, Suite 3320
New York, NY 10017
Telephone: (212) 599-5470

Fax: (212) 599-5476
Offshore Incorporations/Offshore Trusts

Crosby & Farnum, a Professional Law Corporation
2785 Park Avenue
Santa Clara, CA 95050
Telephone: (408) 370-7500
Fax: (408) 984-5063
E-mail: matt@crosbyfarnum.com
Offshore Incorporations/Offshore Trusts

David A. Tanzer & Assoc. PC, Attorneys at Law
2121 N. Frontage Road, #209
Vail, CO 81657
Telephone: (970) 476-6100
E-mail: datlegal@aol.com
Asset Protection/Trusts and Estates/Banking/Passports

Donald MacPherson, JD
7508 N. 59th Avenue
Glendale, AZ 85301
Telephone: (800)-BeatIRS, (800) 232-8477/(623) 209-2003
Web site: www.beatirs.com
Tax and Criminal Lawyer/Offshore Clients

Duke, J. Richard, JD, LLM
Duke Law Firm PC
400 Vestavia Parkway, Suite 100
Birmingham, AL 35216
Telephone: (205) 823-3900
Fax: (205) 823-2630
E-mail: Richard@assetlaw.com
Web site: www.assetlaw.com
Wealth Preservation/Domestic and International Taxation

Dunbar, Breitweiser & Company LLP
202 North Center Street
Bloomington, IL 61701
Telephone: (309) 827-0348
Fax: (309) 827-7858
E-mail: bbreitweiser@dbc-llp.com
Asset Protection and Business Income Tax Strategies

Eric Taylor & Associates P.C.
935 Gardenview Office Parkway
St. Louis, MO 63141
Telephone: (314) 995-3888
Fax: (314) 995-3856
E-mail: erictaylor@swbell.net
Offshore Estate and Tax Planning

Felipe, Marcell, JD
888 Brickell Avenue, 5th Floor
Miami, FL 33131
Telephone: (305) 381-8500
Fax: (305) 381-6225
E-mail: mfelipe@marcellfelipe.com
Web site: www.marcellfelipe.com
Offshore Asset Protection and Estate Planning

FMSI Group Trust
PO Box 801901
Dallas, TX 75380
Tel/Fax: (972) 492-9867
E-mail: fmsigrp@ont.com
Tax and Financial Planning/Accounting

Global Strategic Management
PO Box 6643
Annapolis, MD 21401
Telephone: (410) 224-2037
Fax: (410) 224-8229
Discretionary Account Management

Globalvest Management Company, LP
6000 Estate Charlotte Amalie, Suite 4
St. Thomas, 00802 U.S. Virgin Islands
Telephone: (340) 775-7700
Fax: (340) 777-3880
E-mail: una@globalvest.com
International Investment Advisor

Gary Scott
International Service Center
PO Box 157
Lansing, NC 28643

Fax: (336) 384-1577
E-mail: info@garyscott.com
Web site: www.garyscott.com
Investment Consultant

Grossman, Larry
Sovereign International Asset Management
2706 Alt. 19, Suite 114
Palm Harbor, FL 34683
Telephone: (727) 784-4841
Fax: (727) 784-6181
E-mail: lgrossman@worldwideplanning.com
Domestic and International Financial Planning

Guardian Financial Services Inc.
6621 E. Pacific Coast Highway, Suite 260
Long Beach, CA 90803
Telephone: (562) 431-1140
Fax: (562) 684-4634
Web site: www.guardianfinance.com
Offshore Financial Services

Haddleton & Associates, PC
251 South Street
PO Box 1298
Hyannis, MA 02601-1298
Telephone: (508) 771-3132
Fax: (508) 790-3760
Asset Protection Planning/Tax and Estate Planning

Hadley Donenberg, President
Haddon Corporation
2001 Churchill Lane
Highland Park, IL 60035
Telephone: (847) 831-2997
Fax: (847) 831-2998
E-mail: hdonenberg@aol.com
Offshore Incorporations/Management/Asset Protection/Offshore Financial Services

Hebert Schenk P.C.
1440 E. Missouri Avenue, Suite 125
Phoenix, AZ 85014

Telephone: (602) 248-8203
Fax: (602) 248-8840
E-mail: prr@hs-law.com
Offshore Asset and Estate Planning

Vernon K. Jacobs, CPA
PO Box 8194
Prairie Village, KS 66208
Telephone: (913) 362-9667
Fax: (913) 432-7174
E-mail: jacobs1@kc.rr.com
Web site: www.vernonjacobs.com
Domestic and Offshore Tax Planning

Jahde, Alan, LLM
Anderson & Jahde, PC
950 South Cherry Street, Suite 1000
Denver, CO 80222
Telephone: (303) 782-0003
Fax: (303) 691-9719
Offshore Legal Services

Jeffer, Mangels, Butler & Marmaro LLP
Two Embarcadero Center, 5th Floor
San Francisco, CA 94111
Telephone: (415) 398-8080
Fax: (415) 398-5584
International Estate and Tax Planning

Jeffery R. Matsen & Associates
5001 Birch Street
Newport Beach, CA 92660
Telephone: (949) 442-9191
Fax: (949) 442-9199
E-mail: jeff@jrmatsen.com
Web site: www.jrmatsen.com
Tax, Trust, and Estate Planning/Asset Protection

Karp & Genauer, PA
2 Alhambra Plaza, Suite 1202
Coral Gables, FL 33134
Telephone: (305) 445-3545
Fax: (305) 461-3545
E-mail: kandgpa@karpandgenauer.com
International Tax Planning

Kessler Development Corp.
980 N. Michigan Avenue #1125
Chicago, IL 60611
Telephone: (312) 642-9595
Fax: (312) 642-0733
Private Investment Banking/Asset Protection

Kutchins & Bishop, PA
3974 Tampa Road, Suite A
PO Box 1063
Oldsmar, FL 34677
Telephone: (813) 855-4663
Fax: (813) 855-4893
E-mail: kutchins@msn.com
Offshore Commercial and Estate Planning

Lampf, Lipkind, Prupis & Petigrow
80 Main Street, 3rd Floor
West Orange, NJ 07052
Telephone: (973) 325-2100
Fax: (973) 325-2839
Estate and Tax Planning/Asset Protection

Landman Law Firm, LLC
800 First Capitol Drive, Suite 200
St. Charles, MO 63301
Telephone: (636) 946-0330
Fax: (636) 946-3711
E-mail: nlandman@mail.win.org
Offshore Estate and Tax Planning/Asset Protection

Larsen & Risley, Attorneys at Law
3200 Park Center Drive, Suite 720
Costa Mesa, CA 92626
Telephone: (714) 540-1770
Fax: (714) 540-1020
E-mail: info@larsenandrisley.com
Offshore Legal Services

Law Offices of Robert D. Gillen Ltd.
400 E. Diehl Road, Suite 310
Naperville, IL 60563
Telephone: (630) 955-9400
Fax: (630) 955-9560

E-mail: bob@gillenlaw.com
Offshore Incorporations/Trusts/Asset Protection

Law Offices of Robert D. Gillen Ltd.
7500 Pinnacle Peak Road, Suite A106
Scottsdale, AZ 85255
Telephone: (480) 513-3300
Fax: (480) 513-3301
E-mail: bob@gillenlaw.com
Offshore Incorporations/Trusts/Asset Protection

Law Offices of Stephen A. Malley
12424 Wilshire Boulevard, Suite 1200
Los Angeles, CA 90025
Telephone: (310) 820-7772
Fax: (310) 820-8870
E-mail: samalley@earthlink.net
International Tax and Estate Planning/Asset Protection

Leeb Brokerage Services
500 Fifth Avenue, Suite 3120
New York, NY 10110
Telephone: (212) 653-1504
Fax: (212) 246-3696
E-mail: engorge@leeb.net or engorge@att.net
Global Markets and Economies

Robert B. Martin Jr., JD
140 South Lake Avenue, Suite 249
Pasadena, CA 91101
Telephone: (626) 793-8500
Fax: (626) 793-8779
E-mail: petrose@aol.com
Offshore Legal Services

The McKiernan Law Firm
21 Santa Rosa Street
San Luis Obispo, CA 93405
Telephone: (805) 541-5411
Fax: (805) 544-8329

E-mail: jamesmck@pacbell.ne
International Estate and Asset Protection Planning

Mary Simon
Attorney at Law
Vigal & Simon Inc.
One Union Square Building
600 University, Suite 2401
Seattle, WA 98101
Telephone: (206) 728-5150
Fax: (206) 728-5140
E-mail: vigalsimon@aol.com
A Principal of Compass Asset Management/International Tax and Estate Lawyer

Matheson Financial Services
4501 Tamiami Tr. N. #200
Naples, FL 34103
Telephone: (941) 403-8727
Fax: (941) 659-0459
E-mail: Matheson@matheson-financial.com
Offshore Trusts and Annuities/Investment Specialist/CPA

M. R. Weiser & Co, LLP
135 West 50th Street
New York, NY 10020-1299
Telephone: (212) 812-7000
Fax: (212) 375-6888
Sophisticated Tax and Financial Planning

Osborne & Helman LLP
301 Congress Avenue, Suite 1910
Austin, TX 78701
Telephone: (512) 542-2000
Fax: (512) 542-2011
E-mail: deosborne@osbornehelman.com
Offshore Services to High Net Worth Individuals

Pickering Law Corporation
1415 Placer Street
PO Box 992200
Redding, CA 96099
Telephone: (530) 241-5811

Fax: (530) 241-3145
E-mail: pickering@c-zone.net
Offshore Incorporations/Trusts/Foundations/Partnerships

Jeffrey J. Radowich, JD
Veneable, Baetjer & Howard
2 Hopkins Plaza, Suite 800
Baltimore, MD 21202
Telephone: (410) 244-7516
Fax: (410) 244-7742
Offshore Legal Services

Reed Smith LLP
435 Sixth Avenue
Pittsburgh, PA 15219-1886
Telephone: (412) 288-4046
Fax: (412) 288-3063
E-mail: jummer@rssm.com
International Financial and Estate Planning

Richard M. Colombik, JD, CPA
International Tax Associates
1111 Plaza Drive, Suite 430
Schaumburg, IL 60173
Telephone: (847) 619-5700
Fax: (847) 619-0971
E-mail: rcolombik@colombik.com
Comprehensive Domestic and Offshore Estate and Tax Strategies

Ron Holland
Toll free: (888) 550-8779
Fax: (828) 681-8412
E-mail: ronholland@compuserve.com
Web site: www.ronholland.com
International Financial Consultant/Author

Rothschild, Gideon, JD, CPA, CEP
Moses & Singer LLP
1301 Avenue of the Americas
New York, NY 10019
Telephone: (212) 554-7806
Fax: (212) 554-7700
E-mail: grothschild@mosessinger.com

Web site: www.mosessinger.com/attorneys/rothschild_g.shtml.
Offshore Legal Services

Schnecker Van Wyk & Pearson
9709 Counselor Drive
Vienna, VA 22181
Telephone: (603) 281-6112
Fax: (603) 853-5904
International Law Firm

Schwartz & Associates, PLLC
9302 Lee Highway, Suite 1100
Fairfax, VA 22031-1215
Telephone: (703) 218-2321
Fax: (703) 218-2160
E-mail: pschfamlaw@aol.com
International Tax and Estate Planning/Asset Protection

Timothy D. Scrantom, JD
180 East Bay Street
Charleston, SC 29401
Telephone: (843) 937-0110
Fax: (843) 937-4310
E-mail: tenstate@aol.com
Offshore Legal Services

Selwyn Gerber, CPA
Joint Managing Partner
Primeglobal LLC
Beverly Hills, CA 90210
Telephone: (310) 432-4382
E-mail: sg@primeglobal.com
Web site: www.primeglobal.com

Sulzner & Associates
101 West Broadway, Suite 1050
San Diego, CA 92101
Telephone: (619) 238-8550
Fax: (619) 696-3550
E-mail: sulzner@sulzner.com
Offshore Estate Planning/Asset Protection

Swob, Damrath & Associates
11440 W. Bernardo Court, Suite 380

San Diego, CA 92127
Telephone: (858) 673-7500
Fax: (858) 673-9100
E-mail: info@swob.com
International Tax and Estate Planning

Terry Coxon, President
Passport Financial Inc.
PO Box 5697
Austin, TX 78701
(Also Office in Petaluma, CA)
Telephone: (512) 559-2122
Fax: (512) 559-0431
E-mail: Passport@jump.net
Offshore Trusts/Offshore Trust Information

Thomsen and Stephens, PA
2635 Channing Way
Idaho Falls, ID 83404
Telephone: (208) 522-1230
Fax: (208) 522-1277
E-mail: apttelford@ida.net
Offshore Estate and Asset Protection Planning

Timothy W. Holt, Attorney at law
16150 N. Arrowhead Ftn. Ctr. Drive, Suite 185
Peonz, AZ 85381
Telephone: (623) 435-8103
Fax: (623) 934-1576
Offshore Structures Designed to Defer Capital Transfers

Trident Corporate Services Inc.
3210 Peachtree Road, NE
Atlanta, GA 30305
Telephone: (404) 233-5275
Fax: (404) 233-9629
E-mail: usa@tridenttrust.com
Offshore Company, Trust and Mutual Fund Services

Union Bancaire Privee Asset Management LLC
630 Fifth Avenue, 27th Floor
New York, NY 10011
Telephone: (212) 218-6750

Fax: (212) 218-6755
Asset Management

Vincent H. Miller
Moses & Singer LLP
1301 Avenue of the Americas
New York, NY 10019
Telephone: (212) 554-7806
Fax: (212) 554-7700
E-mail: Rothschild@mosessinger.com
Offshore Legal Services

Walter Weiss, A Law Corporation
1901 Avenue of the Stars, Suite 1200
Los Angeles, CA 90067
Telephone: (310) 553-7019
Fax: (310) 557-0750
E-mail: wwwapt@earthlink.net
International Tax Planning/Asset Protection

ABOUT THE AUTHOR

Hoyt Barber has a diverse international business background and has been a recognized authority on tax havens and offshore banking for the past 20 years.

Barber has authored nine books, this being his seventh nonfiction book and sixth business/investment title. He has also written an entertainment reference book, *The Book of Bond, James Bond.* His previous offshore book, *Tax Havens: How to Bank, Invest and Do Business—Offshore and Tax Free,* was published by McGraw-Hill for 10 consecutive years and went through nine printings between 1993 and 2002.

Barber has completed two international thrillers, the first of which is scheduled for release in October 2006, entitled *From Hell to Havana,* Durban House Press, Houston, Texas.

Meanwhile, Barber is writing his next nonfiction book, *Secrets of Swiss Banking: An Owner's Guide to Quietly Building a Fortune,* planned for publication in 2007.

Today, Barber is President of Barber Financial Advisors in Vancouver, British Columbia, Canada, a provider of offshore financial services, and is publisher of *Offshore Dossier* newsletter, written for offshore investors and expatriates.

His other interests have included flying, boating, diving, fishing, horses, cooking, travel, books, and his three daughters.

Visit the author's web site at www.hoytbarber.com.

Author royalties for this book are being donated by Hoyt Barber to the nonprofit educational organization DownsizeDC.org, Inc., and he encourages you to visit their web site at www.downsizedc.org to learn how you can have a direct effect in Washington.

INDEX